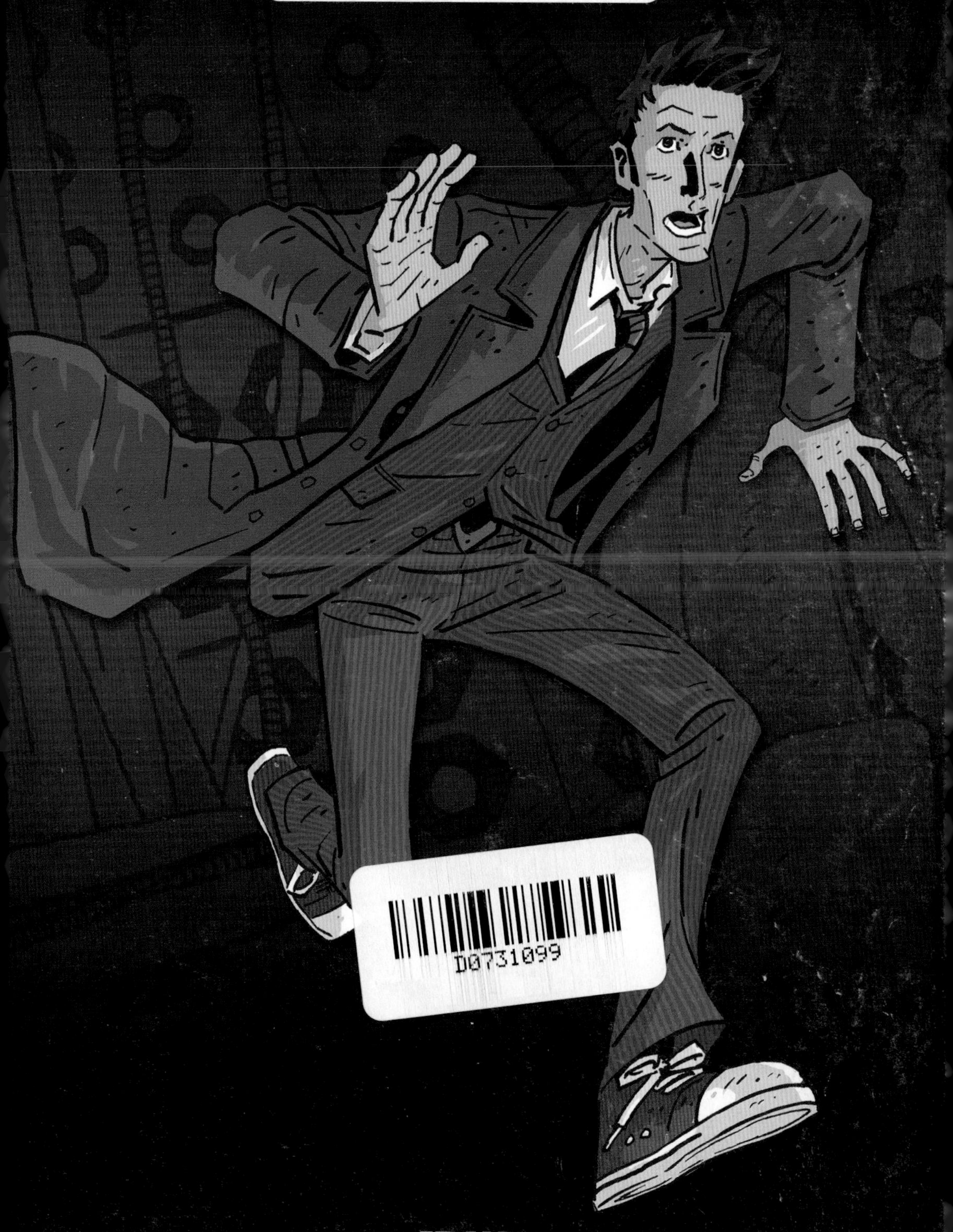

IDW

DOCTOR · WHO

VOLUME 2:
TESSERACT

WRITTEN BY
TONY LEE

ART BY
AL DAVISON &
BLAIR SHEDD

COLORS BY
LOVERN KINDZIERSKI &
CHARLIE KIRCHOFF

LETTERING BY
NEIL UYETAKE &
ROBBIE ROBBINS

ORIGINAL EDITS BY
DENTON J. TIPTON

COLLECTION EDITS BY
JUSTIN EISINGER

COLLECTION DESIGN BY
BILL TORTOLINI

IDW Publishing

Operations:
Ted Adams, CEO & Publisher
Greg Goldstein, Chief Operating Officer
Matthew Ruzicka, CPA, Chief Financial Officer
Alan Payne, VP of Sales
Lorelei Bunjes, Director of Digital Services
Jeff Webber, Director of ePublishing
AnnaMaria White, Dir., Marketing and Public Relations
Dirk Wood, Dir., Retail Marketing
Marci Hubbard, Executive Assistant
Alonzo Simon, Shipping Manager
Angela Loggins, Staff Accountant
Cherrie Go, Assistant Web Designer

Editorial:
Chris Ryall, Chief Creative Officer, Editor-In-Chief
Scott Dunbier, Senior Editor, Special Projects
Andy Schmidt, Senior Editor
Bob Schreck, Senior Editor
Justin Eisinger, Senior Editor, Books
Kris Oprisko, Editor/Foreign Lic.
Denton J. Tipton, Editor
Tom Waltz, Editor
Mariah Huehner, Editor
Carlos Guzman, Assistant Editor
Bobby Curnow, Assistant Editor

Design:
Robbie Robbins, EVP/Sr. Graphic Artist
Neil Uyetake, Senior Art Director
Chris Mowry, Senior Graphic Artist
Amauri Osorio, Graphic Artist
Gilberto Lazcano, Production Assistant
Shawn Lee, Graphic Artist

IDW

ISBN: 978-1-60010-756-6   13 12 11 10   1 2 3 4

To discuss DOCTOR WHO: TESSERACT, join the IDW Insiders,
or to check out exclusive Web offers, check out our site: WWW.IDWPUBLISHING.COM

DOCTOR WHO, VOLUME 2: TESSERACT. OCTOBER 2010. FIRST PRINTING. © 2010 BCC Worldwide. Doctor Who logo ™ and © BBC 2004.
Tardis image © BBC 1963. Licensed by BBC Worldwide Limited. All Rights Reserved. IDW Publishing, a division of Idea and Design Works,
LLC. Editorial offices: 5080 Santa Fe St., San Diego, CA 92109. Any similarities to persons living or dead are purely coincidental. With
the exception of artwork used for review purposes, none of the contents of this publication may be reprinted without the permission
of Idea and Design Works, LLC. Printed in Korea.

IDW Publishing does not read or accept unsolicited submissions of ideas, stories, or artwork.

Originally published as DOCTOR WHO Issues # 7-12.

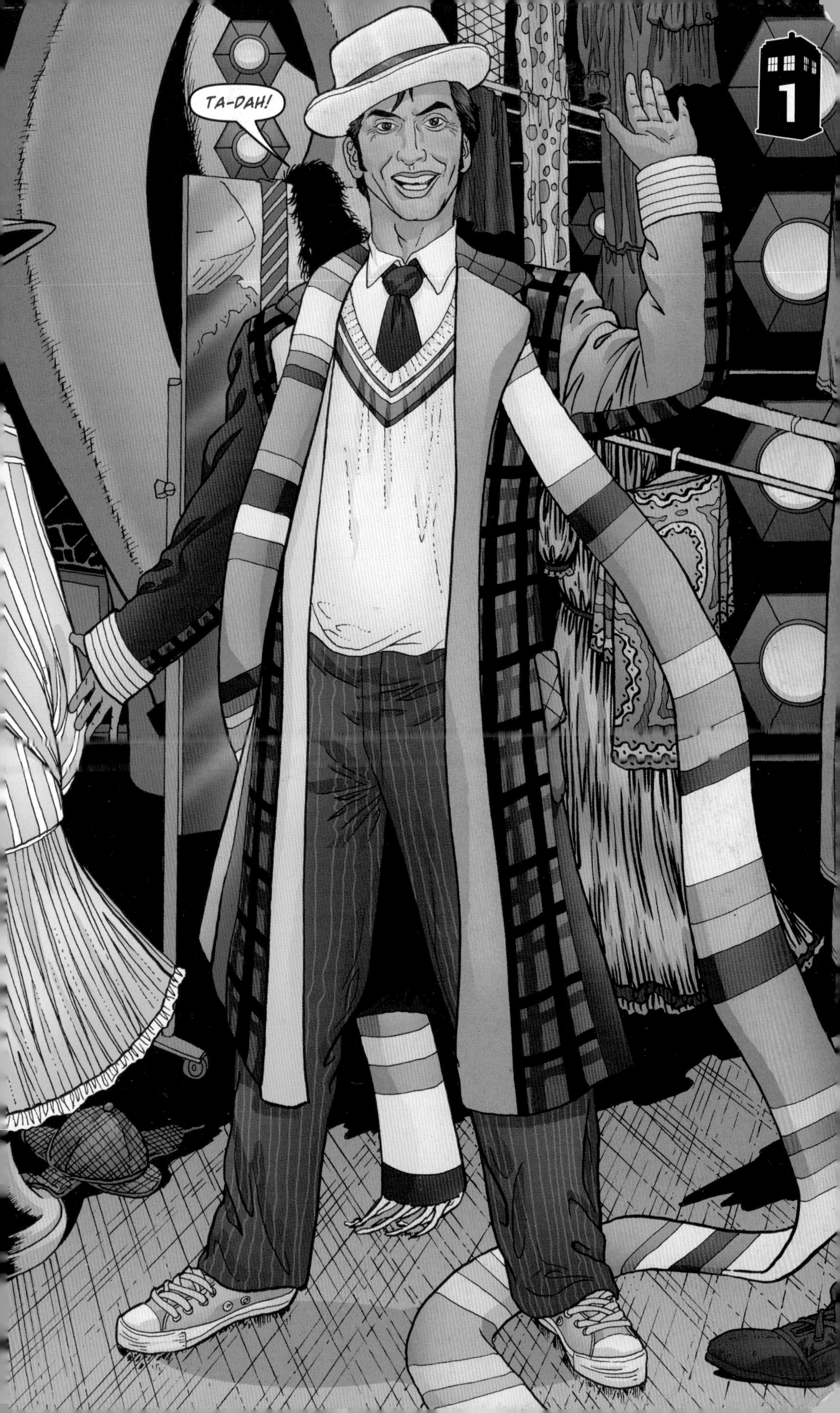
TA-DAH!

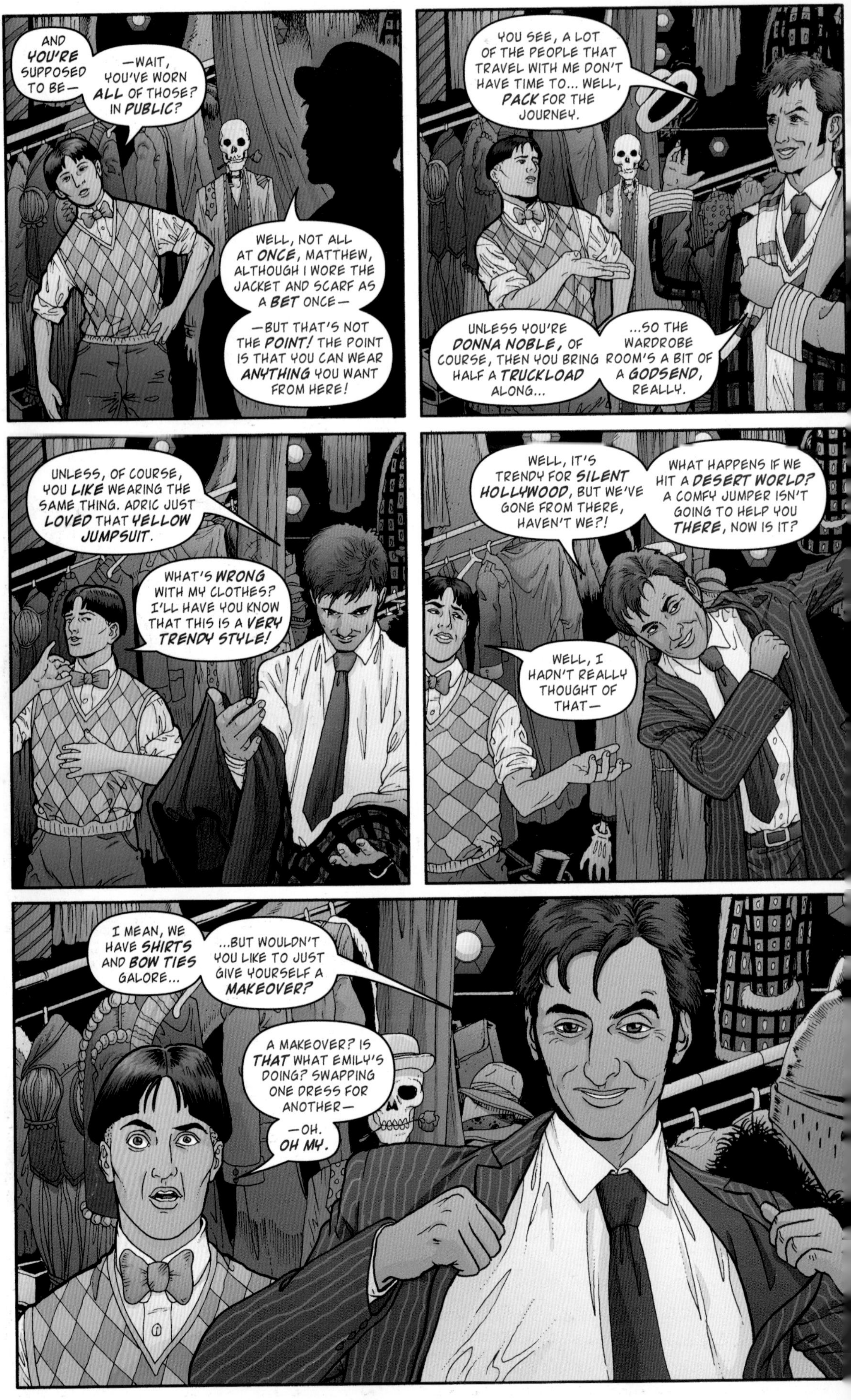
AND YOU'RE SUPPOSED TO BE—
—WAIT, YOU'VE WORN ALL OF THOSE? IN PUBLIC?
WELL, NOT ALL AT ONCE, MATTHEW, ALTHOUGH I WORE THE JACKET AND SCARF AS A BET ONCE—
—BUT THAT'S NOT THE POINT! THE POINT IS THAT YOU CAN WEAR ANYTHING YOU WANT FROM HERE!
YOU SEE, A LOT OF THE PEOPLE THAT TRAVEL WITH ME DON'T HAVE TIME TO... WELL, PACK FOR THE JOURNEY.
UNLESS YOU'RE DONNA NOBLE, OF COURSE, THEN YOU BRING HALF A TRUCKLOAD ALONG...
...SO THE WARDROBE ROOM'S A BIT OF A GODSEND, REALLY.
UNLESS, OF COURSE, YOU LIKE WEARING THE SAME THING. ADRIC JUST LOVED THAT YELLOW JUMPSUIT.
WHAT'S WRONG WITH MY CLOTHES? I'LL HAVE YOU KNOW THAT THIS IS A VERY TRENDY STYLE!
WELL, IT'S TRENDY FOR SILENT HOLLYWOOD, BUT WE'VE GONE FROM THERE, HAVEN'T WE?!
WHAT HAPPENS IF WE HIT A DESERT WORLD? A COMFY JUMPER ISN'T GOING TO HELP YOU THERE, NOW IS IT?
WELL, I HADN'T REALLY THOUGHT OF THAT—
I MEAN, WE HAVE SHIRTS AND BOW TIES GALORE...
...BUT WOULDN'T YOU LIKE TO JUST GIVE YOURSELF A MAKEOVER?
A MAKEOVER? IS THAT WHAT EMILY'S DOING? SWAPPING ONE DRESS FOR ANOTHER—
—OH. OH MY.

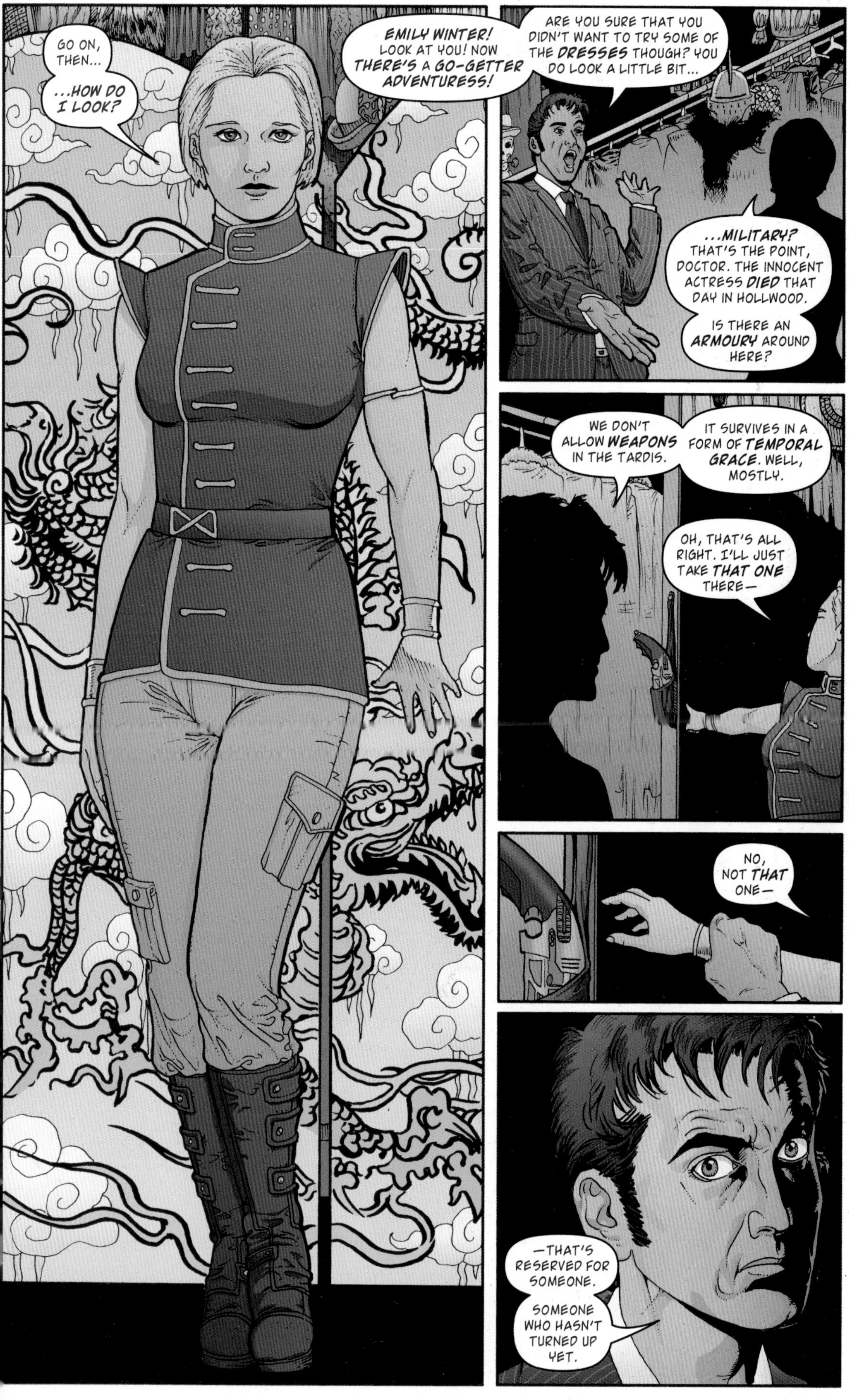
GO ON, THEN...
...HOW DO I LOOK?
EMILY WINTER! LOOK AT YOU! NOW THERE'S A GO-GETTER ADVENTURESS!
ARE YOU SURE THAT YOU DIDN'T WANT TO TRY SOME OF THE DRESSES THOUGH? YOU DO LOOK A LITTLE BIT...
...MILITARY? THAT'S THE POINT, DOCTOR. THE INNOCENT ACTRESS DIED THAT DAY IN HOLLWOOD.
IS THERE AN ARMOURY AROUND HERE?
WE DON'T ALLOW WEAPONS IN THE TARDIS.
IT SURVIVES IN A FORM OF TEMPORAL GRACE. WELL, MOSTLY.
OH, THAT'S ALL RIGHT. I'LL JUST TAKE THAT ONE THERE—
NO, NOT THAT ONE—
—THAT'S RESERVED FOR SOMEONE.
SOMEONE WHO HASN'T TURNED UP YET.

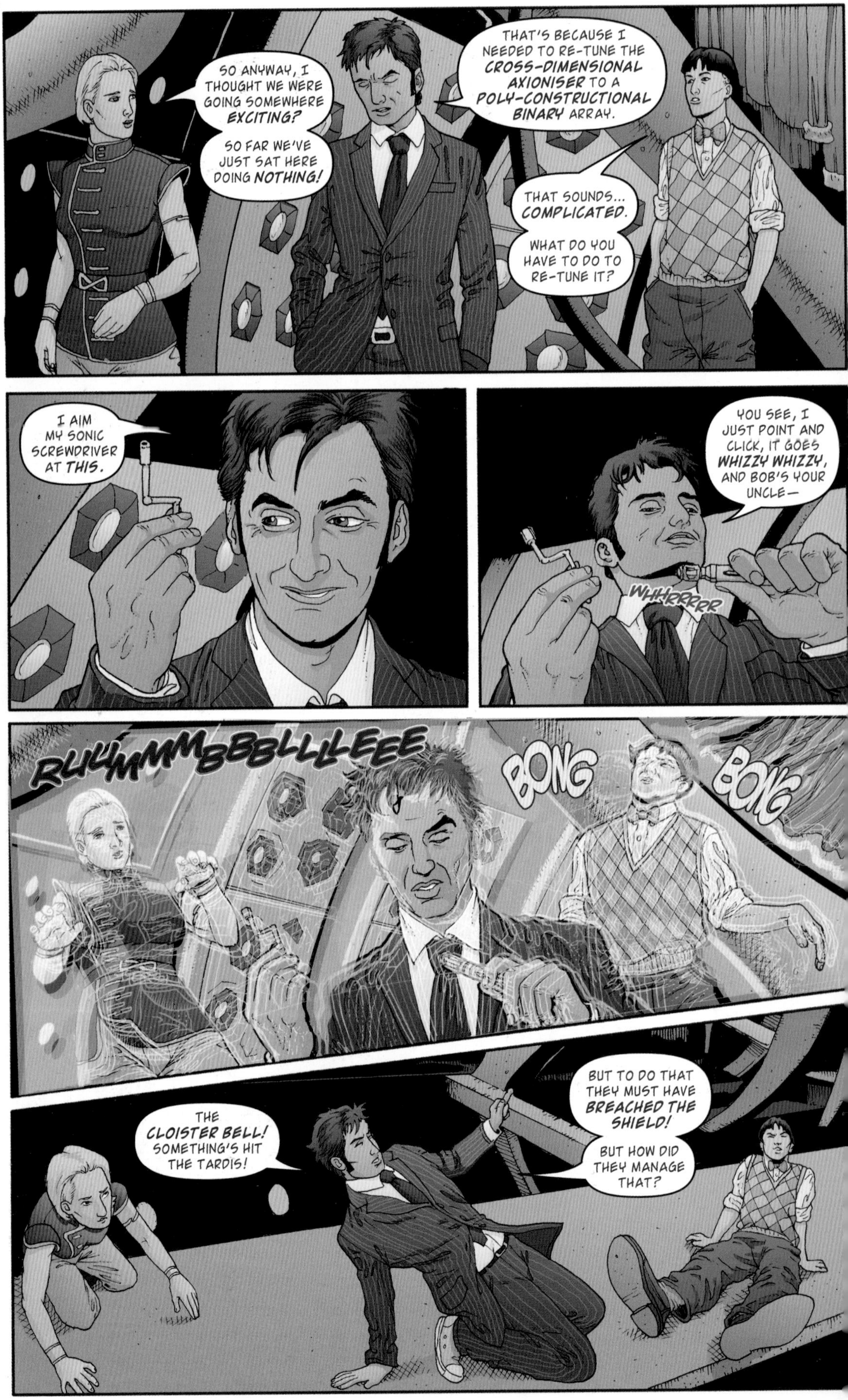
SO ANYWAY, I THOUGHT WE WERE GOING SOMEWHERE **EXCITING?**
SO FAR WE'VE JUST SAT HERE DOING **NOTHING!**
THAT'S BECAUSE I NEEDED TO RE-TUNE THE **CROSS-DIMENSIONAL AXIONISER** TO A **POLY-CONSTRUCTIONAL BINARY** ARRAY.
THAT SOUNDS... **COMPLICATED**.
WHAT DO YOU HAVE TO DO TO RE-TUNE IT?
I AIM MY SONIC SCREWDRIVER AT **THIS**.
YOU SEE, I JUST POINT AND CLICK, IT GOES **WHIZZY WHIZZY**, AND BOB'S YOUR UNCLE—
WHHRRRRR
RUUMMMBBBLLLLEEE
BONG
BONG
THE **CLOISTER BELL!** SOMETHING'S HIT THE TARDIS!
BUT TO DO THAT THEY MUST HAVE **BREACHED THE SHIELD!**
BUT HOW DID THEY MANAGE THAT?

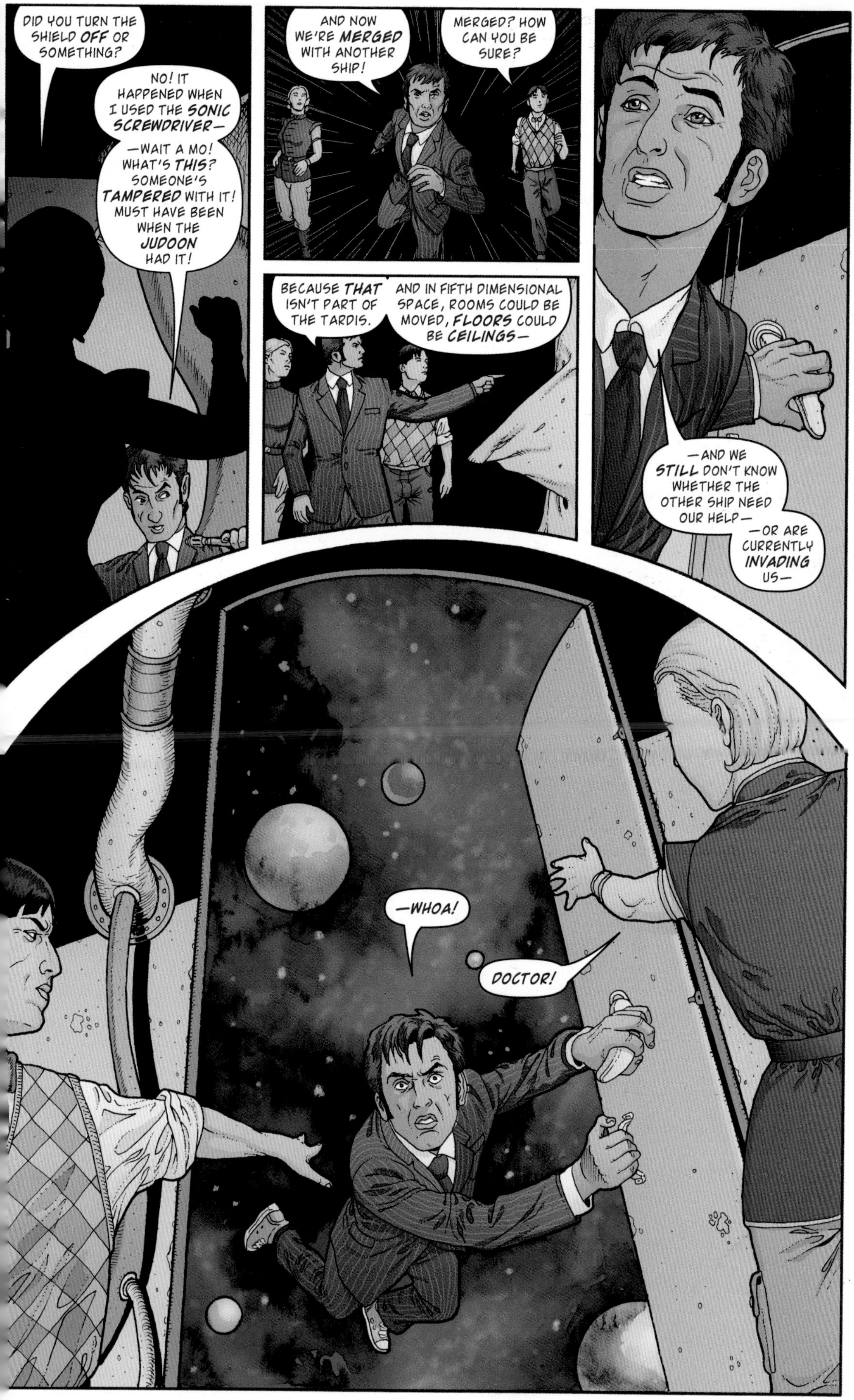
DID YOU TURN THE SHIELD OFF OR SOMETHING?
NO! IT HAPPENED WHEN I USED THE SONIC SCREWDRIVER—
—WAIT A MO! WHAT'S THIS? SOMEONE'S TAMPERED WITH IT! MUST HAVE BEEN WHEN THE JUDOON HAD IT!
AND NOW WE'RE MERGED WITH ANOTHER SHIP!
MERGED? HOW CAN YOU BE SURE?
BECAUSE THAT ISN'T PART OF THE TARDIS.
AND IN FIFTH DIMENSIONAL SPACE, ROOMS COULD BE MOVED, FLOORS COULD BE CEILINGS—
—AND WE STILL DON'T KNOW WHETHER THE OTHER SHIP NEED OUR HELP—
—OR ARE CURRENTLY INVADING US—
—WHOA!
DOCTOR!

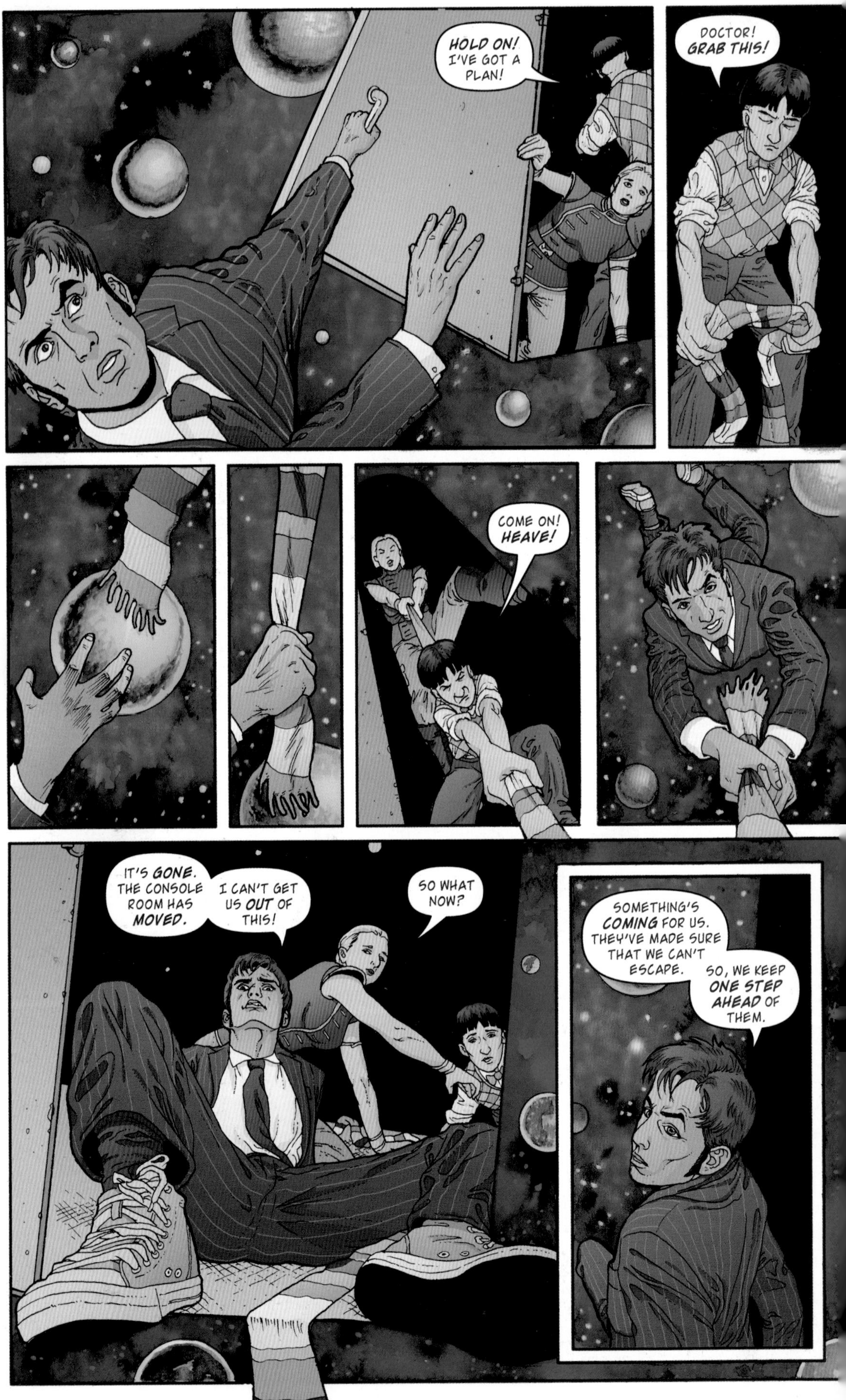
HOLD ON! I'VE GOT A PLAN!
DOCTOR! GRAB THIS!
COME ON! HEAVE!
IT'S GONE. THE CONSOLE ROOM HAS MOVED.
I CAN'T GET US OUT OF THIS!
SO WHAT NOW?
SOMETHING'S COMING FOR US. THEY'VE MADE SURE THAT WE CAN'T ESCAPE.
SO, WE KEEP ONE STEP AHEAD OF THEM.

ELSEWHERE.

CLANG

〈 TIME IS **SHORT**. FULFIL THE MISSION. 〉

〈 EXTRACT THE **PACKAGE** AND THEN FULFIL SECONDARY TARGET... 〉

〈 ...**KILL** THE DOCTOR. 〉

BREACH IS **SECURE**, MA'AM.

THE DOCTOR'S CONSOLE ROOM HAS BEEN **MOVED**. HE CANNOT REACH IT.

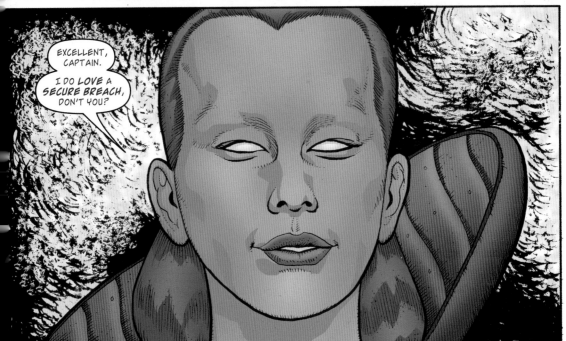

EXCELLENT, CAPTAIN.

I DO **LOVE** A SECURE BREACH, DON'T YOU?

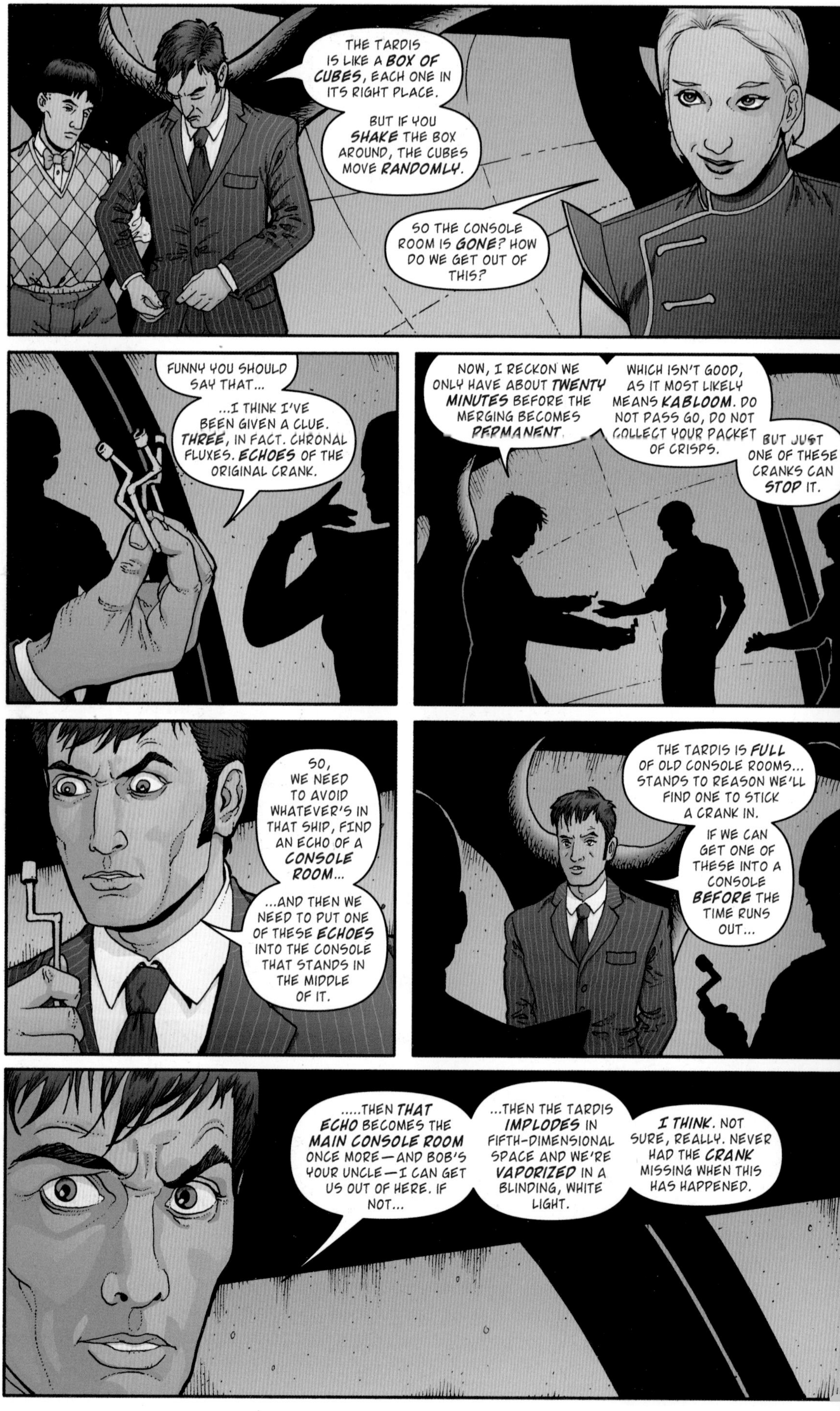
THE TARDIS IS LIKE A BOX OF CUBES, EACH ONE IN ITS RIGHT PLACE.
BUT IF YOU SHAKE THE BOX AROUND, THE CUBES MOVE RANDOMLY.
SO THE CONSOLE ROOM IS GONE? HOW DO WE GET OUT OF THIS?
FUNNY YOU SHOULD SAY THAT...
...I THINK I'VE BEEN GIVEN A CLUE. THREE, IN FACT. CHRONAL FLUXES. ECHOES OF THE ORIGINAL CRANK.
NOW, I RECKON WE ONLY HAVE ABOUT TWENTY MINUTES BEFORE THE MERGING BECOMES PERMANENT.
WHICH ISN'T GOOD, AS IT MOST LIKELY MEANS KABLOOM. DO NOT PASS GO, DO NOT COLLECT YOUR PACKET OF CRISPS.
BUT JUST ONE OF THESE CRANKS CAN STOP IT.
SO, WE NEED TO AVOID WHATEVER'S IN THAT SHIP, FIND AN ECHO OF A CONSOLE ROOM...
...AND THEN WE NEED TO PUT ONE OF THESE ECHOES INTO THE CONSOLE THAT STANDS IN THE MIDDLE OF IT.
THE TARDIS IS FULL OF OLD CONSOLE ROOMS... STANDS TO REASON WE'LL FIND ONE TO STICK A CRANK IN.
IF WE CAN GET ONE OF THESE INTO A CONSOLE BEFORE THE TIME RUNS OUT...
.....THEN THAT ECHO BECOMES THE MAIN CONSOLE ROOM ONCE MORE—AND BOB'S YOUR UNCLE—I CAN GET US OUT OF HERE. IF NOT...
...THEN THE TARDIS IMPLODES IN FIFTH-DIMENSIONAL SPACE AND WE'RE VAPORIZED IN A BLINDING, WHITE LIGHT.
I THINK. NOT SURE, REALLY. NEVER HAD THE CRANK MISSING WHEN THIS HAS HAPPENED.

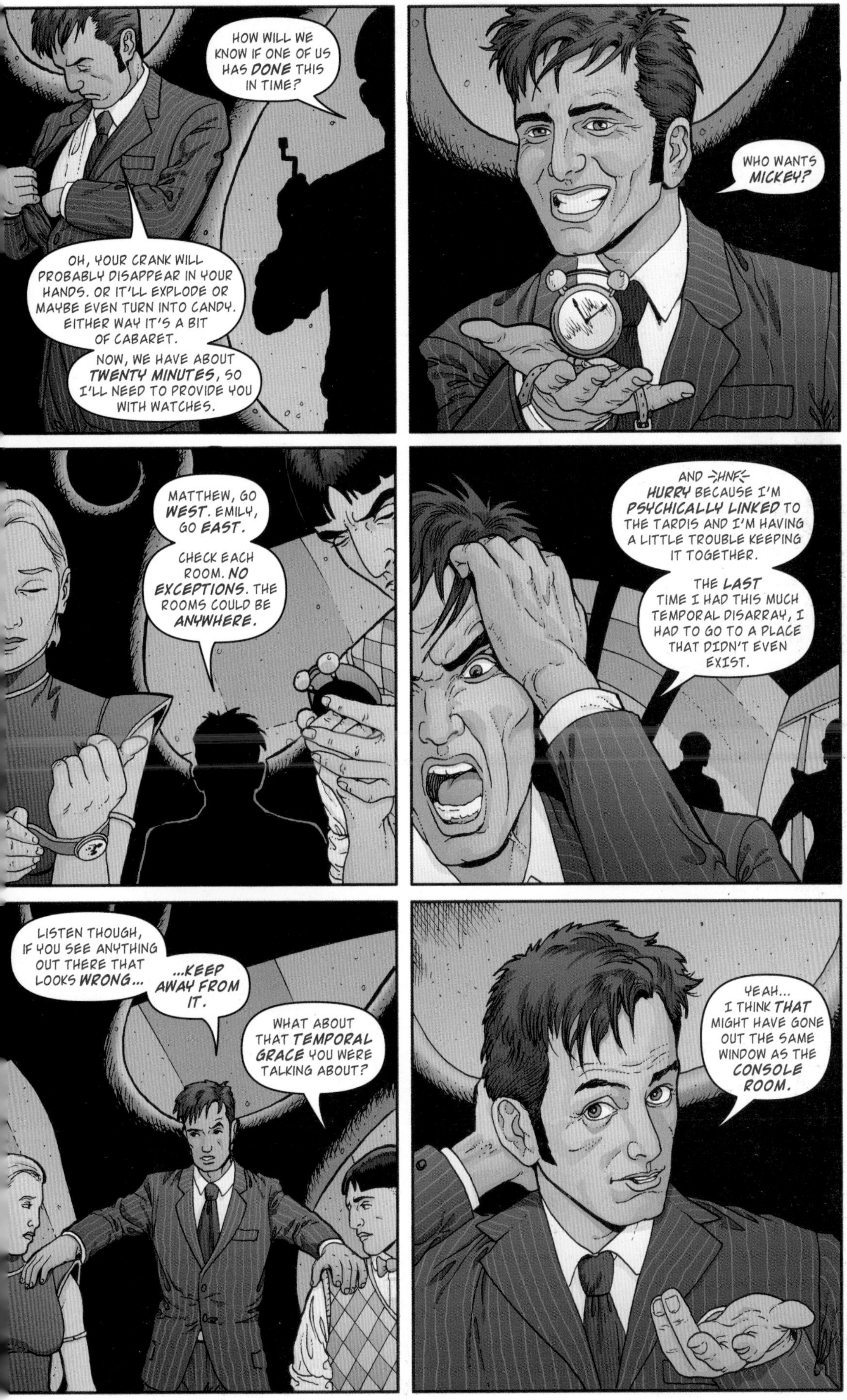
HOW WILL WE KNOW IF ONE OF US HAS DONE THIS IN TIME?
OH, YOUR CRANK WILL PROBABLY DISAPPEAR IN YOUR HANDS. OR IT'LL EXPLODE OR MAYBE EVEN TURN INTO CANDY. EITHER WAY IT'S A BIT OF CABARET.
NOW, WE HAVE ABOUT TWENTY MINUTES, SO I'LL NEED TO PROVIDE YOU WITH WATCHES.
WHO WANTS MICKEY?
MATTHEW, GO WEST. EMILY, GO EAST.
CHECK EACH ROOM. NO EXCEPTIONS. THE ROOMS COULD BE ANYWHERE.
AND -HNF- HURRY BECAUSE I'M PSYCHICALLY LINKED TO THE TARDIS AND I'M HAVING A LITTLE TROUBLE KEEPING IT TOGETHER.
THE LAST TIME I HAD THIS MUCH TEMPORAL DISARRAY, I HAD TO GO TO A PLACE THAT DIDN'T EVEN EXIST.
LISTEN THOUGH, IF YOU SEE ANYTHING OUT THERE THAT LOOKS WRONG...
...KEEP AWAY FROM IT.
WHAT ABOUT THAT TEMPORAL GRACE YOU WERE TALKING ABOUT?
YEAH... I THINK THAT MIGHT HAVE GONE OUT THE SAME WINDOW AS THE CONSOLE ROOM.

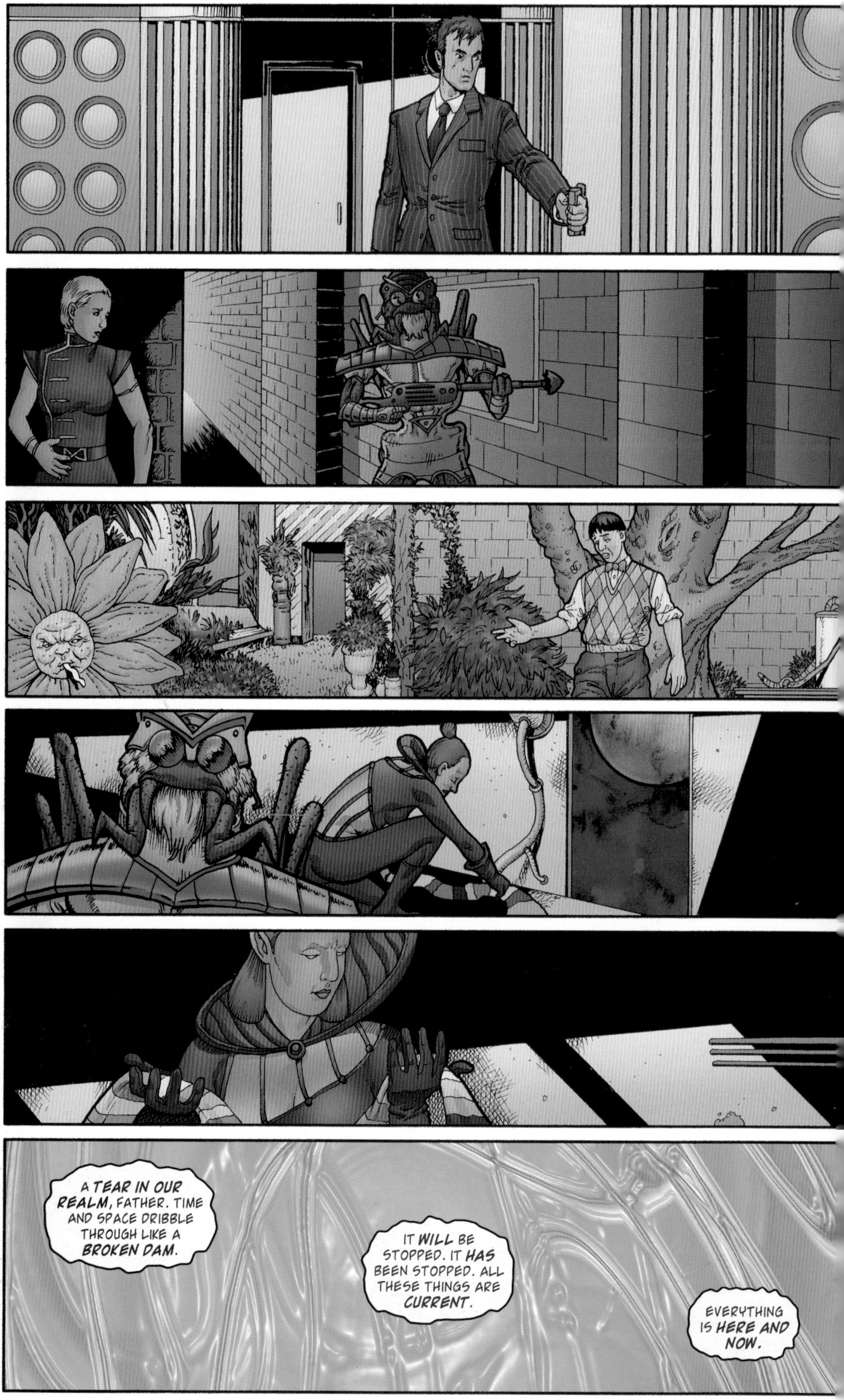
A TEAR IN OUR REALM, FATHER. TIME AND SPACE DRIBBLE THROUGH LIKE A BROKEN DAM.
IT WILL BE STOPPED. IT HAS BEEN STOPPED. ALL THESE THINGS ARE CURRENT.
EVERYTHING IS HERE AND NOW.

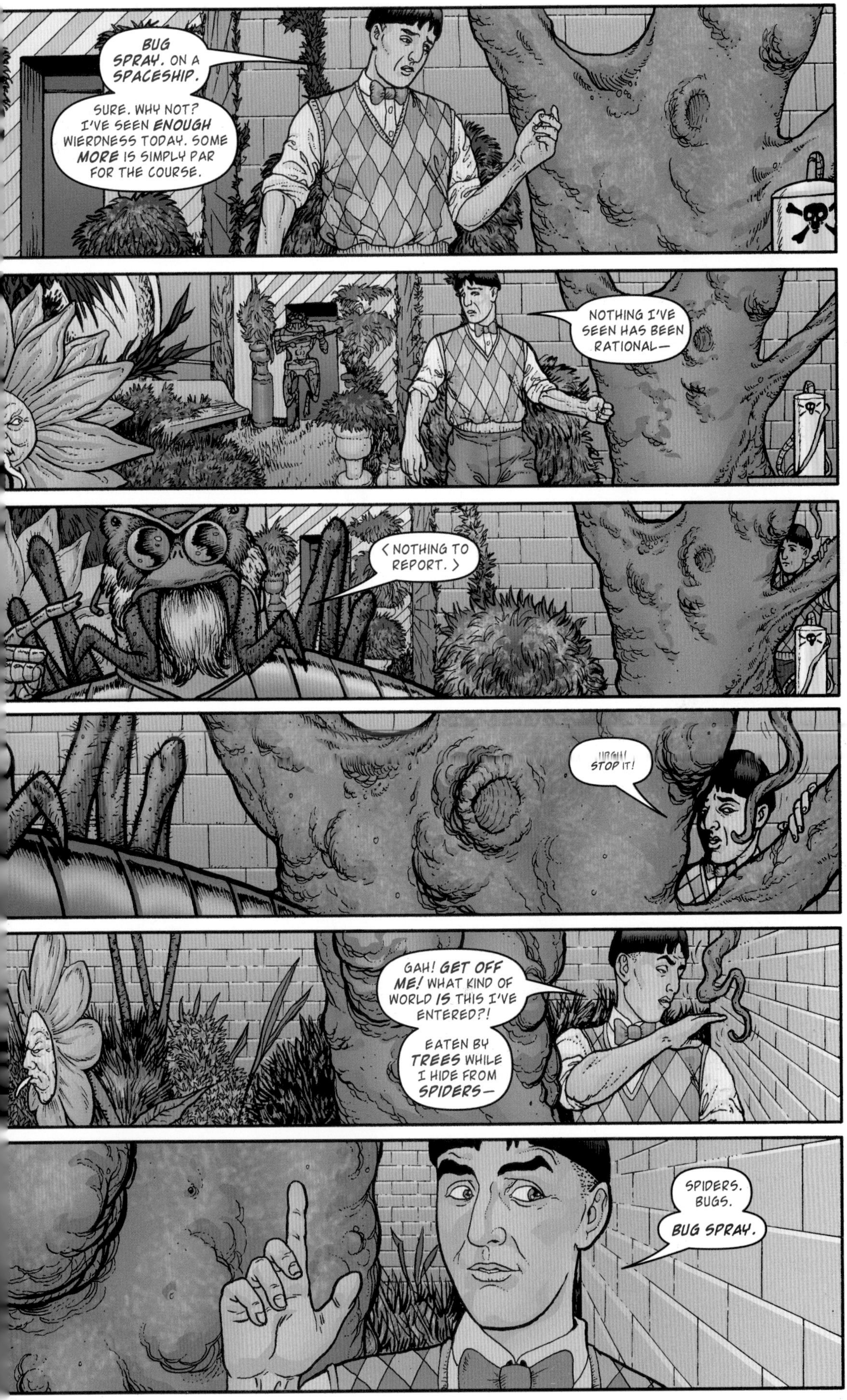

BUG SPRAY. ON A SPACESHIP.
SURE. WHY NOT? I'VE SEEN ENOUGH WIERDNESS TODAY. SOME MORE IS SIMPLY PAR FOR THE COURSE.
NOTHING I'VE SEEN HAS BEEN RATIONAL—
< NOTHING TO REPORT. >
URGH! STOP IT!
GAH! GET OFF ME! WHAT KIND OF WORLD IS THIS I'VE ENTERED?!
EATEN BY TREES WHILE I HIDE FROM SPIDERS—
SPIDERS. BUGS.
BUG SPRAY.

YUP. FIGURES THAT YOU'RE A *CRICKET* MAN.

STILL, IF YOU WON'T LET ME HAVE A *GUN...*

...*THIS* COULD COME IN HANDY.

WHAT THE—

BRAKKAA

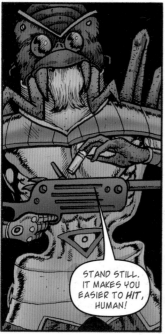

STAND STILL. IT MAKES YOU EASIER TO *HIT,* HUMAN!

SIR! I HAVE ONE OF THE TRAVELLERS. DO I HAVE A KILL ORDER?

AH.

WHACK

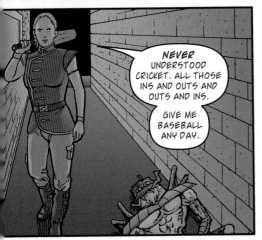
NEVER UNDERSTOOD CRICKET. ALL THOSE INS AND OUTS AND OUTS AND INS.

GIVE ME BASEBALL ANY DAY.

OOH. I CAN TAKE HIS GUN.

THERE SHE IS! KILL HER!

BRAKKA

I DON'T NEED A GUN! I DON'T NEED A GUN!

< WHY DO **WE** HAVE TO GUARD THE DOOR? >

< I WANT TO **KILL HUMANS!** >

< WE **COULD** KILL HUMANS IF WE WANTED. WE **CHOOSE** TO GUARD THE DOOR. >

ACARI. COUSINS TO HALF A DOZEN SPIDER RACES I'VE MET. HALF AS BRIGHT, TOO, IF I REMEMBER RIGHT.

BUT THERE'S **NO WAY** THAT THEY COULD HAVE DEVELOPED **FIFTH-DIMENSIONAL** TRAVEL!

I NEED TO GET IN **THERE**... SEE WHAT'S GOING ON.

PERHAPS I CAN EVEN **BYPASS** THE NEED FOR A **CONTROL ROOM** IF I—

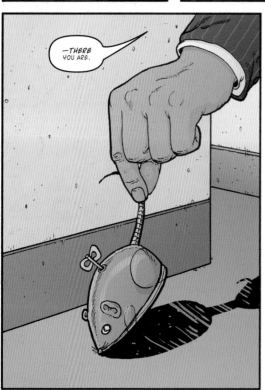

—THERE YOU ARE.

WIND IT UP AND WATCH IT GO.

SQUEAK FOR ME, MOUSEY.

COME ON... COME AND HAVE A LOOK AT THE **EXCITING, NEW SHINY THING.**

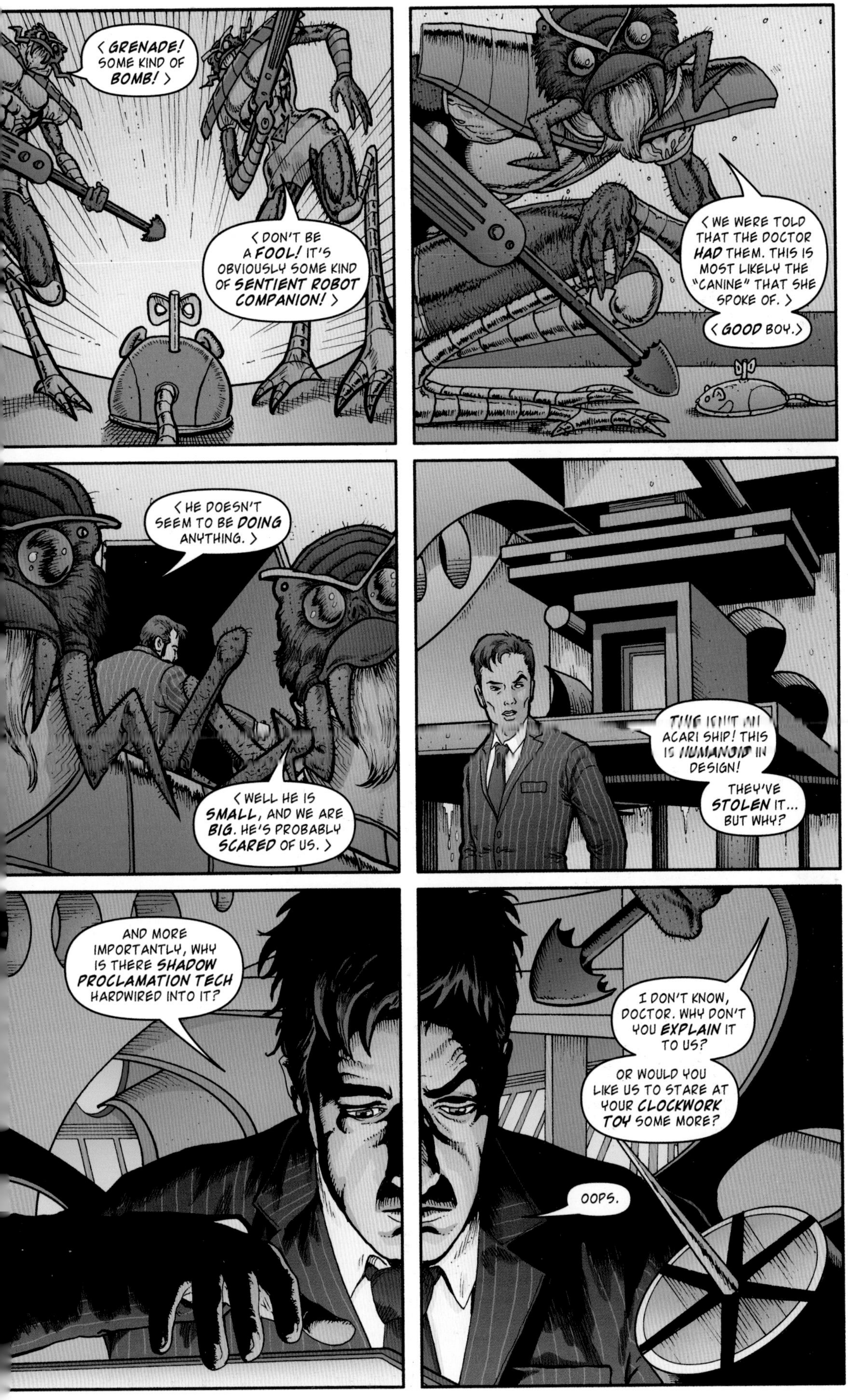
< GRENADE! SOME KIND OF BOMB! >
< DON'T BE A FOOL! IT'S OBVIOUSLY SOME KIND OF SENTIENT ROBOT COMPANION! >
< WE WERE TOLD THAT THE DOCTOR HAD THEM. THIS IS MOST LIKELY THE "CANINE" THAT SHE SPOKE OF. >
< GOOD BOY. >
< HE DOESN'T SEEM TO BE DOING ANYTHING. >
< WELL HE IS SMALL, AND WE ARE BIG. HE'S PROBABLY SCARED OF US. >
THIS ISN'T AN ACARI SHIP! THIS IS HUMANOID IN DESIGN!
THEY'VE STOLEN IT... BUT WHY?
AND MORE IMPORTANTLY, WHY IS THERE SHADOW PROCLAMATION TECH HARDWIRED INTO IT?
I DON'T KNOW, DOCTOR. WHY DON'T YOU EXPLAIN IT TO US?
OR WOULD YOU LIKE US TO STARE AT YOUR CLOCKWORK TOY SOME MORE?
OOPS.

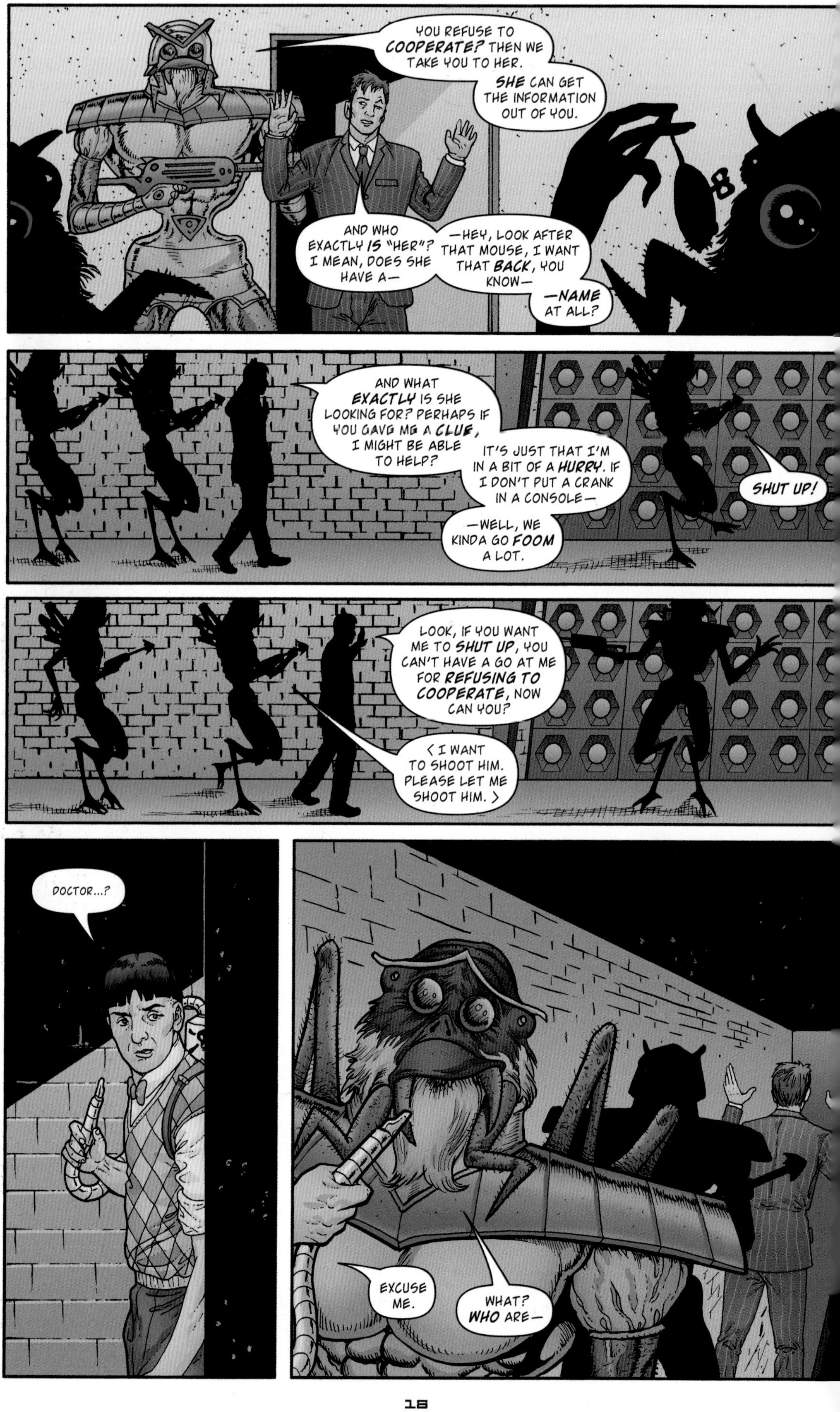

YOU REFUSE TO COOPERATE? THEN WE TAKE YOU TO HER.
SHE CAN GET THE INFORMATION OUT OF YOU.
AND WHO EXACTLY IS "HER"? I MEAN, DOES SHE HAVE A—
—HEY, LOOK AFTER THAT MOUSE, I WANT THAT BACK, YOU KNOW—
—NAME AT ALL?
AND WHAT EXACTLY IS SHE LOOKING FOR? PERHAPS IF YOU GAVE ME A CLUE, I MIGHT BE ABLE TO HELP?
IT'S JUST THAT I'M IN A BIT OF A HURRY. IF I DON'T PUT A CRANK IN A CONSOLE—
—WELL, WE KINDA GO FOOM A LOT.
SHUT UP!
LOOK, IF YOU WANT ME TO SHUT UP, YOU CAN'T HAVE A GO AT ME FOR REFUSING TO COOPERATE, NOW CAN YOU?
< I WANT TO SHOOT HIM. PLEASE LET ME SHOOT HIM. >
DOCTOR...?
EXCUSE ME.
WHAT? WHO ARE—

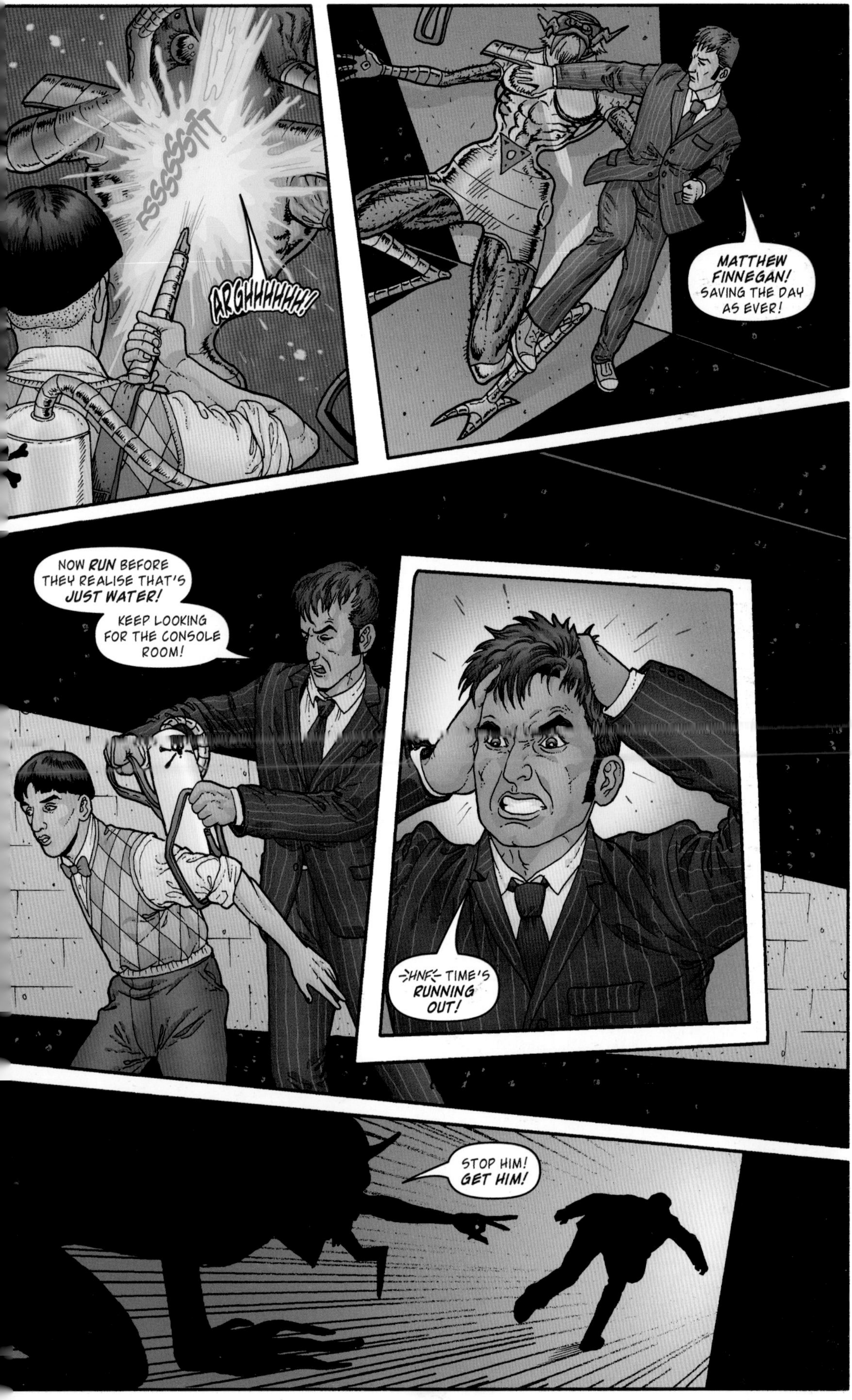

FSSSSSSTT!
ARGHHHHHH!
MATTHEW FINNEGAN! SAVING THE DAY AS EVER!
NOW RUN BEFORE THEY REALISE THAT'S JUST WATER!
KEEP LOOKING FOR THE CONSOLE ROOM!
HNF TIME'S RUNNING OUT!
STOP HIM! GET HIM!

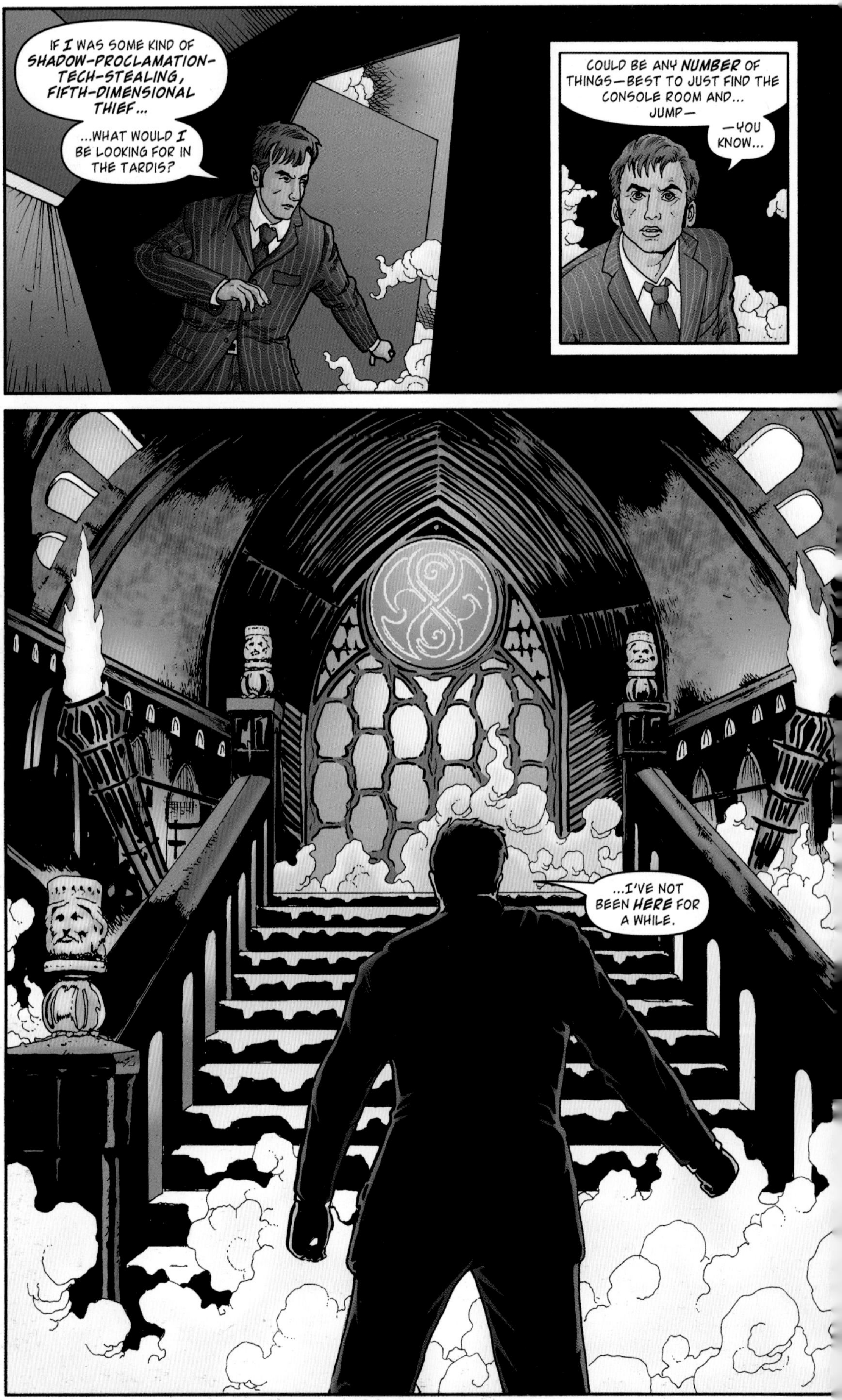
IF I WAS SOME KIND OF SHADOW-PROCLAMATION-TECH-STEALING, FIFTH-DIMENSIONAL THIEF...
...WHAT WOULD I BE LOOKING FOR IN THE TARDIS?
COULD BE ANY NUMBER OF THINGS—BEST TO JUST FIND THE CONSOLE ROOM AND... JUMP—
—YOU KNOW...
...I'VE NOT BEEN HERE FOR A WHILE.

SPIDERS! GREAT BIG, *GUN-CARRYING* SPIDERS!

WHY DID I *EVER* AGREE TO THIS?!

OH YES. *EMILY.* RIGHT THEN. CONSOLE ROOM? NO?

ONWARDS AND UPWARDS THEN, MATTHEW FINNEGAN. ONLY ANOTHER *HUNDRED* OR SO—

THIS WAS *ADRIC'S* ROOM, MATTHEW FINNEGAN.

HE WAS A *COMPANION* OF THE DOCTOR, BUT HE DIED A POINTLESS *DEATH...*

...PLUMMETING TO EARTH IN A *BURNING CRAFT* WITH *ALL THE TIME IN THE WORLD* TO BE RESCUED.

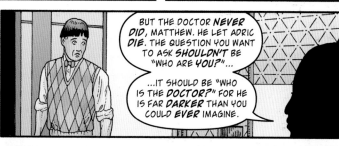

BUT THE DOCTOR *NEVER DID,* MATTHEW. HE LET ADRIC *DIE.* THE QUESTION YOU WANT TO ASK *SHOULDN'T* BE "WHO ARE *YOU?*"...

...IT SHOULD BE "WHO IS THE *DOCTOR?*" FOR HE IS FAR *DARKER* THAN YOU COULD *EVER* IMAGINE.

COME, *SIT* WITH ME. I'LL TELL YOU THE STORY OF *ADRIC...*

...AND HOW *VISLOR TURLOUGH* ALMOST SAVED THE UNIVERSE BEFORE THE DOCTOR *TRICKED* HIM.

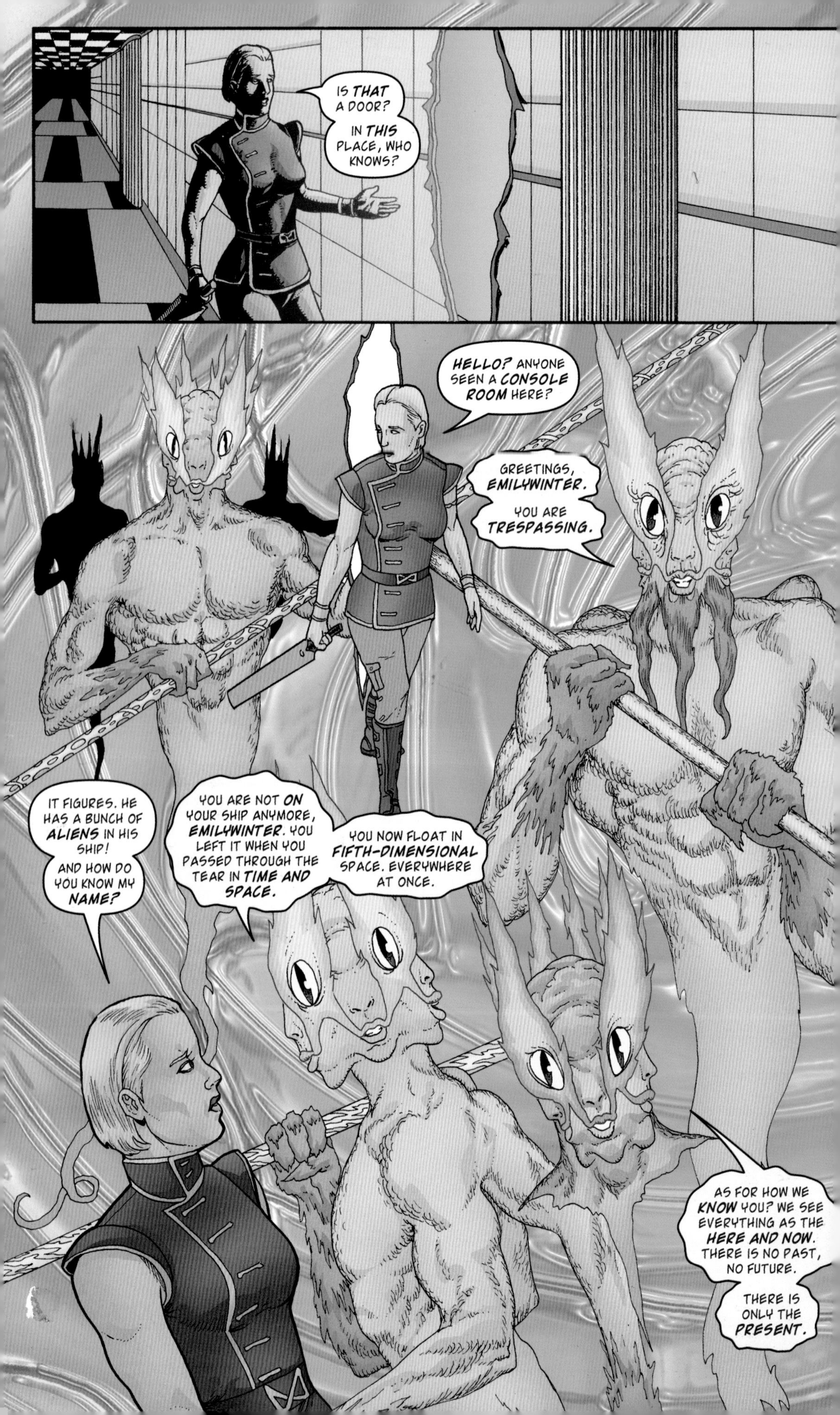

IS THAT A DOOR? IN THIS PLACE, WHO KNOWS?
HELLO? ANYONE SEEN A CONSOLE ROOM HERE?
GREETINGS, EMILYWINTER. YOU ARE TRESPASSING.
IT FIGURES. HE HAS A BUNCH OF ALIENS IN HIS SHIP! AND HOW DO YOU KNOW MY NAME?
YOU ARE NOT ON YOUR SHIP ANYMORE, EMILYWINTER. YOU LEFT IT WHEN YOU PASSED THROUGH THE TEAR IN TIME AND SPACE.
YOU NOW FLOAT IN FIFTH-DIMENSIONAL SPACE. EVERYWHERE AT ONCE.
AS FOR HOW WE KNOW YOU? WE SEE EVERYTHING AS THE HERE AND NOW. THERE IS NO PAST, NO FUTURE.
THERE IS ONLY THE PRESENT.

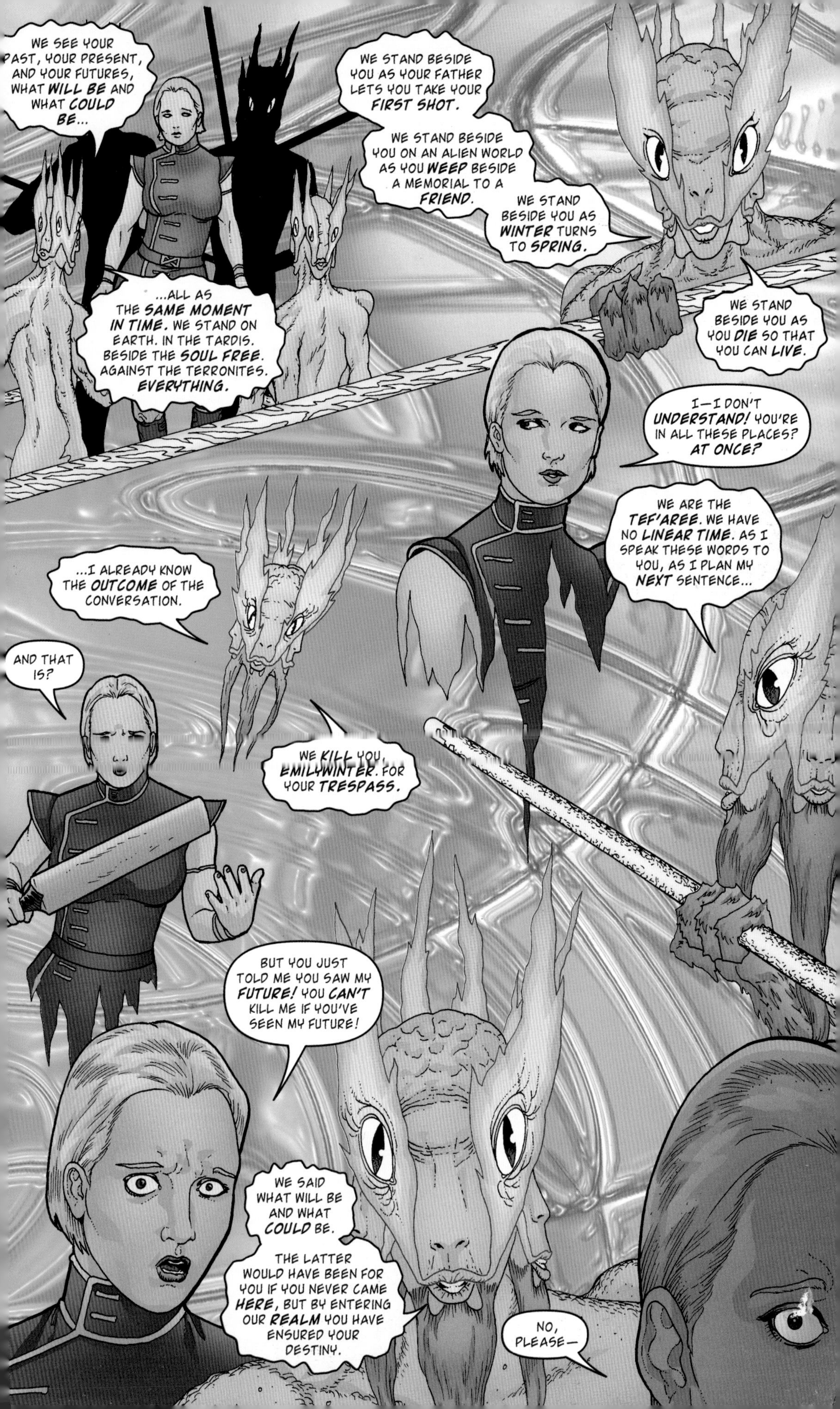
WE SEE YOUR PAST, YOUR PRESENT, AND YOUR FUTURES, WHAT WILL BE AND WHAT COULD BE...
WE STAND BESIDE YOU AS YOUR FATHER LETS YOU TAKE YOUR FIRST SHOT.
WE STAND BESIDE YOU ON AN ALIEN WORLD AS YOU WEEP BESIDE A MEMORIAL TO A FRIEND.
WE STAND BESIDE YOU AS WINTER TURNS TO SPRING.
WE STAND BESIDE YOU AS YOU DIE SO THAT YOU CAN LIVE.
...ALL AS THE SAME MOMENT IN TIME. WE STAND ON EARTH. IN THE TARDIS. BESIDE THE SOUL FREE. AGAINST THE TERRONITES. EVERYTHING.
I—I DON'T UNDERSTAND! YOU'RE IN ALL THESE PLACES? AT ONCE?
WE ARE THE TEF'AREE. WE HAVE NO LINEAR TIME. AS I SPEAK THESE WORDS TO YOU, AS I PLAN MY NEXT SENTENCE...
...I ALREADY KNOW THE OUTCOME OF THE CONVERSATION.
AND THAT IS?
WE KILL YOU, EMILY WINTER. FOR YOUR TRESPASS.
BUT YOU JUST TOLD ME YOU SAW MY FUTURE! YOU CAN'T KILL ME IF YOU'VE SEEN MY FUTURE!
WE SAID WHAT WILL BE AND WHAT COULD BE.
THE LATTER WOULD HAVE BEEN FOR YOU IF YOU NEVER CAME HERE, BUT BY ENTERING OUR REALM YOU HAVE ENSURED YOUR DESTINY.
NO, PLEASE—

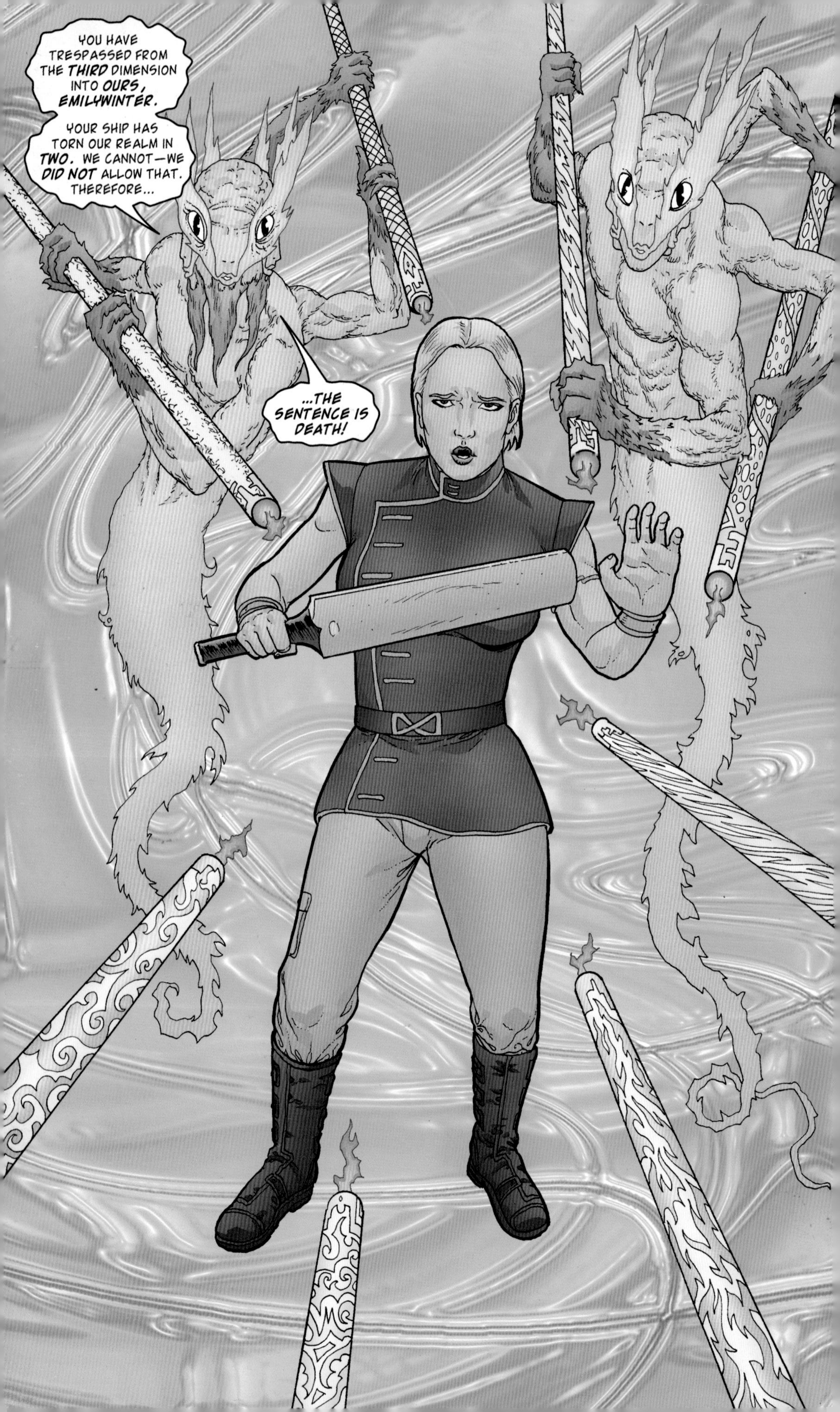
YOU HAVE TRESPASSED FROM THE THIRD DIMENSION INTO OURS, EMILYWINTER.
YOUR SHIP HAS TORN OUR REALM IN TWO. WE CANNOT—WE DID NOT ALLOW THAT. THEREFORE...
...THE SENTENCE IS DEATH!

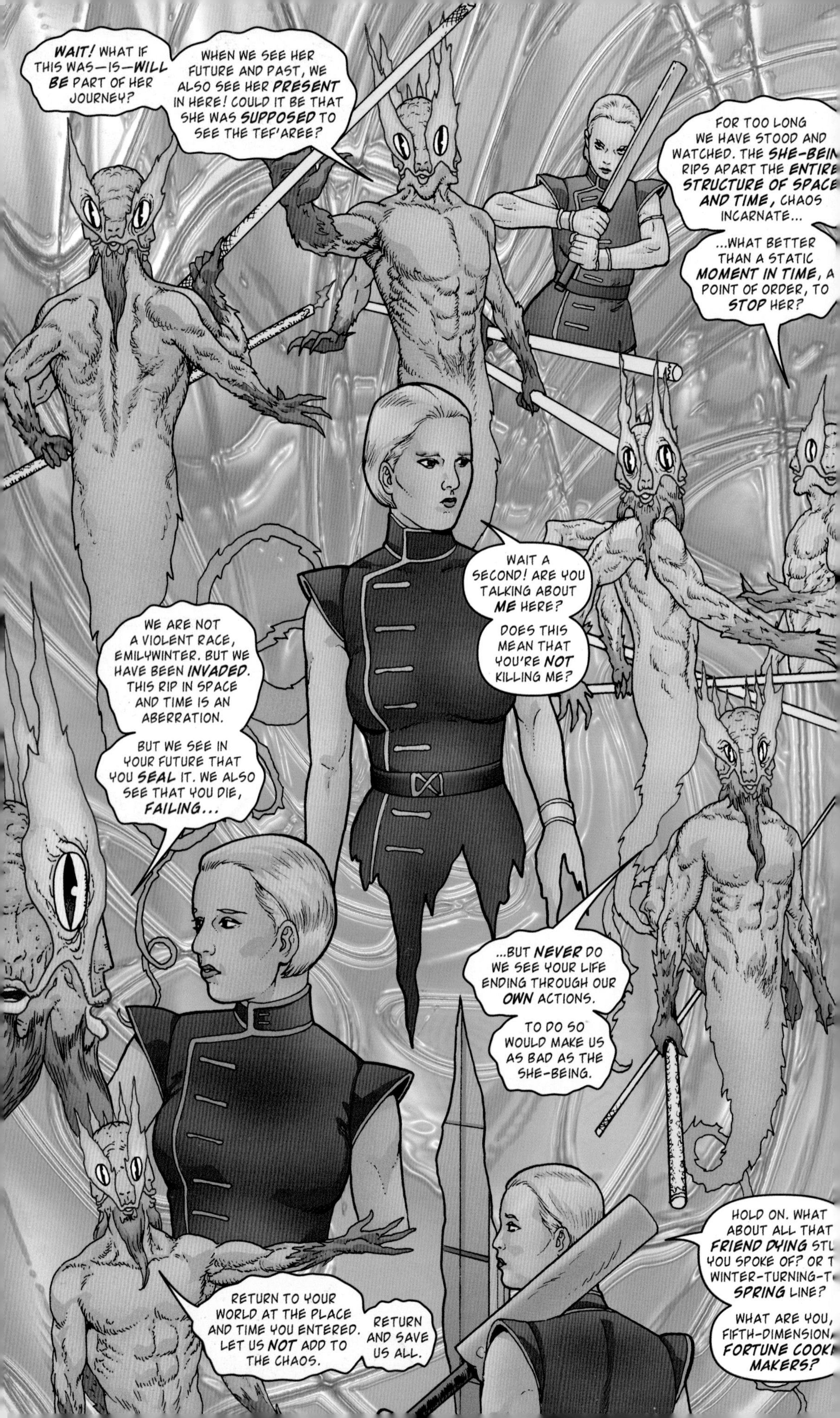
WAIT! WHAT IF THIS WAS—IS—WILL BE PART OF HER JOURNEY?
WHEN WE SEE HER FUTURE AND PAST, WE ALSO SEE HER PRESENT IN HERE! COULD IT BE THAT SHE WAS SUPPOSED TO SEE THE TEF'AREE?
FOR TOO LONG WE HAVE STOOD AND WATCHED. THE SHE-BEIN RIPS APART THE ENTIRE STRUCTURE OF SPACE AND TIME, CHAOS INCARNATE...
...WHAT BETTER THAN A STATIC MOMENT IN TIME, A POINT OF ORDER, TO STOP HER?
WAIT A SECOND! ARE YOU TALKING ABOUT ME HERE?
DOES THIS MEAN THAT YOU'RE NOT KILLING ME?
WE ARE NOT A VIOLENT RACE, EMILYWINTER. BUT WE HAVE BEEN INVADED. THIS RIP IN SPACE AND TIME IS AN ABERRATION.
BUT WE SEE IN YOUR FUTURE THAT YOU SEAL IT. WE ALSO SEE THAT YOU DIE, FAILING...
...BUT NEVER DO WE SEE YOUR LIFE ENDING THROUGH OUR OWN ACTIONS.
TO DO SO WOULD MAKE US AS BAD AS THE SHE-BEING.
RETURN TO YOUR WORLD AT THE PLACE AND TIME YOU ENTERED. LET US NOT ADD TO THE CHAOS.
RETURN AND SAVE US ALL.
HOLD ON. WHAT ABOUT ALL THAT FRIEND DYING STU YOU SPOKE OF? OR T WINTER-TURNING-T SPRING LINE?
WHAT ARE YOU, FIFTH-DIMENSION, FORTUNE COOKI MAKERS?

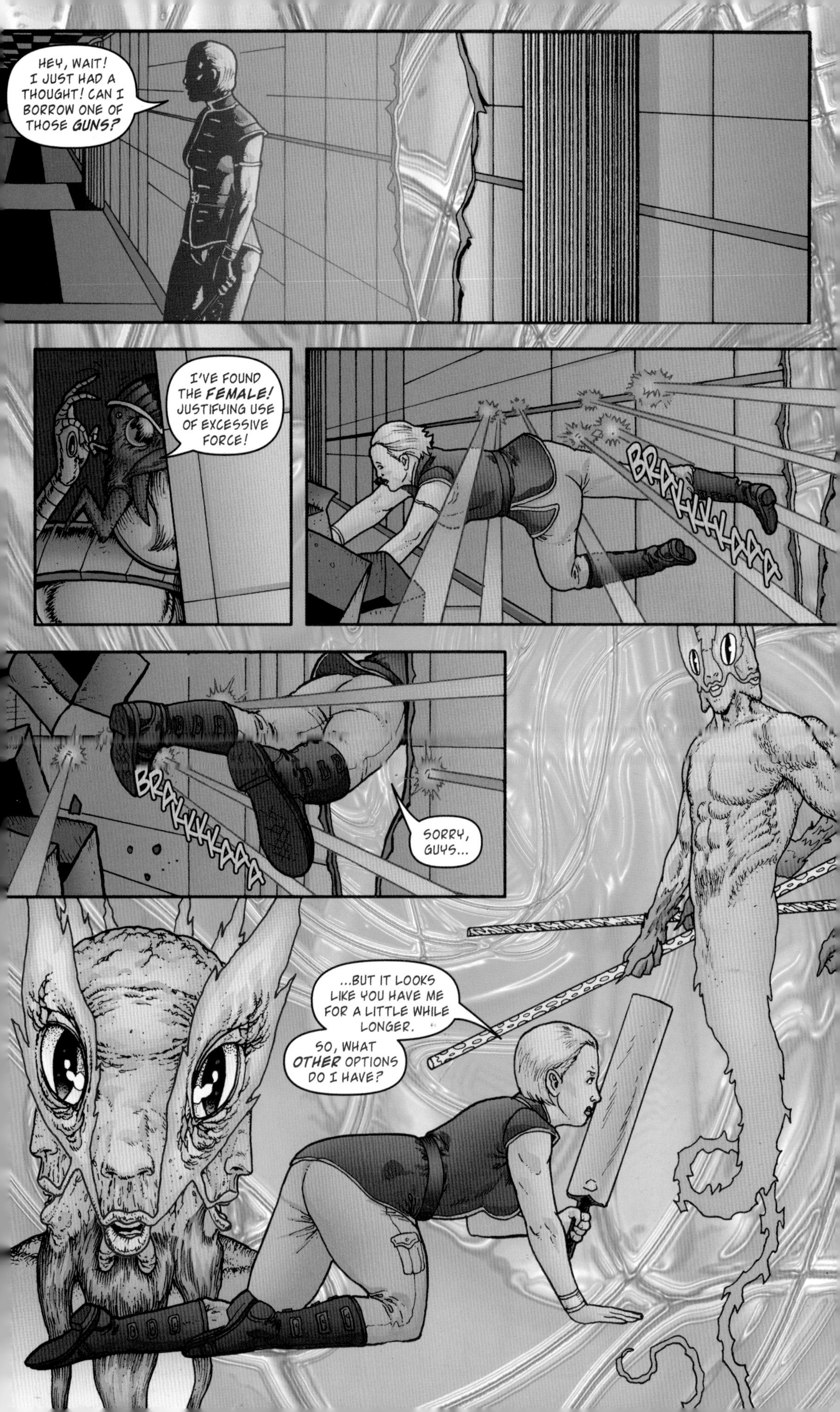
HEY, WAIT! I JUST HAD A THOUGHT! CAN I BORROW ONE OF THOSE GUNS?
I'VE FOUND THE FEMALE! JUSTIFYING USE OF EXCESSIVE FORCE!
BRAKKKKAAAA
BRAKKKKAAAA
SORRY, GUYS...
...BUT IT LOOKS LIKE YOU HAVE ME FOR A LITTLE WHILE LONGER.
SO, WHAT OTHER OPTIONS DO I HAVE?

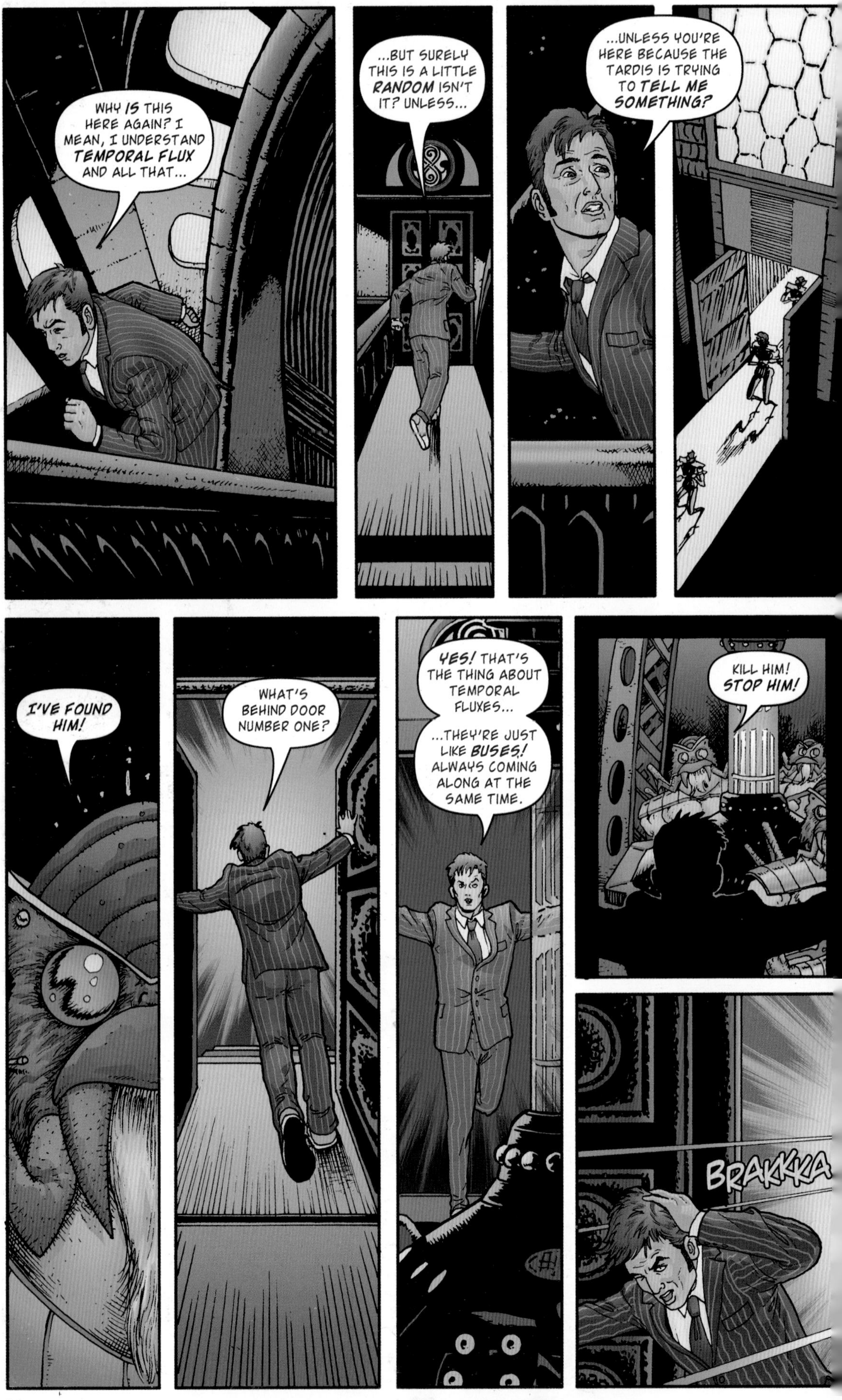
WHY IS THIS HERE AGAIN? I MEAN, I UNDERSTAND TEMPORAL FLUX AND ALL THAT...
...BUT SURELY THIS IS A LITTLE RANDOM ISN'T IT? UNLESS...
...UNLESS YOU'RE HERE BECAUSE THE TARDIS IS TRYING TO TELL ME SOMETHING?
I'VE FOUND HIM!
WHAT'S BEHIND DOOR NUMBER ONE?
YES! THAT'S THE THING ABOUT TEMPORAL FLUXES...
...THEY'RE JUST LIKE BUSES! ALWAYS COMING ALONG AT THE SAME TIME.
KILL HIM! STOP HIM!
BRAKKKA

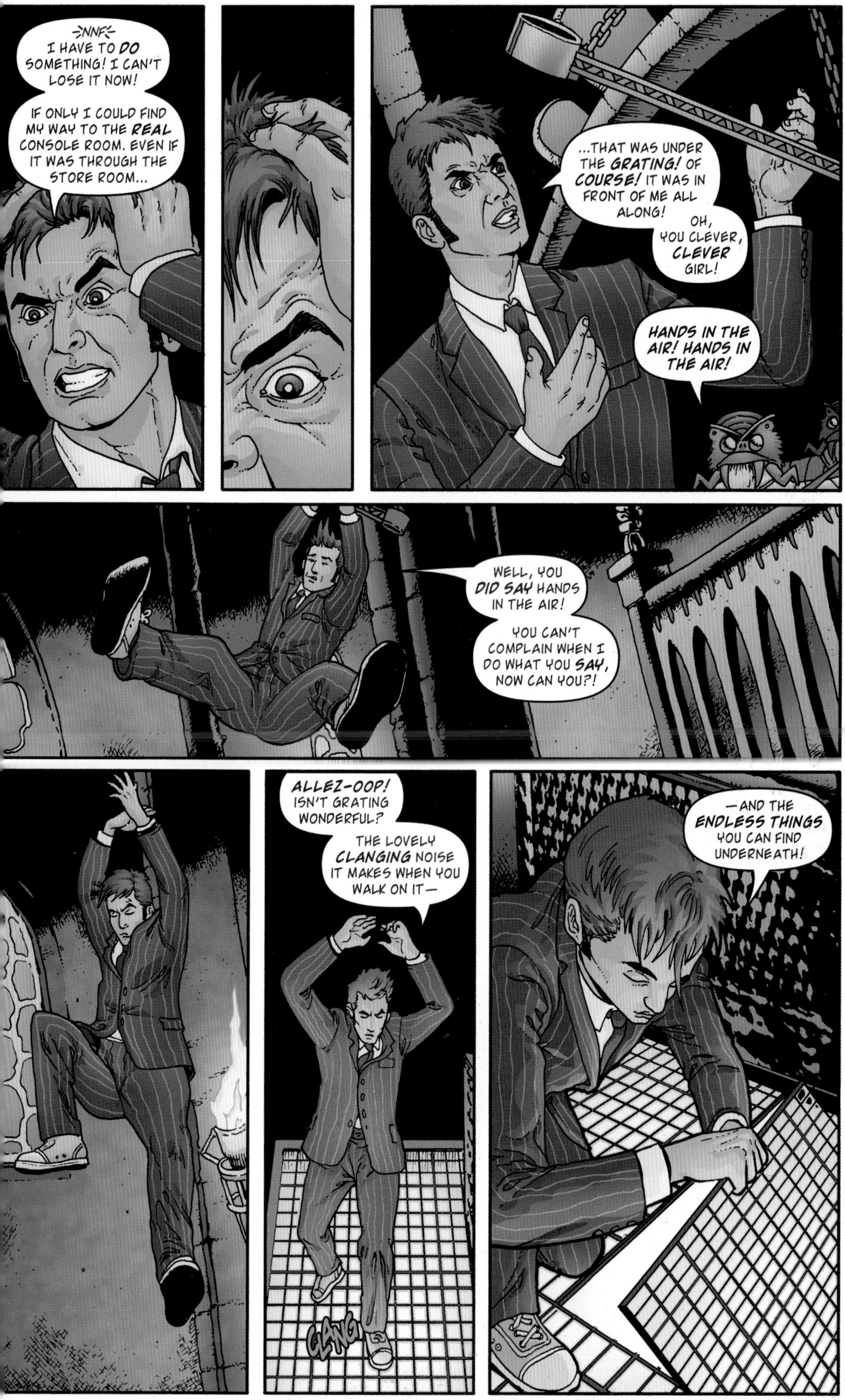

-NNF-
I HAVE TO DO SOMETHING! I CAN'T LOSE IT NOW!
IF ONLY I COULD FIND MY WAY TO THE REAL CONSOLE ROOM. EVEN IF IT WAS THROUGH THE STORE ROOM...
...THAT WAS UNDER THE GRATING! OF COURSE! IT WAS IN FRONT OF ME ALL ALONG!
OH, YOU CLEVER, CLEVER GIRL!
HANDS IN THE AIR! HANDS IN THE AIR!
WELL, YOU DID SAY HANDS IN THE AIR!
YOU CAN'T COMPLAIN WHEN I DO WHAT YOU SAY, NOW CAN YOU?!
ALLEZ-OOP! ISN'T GRATING WONDERFUL?
THE LOVELY CLANGING NOISE IT MAKES WHEN YOU WALK ON IT—
CLANG
—AND THE ENDLESS THINGS YOU CAN FIND UNDERNEATH!

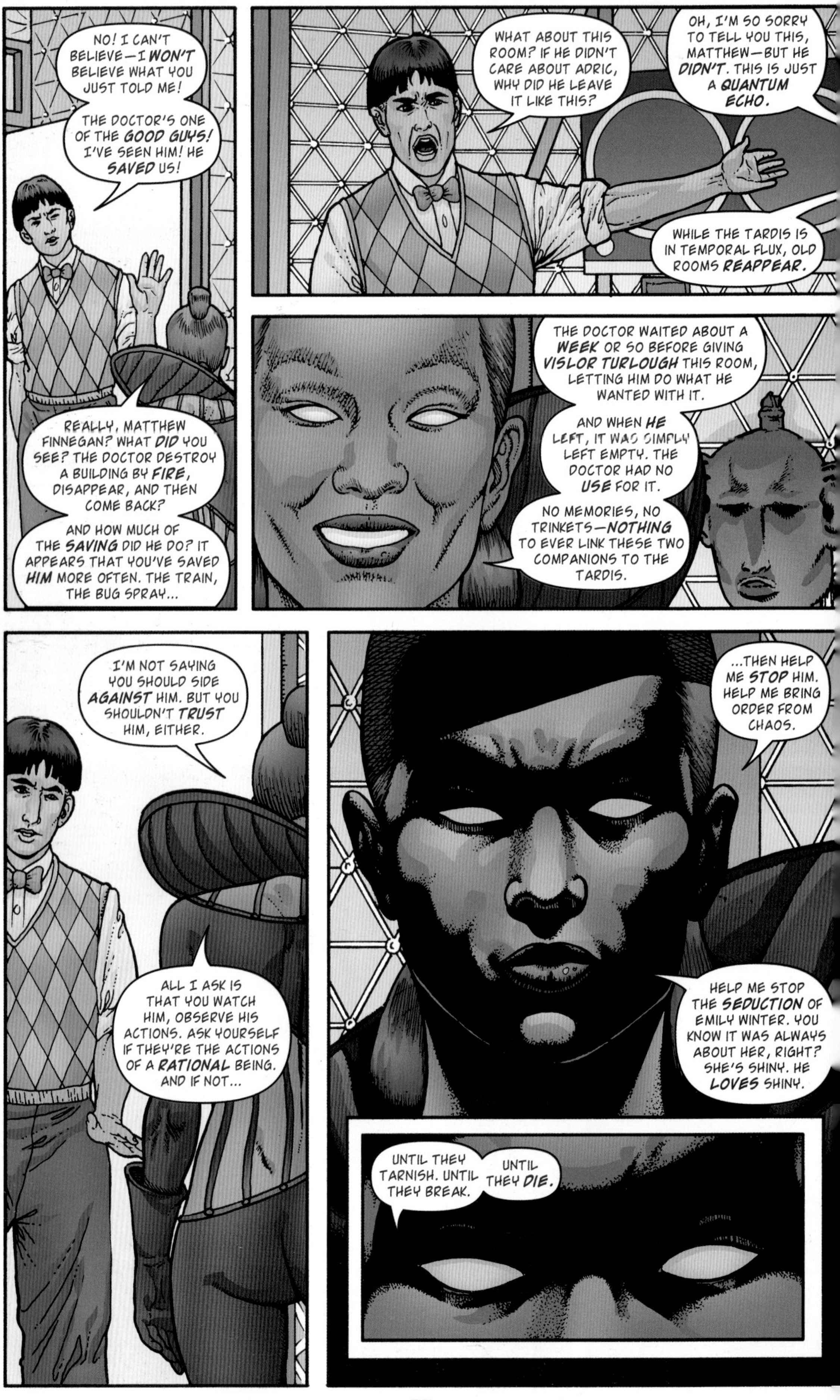
NO! I CAN'T BELIEVE—I WON'T BELIEVE WHAT YOU JUST TOLD ME!
THE DOCTOR'S ONE OF THE GOOD GUYS! I'VE SEEN HIM! HE SAVED US!
REALLY, MATTHEW FINNEGAN? WHAT DID YOU SEE? THE DOCTOR DESTROY A BUILDING BY FIRE, DISAPPEAR, AND THEN COME BACK?
AND HOW MUCH OF THE SAVING DID HE DO? IT APPEARS THAT YOU'VE SAVED HIM MORE OFTEN. THE TRAIN, THE BUG SPRAY...
WHAT ABOUT THIS ROOM? IF HE DIDN'T CARE ABOUT ADRIC, WHY DID HE LEAVE IT LIKE THIS?
OH, I'M SO SORRY TO TELL YOU THIS, MATTHEW—BUT HE DIDN'T. THIS IS JUST A QUANTUM ECHO.
WHILE THE TARDIS IS IN TEMPORAL FLUX, OLD ROOMS REAPPEAR.
THE DOCTOR WAITED ABOUT A WEEK OR SO BEFORE GIVING VISLOR TURLOUGH THIS ROOM, LETTING HIM DO WHAT HE WANTED WITH IT.
AND WHEN HE LEFT, IT WAS SIMPLY LEFT EMPTY. THE DOCTOR HAD NO USE FOR IT.
NO MEMORIES, NO TRINKETS—NOTHING TO EVER LINK THESE TWO COMPANIONS TO THE TARDIS.
I'M NOT SAYING YOU SHOULD SIDE AGAINST HIM. BUT YOU SHOULDN'T TRUST HIM, EITHER.
ALL I ASK IS THAT YOU WATCH HIM, OBSERVE HIS ACTIONS. ASK YOURSELF IF THEY'RE THE ACTIONS OF A RATIONAL BEING. AND IF NOT...
...THEN HELP ME STOP HIM. HELP ME BRING ORDER FROM CHAOS.
HELP ME STOP THE SEDUCTION OF EMILY WINTER. YOU KNOW IT WAS ALWAYS ABOUT HER, RIGHT? SHE'S SHINY. HE LOVES SHINY.
UNTIL THEY TARNISH. UNTIL THEY BREAK.
UNTIL THEY DIE.

DON'T MAKE A DECISION NOW. ALL I ASK IS THAT YOU *QUESTION* EVERY TASK HE GIVES YOU.

AFTER ALL, WE *BOTH* KNOW THAT YOU WERE JUST BROUGHT ON BOARD TO PLACATE THE WOMAN...

...SO WILL YOU BE A *TURLOUGH*... OR JUST ANOTHER *ADRIC*?

NO! THESE ARE *LIES!* HE TOOK US BOTH BECAUSE HE WANTED TO!

I *WASN'T* A MERCY CHOICE! I WON'T LISTEN!

HUMANS. SUCH FUN.

SO... *PLIABLE.*

REPORT! HAVE YOU KILLED THE DOCTOR YET?

NEGATIVE. HE HAS A HOME ADVANTAGE. IT IS PROVING *HARDER* THAN WE THOUGHT.

OR YOU'RE MORE *STUPID* THAN I THOUGHT.

BELAY THAT ORDER. I NEED THE DOCTOR KEPT *ALIVE.* I HAVE THE ITEM... AND A *NEW* PLAN.

THIS ONE IS GOING TO BE *SO MUCH MORE FUN.*

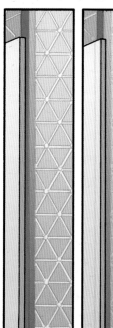

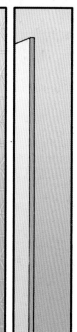

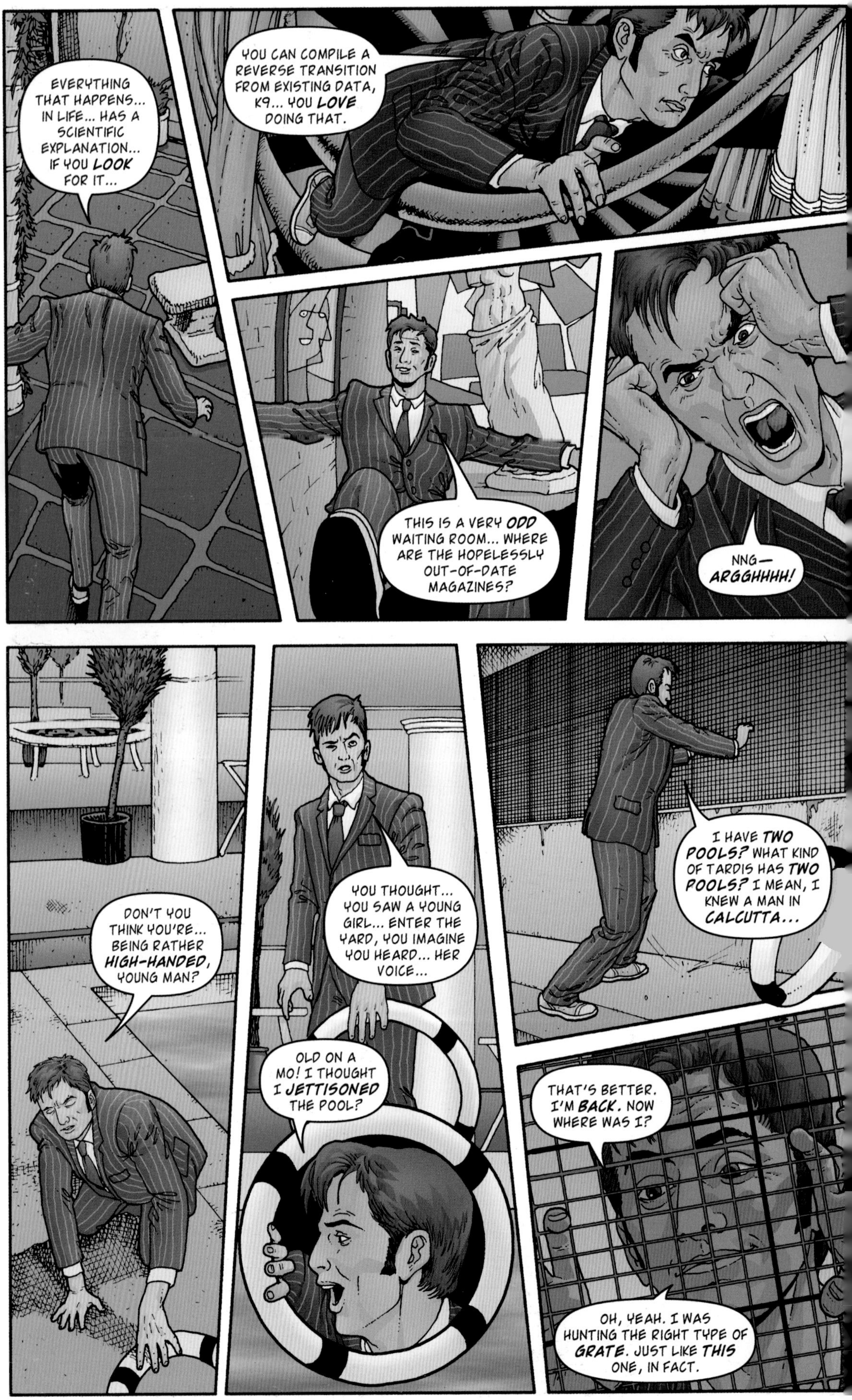
EVERYTHING THAT HAPPENS... IN LIFE... HAS A SCIENTIFIC EXPLANATION... IF YOU LOOK FOR IT...
YOU CAN COMPILE A REVERSE TRANSITION FROM EXISTING DATA, K9... YOU LOVE DOING THAT.
THIS IS A VERY ODD WAITING ROOM... WHERE ARE THE HOPELESSLY OUT-OF-DATE MAGAZINES?
NNG— ARGGHHHH!
DON'T YOU THINK YOU'RE... BEING RATHER HIGH-HANDED, YOUNG MAN?
YOU THOUGHT... YOU SAW A YOUNG GIRL... ENTER THE YARD, YOU IMAGINE YOU HEARD... HER VOICE...
OLD ON A MO! I THOUGHT I JETTISONED THE POOL?
I HAVE TWO POOLS? WHAT KIND OF TARDIS HAS TWO POOLS? I MEAN, I KNEW A MAN IN CALCUTTA...
THAT'S BETTER. I'M BACK. NOW WHERE WAS I?
OH, YEAH. I WAS HUNTING THE RIGHT TYPE OF GRATE. JUST LIKE THIS ONE, IN FACT.

THIS PLACE IS AN *INSANE ASYLUM*... AND *I'M* THE INMATE.

HOW MANY *ROOMS* DOES IT HAVE, ANYWAY? AND HOW MANY BEFORE I FIND THE—

—AH.

THIS IS IT, MATTHEW. YOUR CHANCE TO BE THE *HERO*.

ALL YOU HAVE TO DO IS PUT THE CRANK THING INTO THE HOLE WHATSIT AND YOU *SAVE EVERYONE.* IT'S EASY.

IF IT'S SO *EASY,* WHY HASN'T THE DOCTOR ALREADY *DONE* IT?

IS IT A TRICK? A *TRICK* TO GET RID OF ME SO HE CAN KEEP EMILY TO HIMSELF?

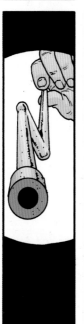

I—I *DON'T KNOW WHAT TO DO!*

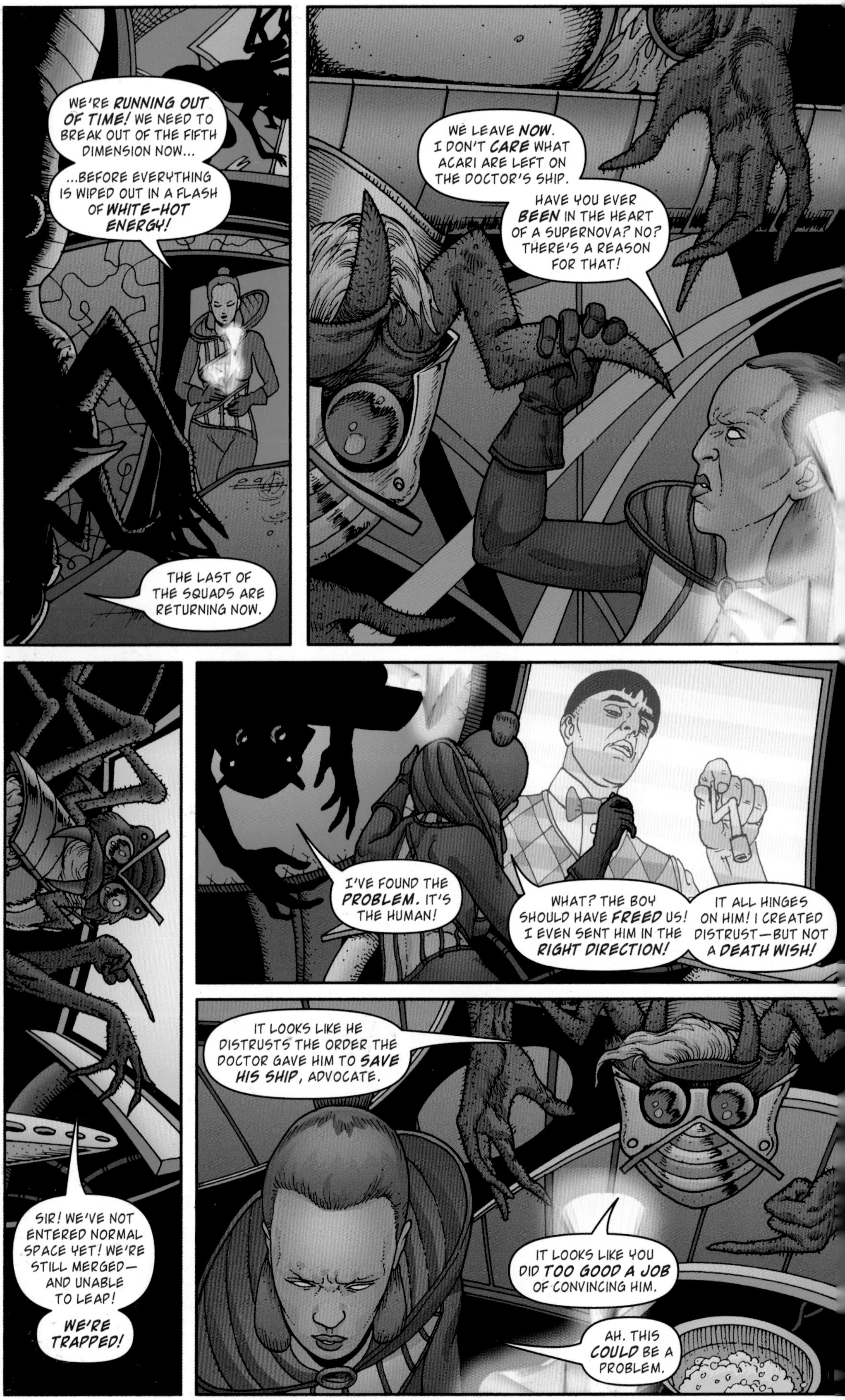
WE'RE **RUNNING OUT OF TIME!** WE NEED TO BREAK OUT OF THE FIFTH DIMENSION NOW...
...BEFORE EVERYTHING IS WIPED OUT IN A FLASH OF **WHITE-HOT ENERGY!**
THE LAST OF THE SQUADS ARE RETURNING NOW.
WE LEAVE **NOW**. I DON'T **CARE** WHAT ACARI ARE LEFT ON THE DOCTOR'S SHIP.
HAVE YOU EVER **BEEN** IN THE HEART OF A SUPERNOVA? NO? THERE'S A REASON FOR THAT!
I'VE FOUND THE **PROBLEM.** IT'S THE HUMAN!
WHAT? THE BOY SHOULD HAVE **FREED** US! I EVEN SENT HIM IN THE **RIGHT DIRECTION!**
IT ALL HINGES ON HIM! I CREATED DISTRUST—BUT NOT A **DEATH WISH!**
SIR! WE'VE NOT ENTERED NORMAL SPACE YET! WE'RE STILL MERGED—AND UNABLE TO LEAP!
WE'RE TRAPPED!
IT LOOKS LIKE HE DISTRUSTS THE ORDER THE DOCTOR GAVE HIM TO **SAVE HIS SHIP**, ADVOCATE.
IT LOOKS LIKE YOU DID **TOO GOOD A JOB** OF CONVINCING HIM.
AH. THIS **COULD** BE A PROBLEM.

CLANK

BONG

BONG

THE *CLOISTER BELL!* WE'RE ALMOST OUT OF TIME!

BONG BONG

CAN'T... THINK... NEED TO— *ARRGHH!* MUSTN'T... STOP NOW...

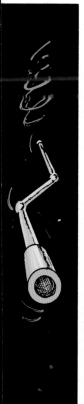

CLANK

IF CAPTAIN... JACK COULD... SEE ME NOW... ...IT'D MAKE HIS...

BONG BONG

I—I DON'T BELIEVE IT. I'M *TOO LATE!*

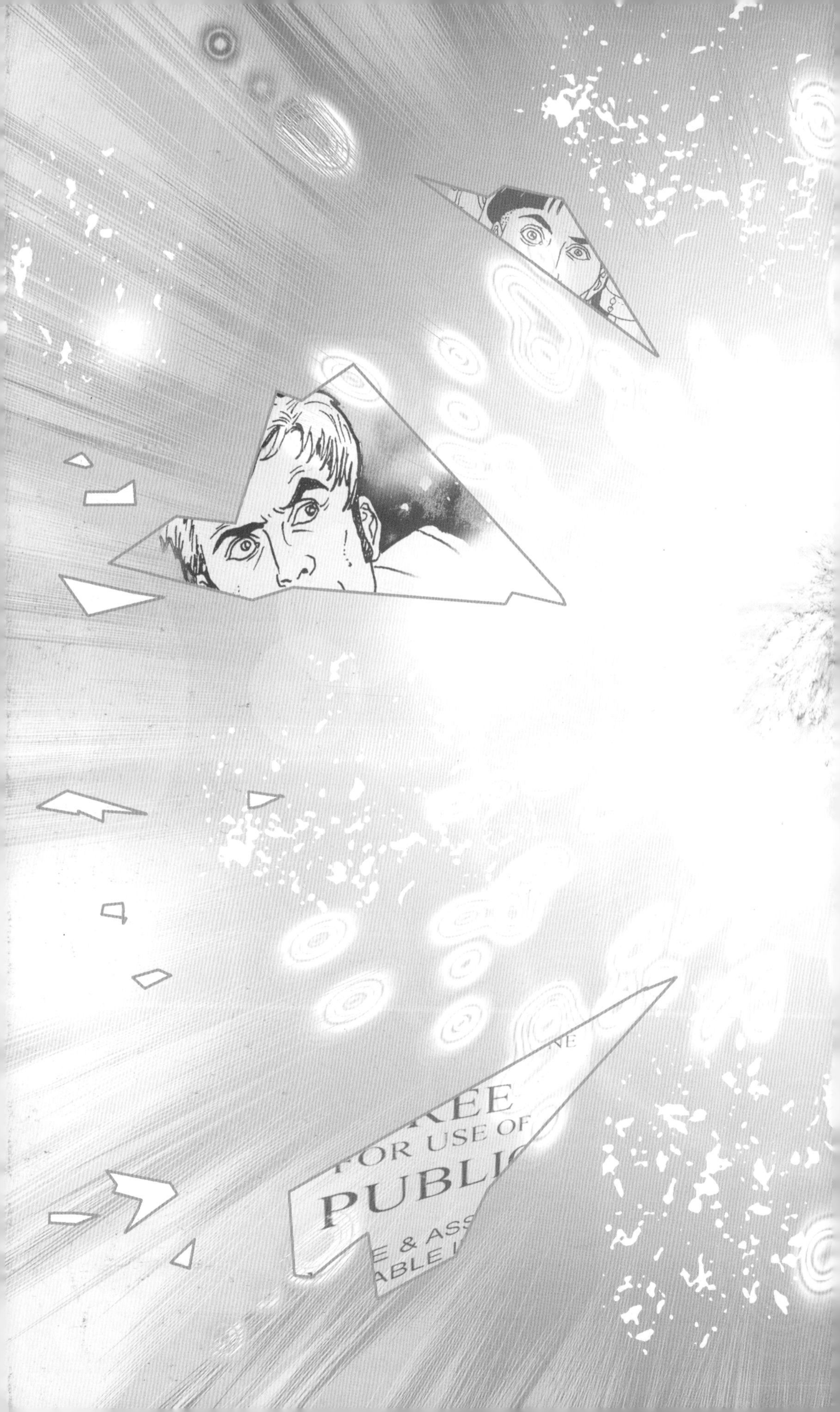
NE
REE
FOR USE OF
PUBLI
E & ASS
ABLE L

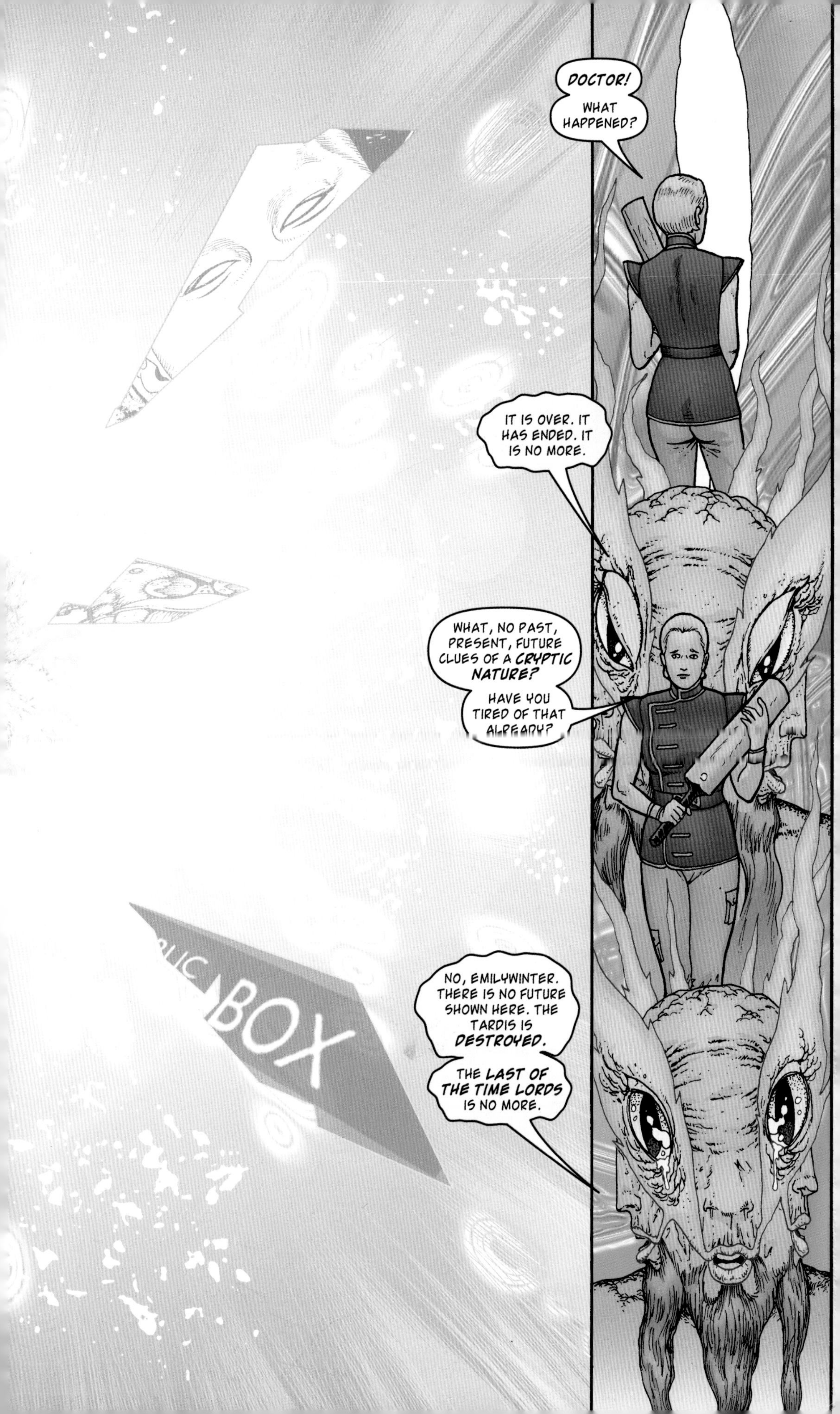
BOX
DOCTOR!
WHAT HAPPENED?
IT IS OVER. IT HAS ENDED. IT IS NO MORE.
WHAT, NO PAST, PRESENT, FUTURE CLUES OF A CRYPTIC NATURE?
HAVE YOU TIRED OF THAT ALREADY?
NO, EMILYWINTER. THERE IS NO FUTURE SHOWN HERE. THE TARDIS IS DESTROYED.
THE LAST OF THE TIME LORDS IS NO MORE.

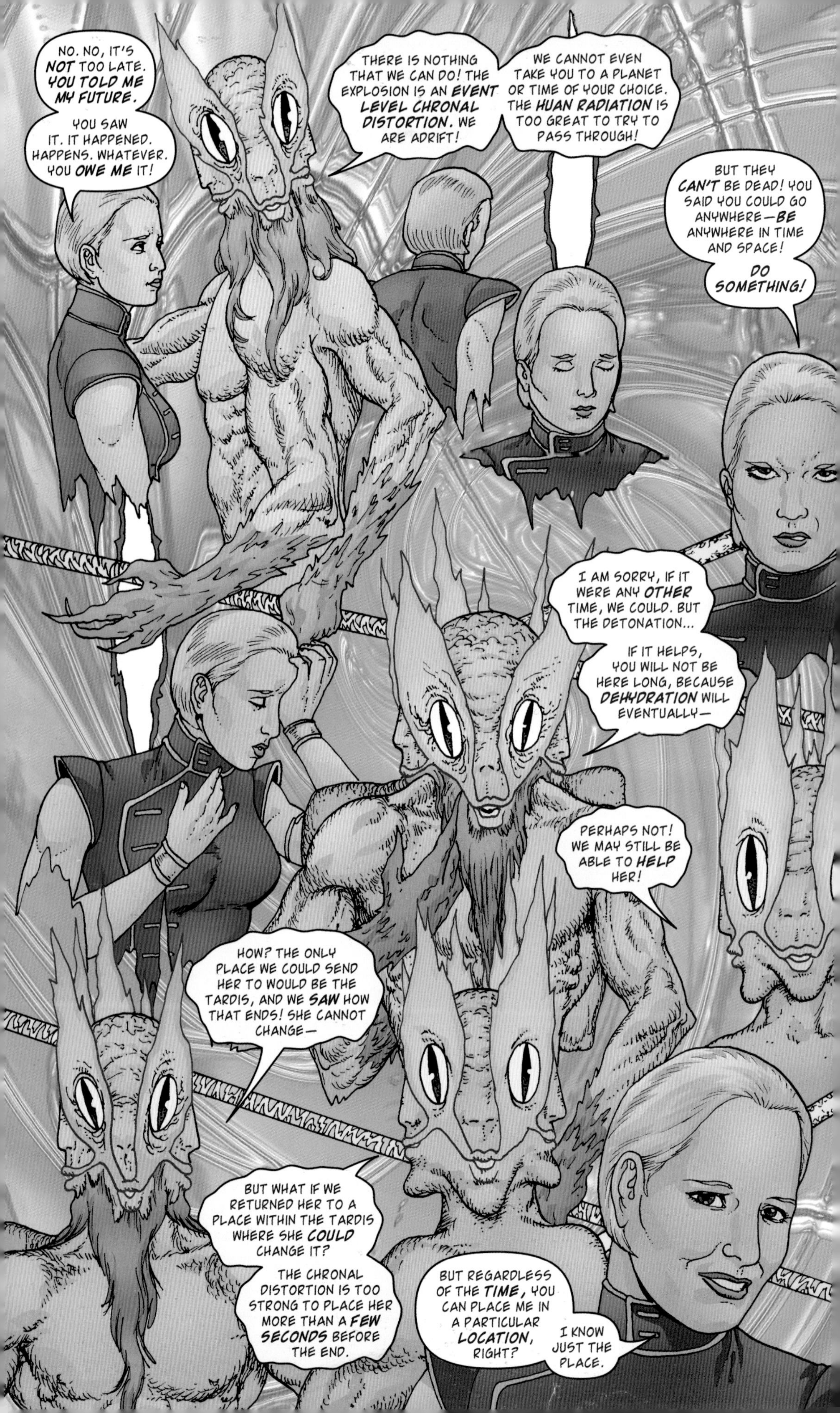
NO. NO, IT'S NOT TOO LATE. YOU TOLD ME MY FUTURE.
YOU SAW IT. IT HAPPENED. HAPPENS. WHATEVER. YOU OWE ME IT!
THERE IS NOTHING THAT WE CAN DO! THE EXPLOSION IS AN EVENT LEVEL CHRONAL DISTORTION. WE ARE ADRIFT!
WE CANNOT EVEN TAKE YOU TO A PLANET OR TIME OF YOUR CHOICE. THE HUAN RADIATION IS TOO GREAT TO TRY TO PASS THROUGH!
BUT THEY CAN'T BE DEAD! YOU SAID YOU COULD GO ANYWHERE—BE ANYWHERE IN TIME AND SPACE!
DO SOMETHING!
I AM SORRY, IF IT WERE ANY OTHER TIME, WE COULD. BUT THE DETONATION...
IF IT HELPS, YOU WILL NOT BE HERE LONG, BECAUSE DEHYDRATION WILL EVENTUALLY—
PERHAPS NOT! WE MAY STILL BE ABLE TO HELP HER!
HOW? THE ONLY PLACE WE COULD SEND HER TO WOULD BE THE TARDIS, AND WE SAW HOW THAT ENDS! SHE CANNOT CHANGE—
BUT WHAT IF WE RETURNED HER TO A PLACE WITHIN THE TARDIS WHERE SHE COULD CHANGE IT?
THE CHRONAL DISTORTION IS TOO STRONG TO PLACE HER MORE THAN A FEW SECONDS BEFORE THE END.
BUT REGARDLESS OF THE TIME, YOU CAN PLACE ME IN A PARTICULAR LOCATION, RIGHT?
I KNOW JUST THE PLACE.

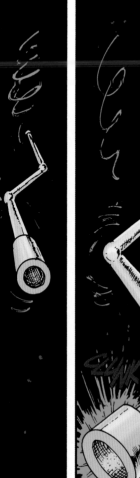

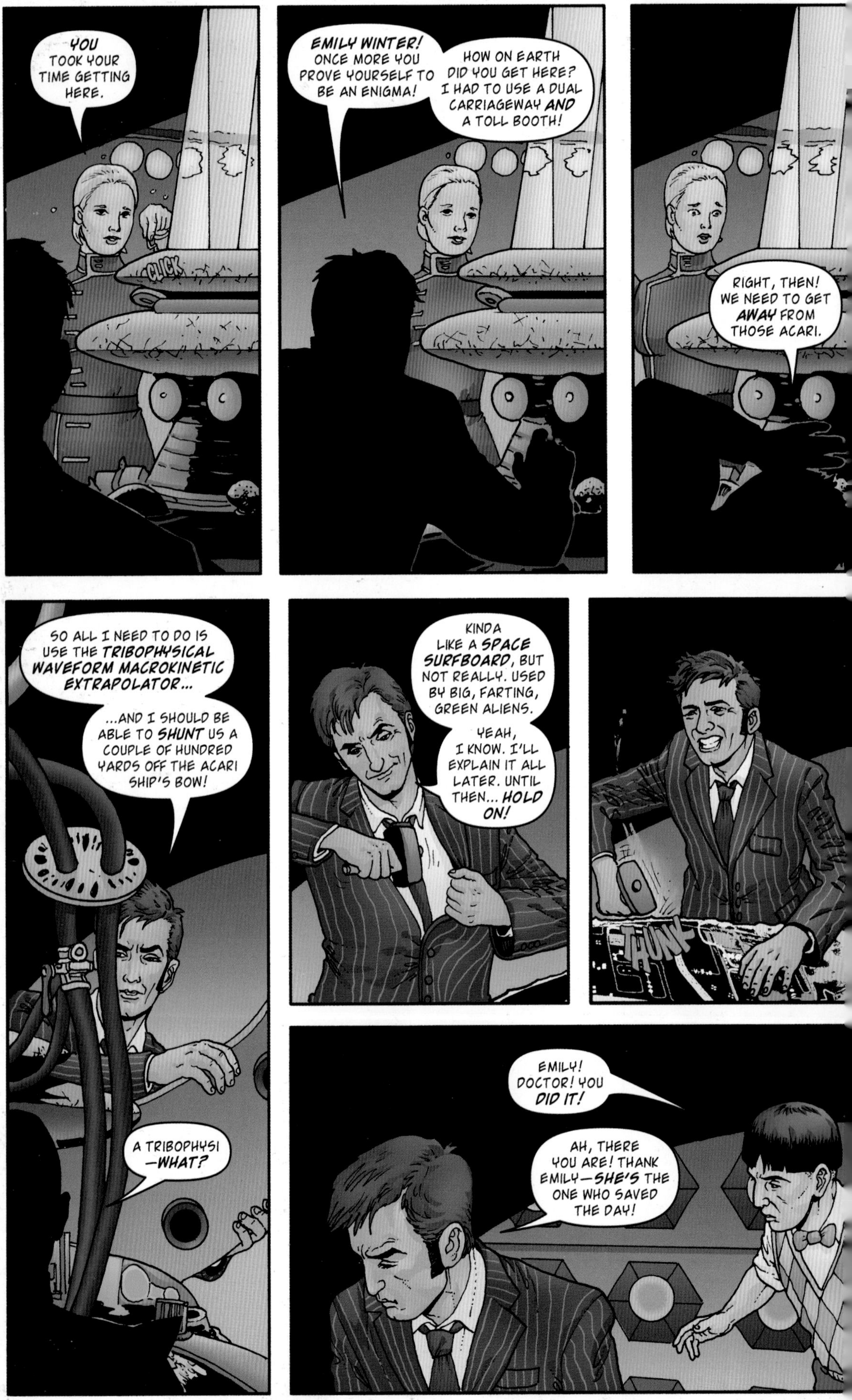

YOU TOOK YOUR TIME GETTING HERE.
CLICK
EMILY WINTER! ONCE MORE YOU PROVE YOURSELF TO BE AN ENIGMA!
HOW ON EARTH DID YOU GET HERE? I HAD TO USE A DUAL CARRIAGEWAY AND A TOLL BOOTH!
RIGHT, THEN! WE NEED TO GET AWAY FROM THOSE ACARI.
SO ALL I NEED TO DO IS USE THE TRIBOPHYSICAL WAVEFORM MACROKINETIC EXTRAPOLATOR...
...AND I SHOULD BE ABLE TO SHUNT US A COUPLE OF HUNDRED YARDS OFF THE ACARI SHIP'S BOW!
A TRIBOPHYSI—WHAT?
KINDA LIKE A SPACE SURFBOARD, BUT NOT REALLY. USED BY BIG, FARTING, GREEN ALIENS.
YEAH, I KNOW. I'LL EXPLAIN IT ALL LATER. UNTIL THEN... HOLD ON!
THUNK
EMILY! DOCTOR! YOU DID IT!
AH, THERE YOU ARE! THANK EMILY—SHE'S THE ONE WHO SAVED THE DAY!

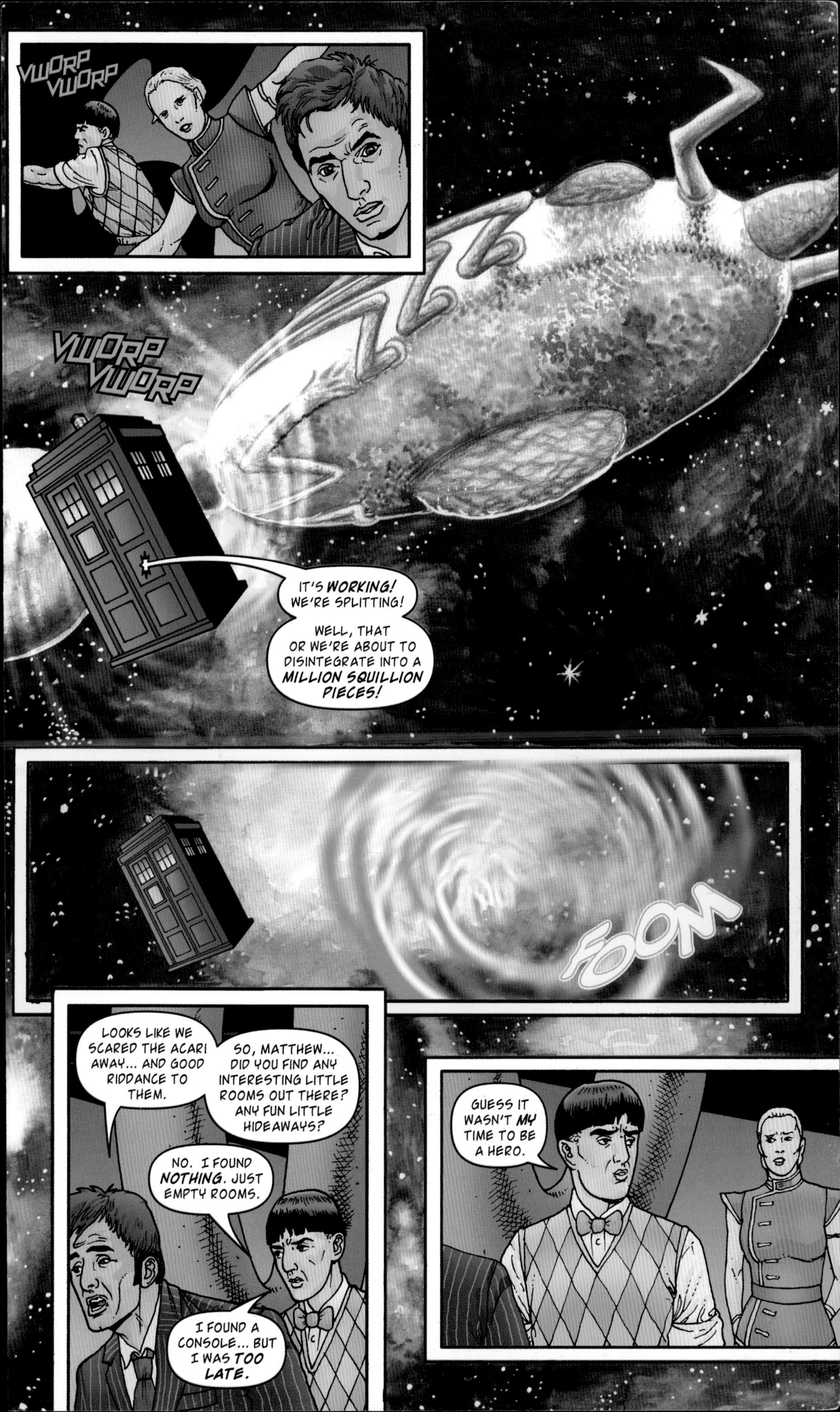
VWORP VWORP
VWORP VWORP
IT'S **WORKING!** WE'RE SPLITTING!
WELL, THAT OR WE'RE ABOUT TO DISINTEGRATE INTO A **MILLION SQUILLION PIECES!**
FOOM
LOOKS LIKE WE SCARED THE ACARI AWAY... AND GOOD RIDDANCE TO THEM.
SO, MATTHEW... DID YOU FIND ANY INTERESTING LITTLE ROOMS OUT THERE? ANY FUN LITTLE HIDEAWAYS?
NO. I FOUND **NOTHING**. JUST EMPTY ROOMS.
I FOUND A CONSOLE... BUT I WAS **TOO LATE**.
GUESS IT WASN'T **MY** TIME TO BE A HERO.

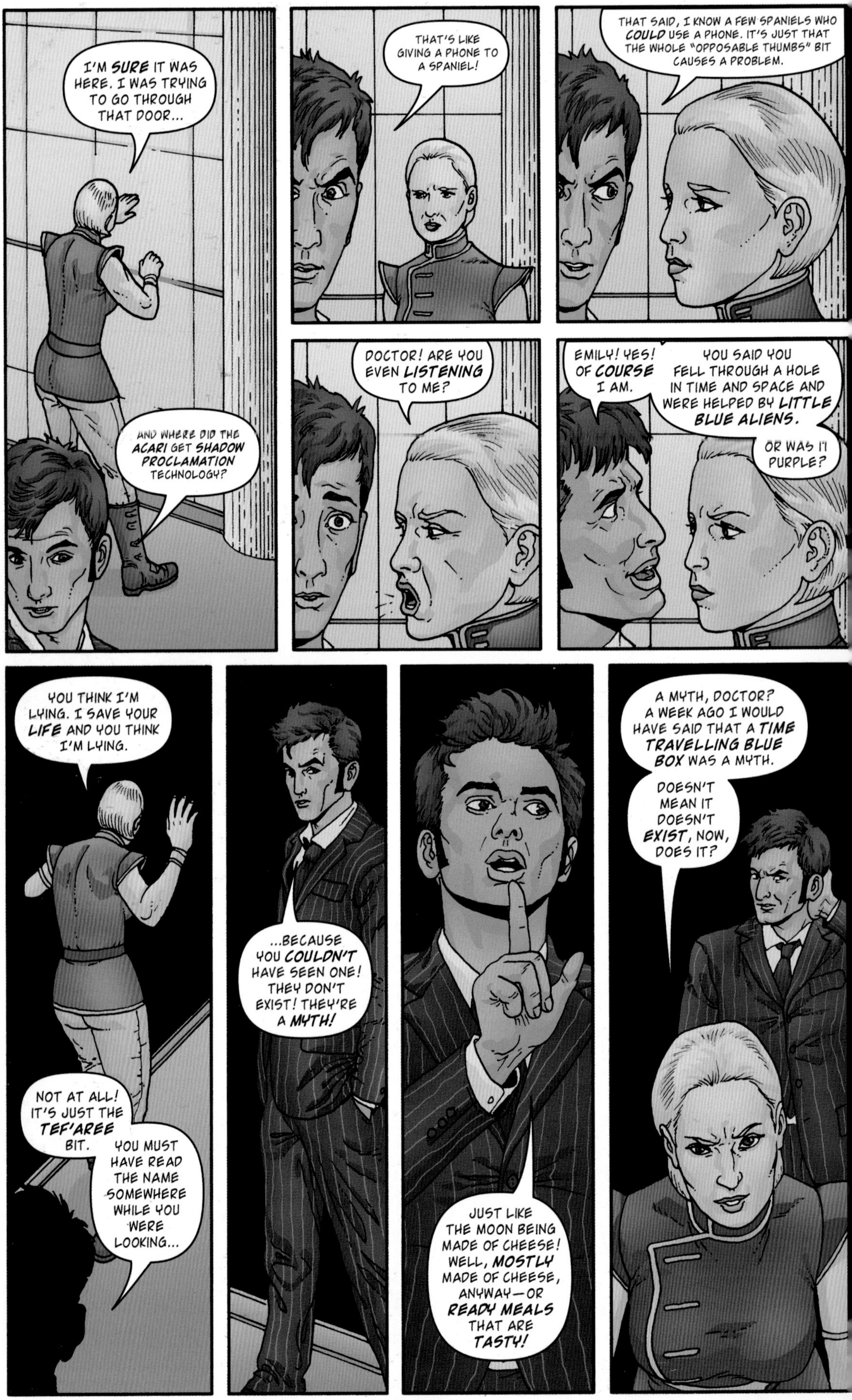

I'M SURE IT WAS HERE. I WAS TRYING TO GO THROUGH THAT DOOR...
AND WHERE DID THE ACARI GET SHADOW PROCLAMATION TECHNOLOGY?
THAT'S LIKE GIVING A PHONE TO A SPANIEL!
THAT SAID, I KNOW A FEW SPANIELS WHO COULD USE A PHONE. IT'S JUST THAT THE WHOLE "OPPOSABLE THUMBS" BIT CAUSES A PROBLEM.
DOCTOR! ARE YOU EVEN LISTENING TO ME?
EMILY! YES! OF COURSE I AM.
YOU SAID YOU FELL THROUGH A HOLE IN TIME AND SPACE AND WERE HELPED BY LITTLE BLUE ALIENS.
OR WAS IT PURPLE?
YOU THINK I'M LYING. I SAVE YOUR LIFE AND YOU THINK I'M LYING.
NOT AT ALL! IT'S JUST THE TEF'AREE BIT.
YOU MUST HAVE READ THE NAME SOMEWHERE WHILE YOU WERE LOOKING...
...BECAUSE YOU COULDN'T HAVE SEEN ONE! THEY DON'T EXIST! THEY'RE A MYTH!
JUST LIKE THE MOON BEING MADE OF CHEESE! WELL, MOSTLY MADE OF CHEESE, ANYWAY—OR READY MEALS THAT ARE TASTY!
A MYTH, DOCTOR? A WEEK AGO I WOULD HAVE SAID THAT A TIME TRAVELLING BLUE BOX WAS A MYTH.
DOESN'T MEAN IT DOESN'T EXIST, NOW, DOES IT?

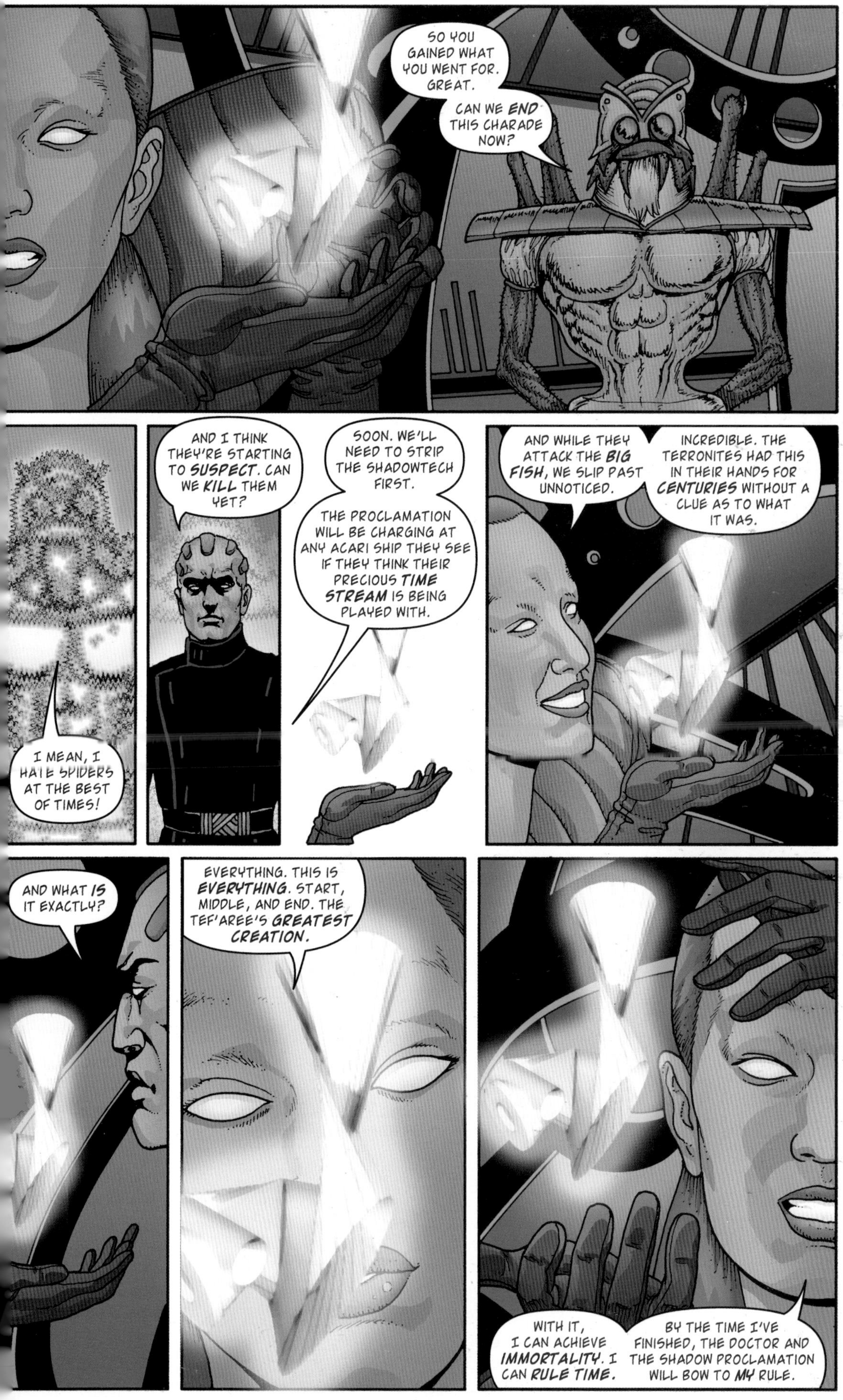
SO YOU GAINED WHAT YOU WENT FOR. GREAT.
CAN WE END THIS CHARADE NOW?
AND I THINK THEY'RE STARTING TO SUSPECT. CAN WE KILL THEM YET?
I MEAN, I HATE SPIDERS AT THE BEST OF TIMES!
SOON. WE'LL NEED TO STRIP THE SHADOWTECH FIRST.
THE PROCLAMATION WILL BE CHARGING AT ANY ACARI SHIP THEY SEE IF THEY THINK THEIR PRECIOUS TIME STREAM IS BEING PLAYED WITH.
AND WHILE THEY ATTACK THE BIG FISH, WE SLIP PAST UNNOTICED.
INCREDIBLE. THE TERRONITES HAD THIS IN THEIR HANDS FOR CENTURIES WITHOUT A CLUE AS TO WHAT IT WAS.
AND WHAT IS IT EXACTLY?
EVERYTHING. THIS IS EVERYTHING. START, MIDDLE, AND END. THE TEF'AREE'S GREATEST CREATION.
WITH IT, I CAN ACHIEVE IMMORTALITY. I CAN RULE TIME.
BY THE TIME I'VE FINISHED, THE DOCTOR AND THE SHADOW PROCLAMATION WILL BOW TO MY RULE.

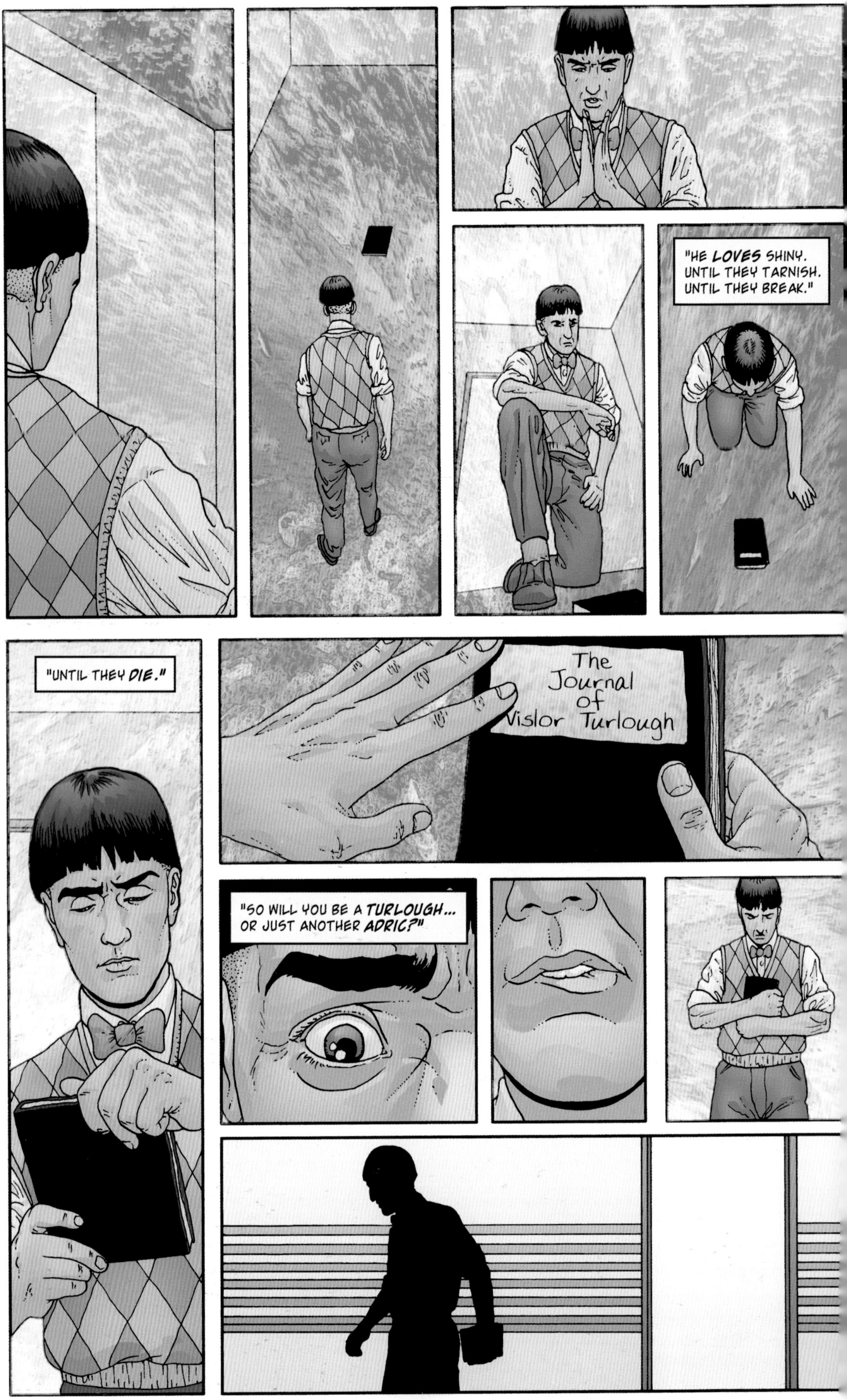
"HE LOVES SHINY.
UNTIL THEY TARNISH.
UNTIL THEY BREAK."
"UNTIL THEY DIE."
The Journal of Vislor Turlough
"SO WILL YOU BE A TURLOUGH... OR JUST ANOTHER ADRIC?"

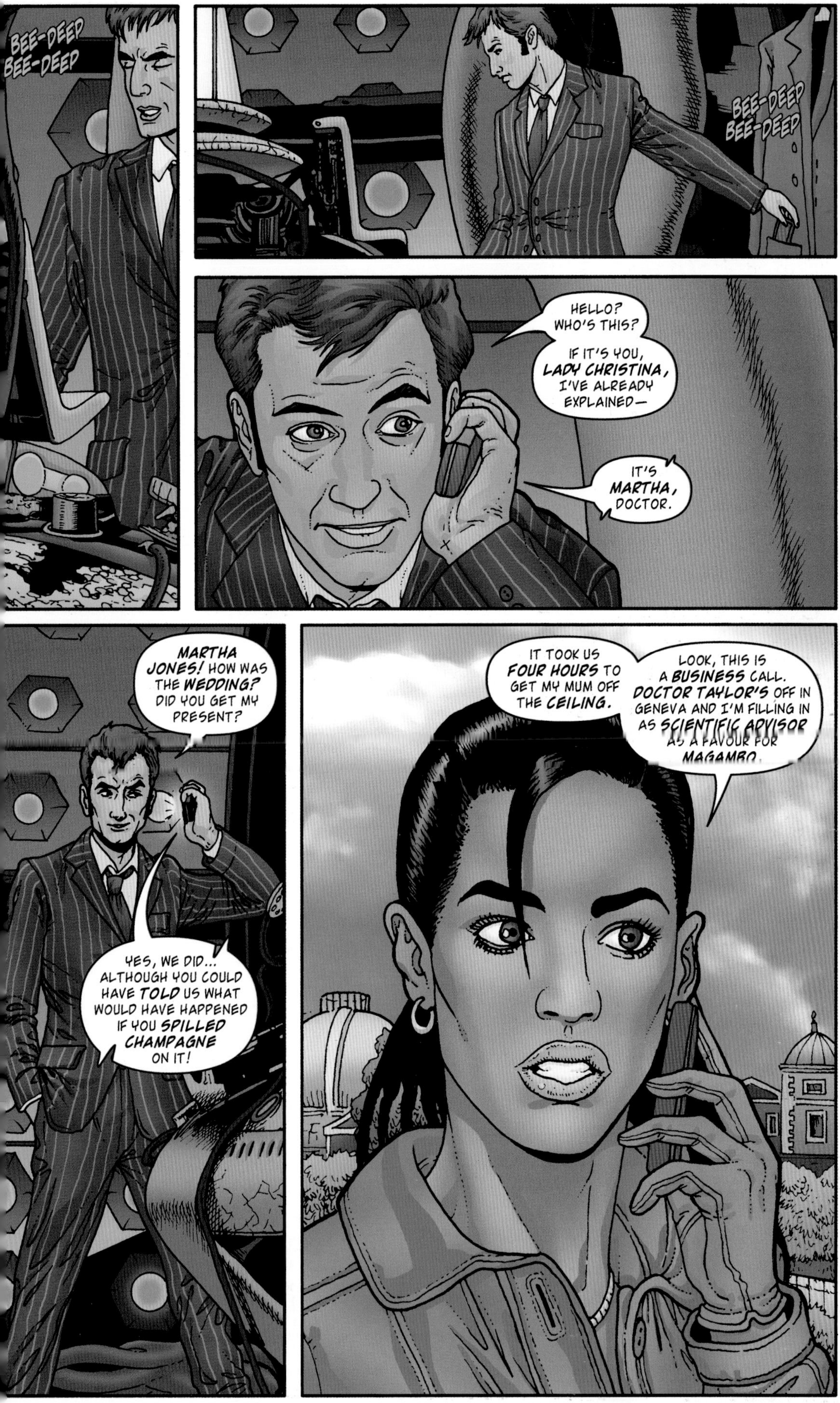
BEE-DEEP BEE-DEEP
BEE-DEEP BEE-DEEP
HELLO? WHO'S THIS?
IF IT'S YOU, LADY CHRISTINA, I'VE ALREADY EXPLAINED—
IT'S MARTHA, DOCTOR.
MARTHA JONES! HOW WAS THE WEDDING? DID YOU GET MY PRESENT?
YES, WE DID... ALTHOUGH YOU COULD HAVE TOLD US WHAT WOULD HAVE HAPPENED IF YOU SPILLED CHAMPAGNE ON IT!
IT TOOK US FOUR HOURS TO GET MY MUM OFF THE CEILING.
LOOK, THIS IS A BUSINESS CALL. DOCTOR TAYLOR'S OFF IN GENEVA AND I'M FILLING IN AS SCIENTIFIC ADVISOR AS A FAVOUR FOR MAGAMBO.

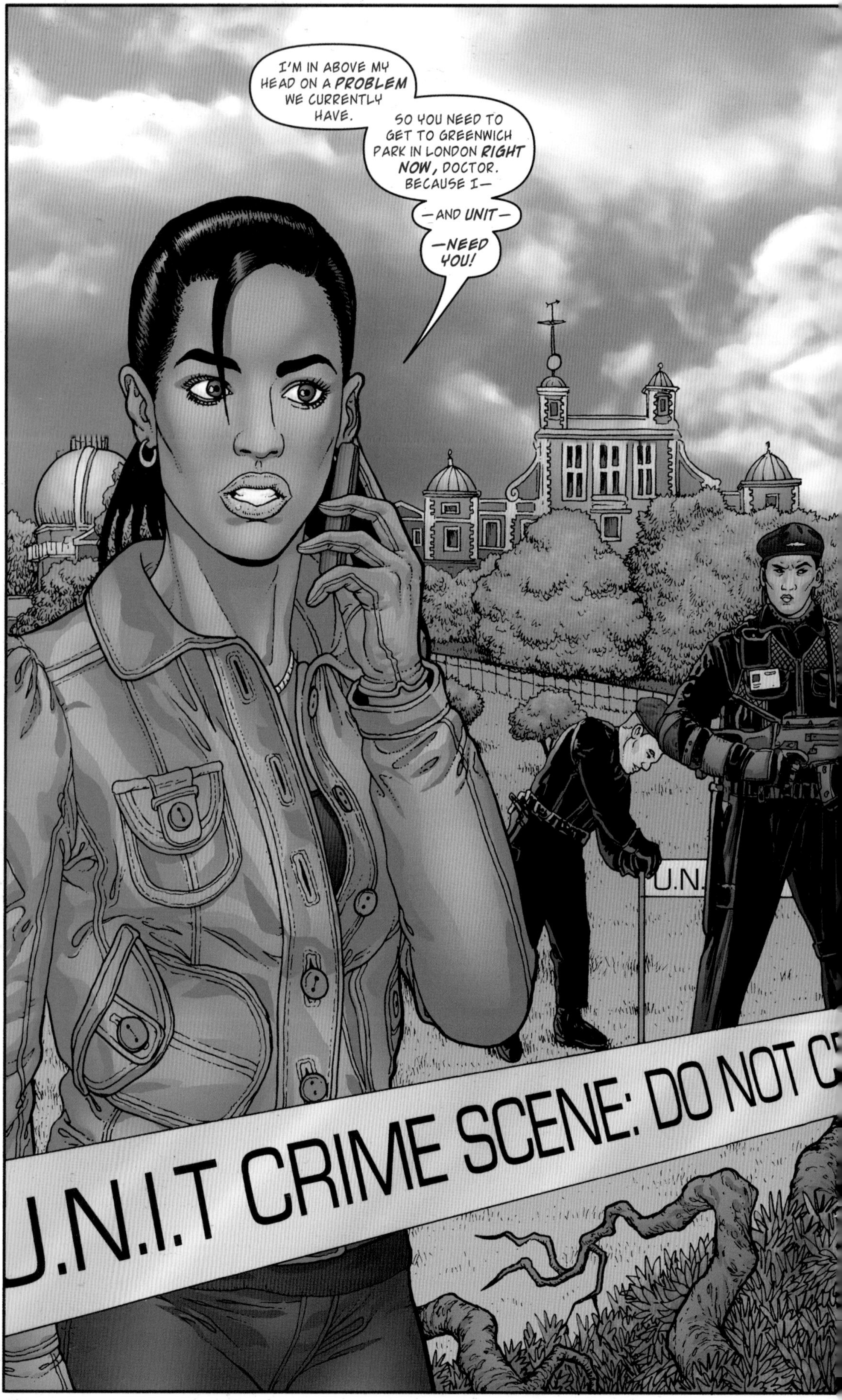

I'M IN ABOVE MY HEAD ON A PROBLEM WE CURRENTLY HAVE.
SO YOU NEED TO GET TO GREENWICH PARK IN LONDON RIGHT NOW, DOCTOR. BECAUSE I—
—AND UNIT—
—NEED YOU!
U.N.
U.N.I.T CRIME SCENE: DO NOT C

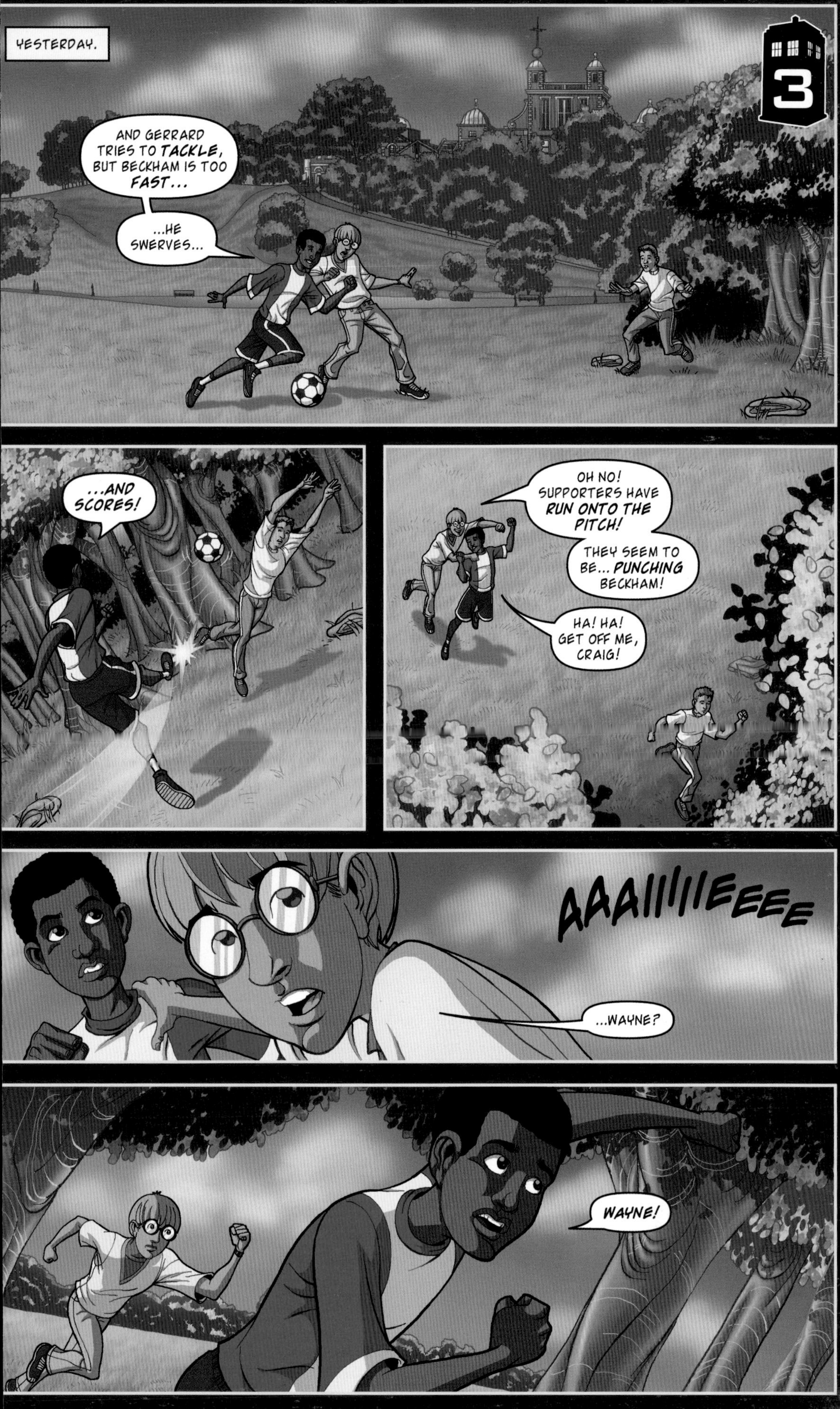

YESTERDAY.
3
AND GERRARD TRIES TO TACKLE, BUT BECKHAM IS TOO FAST...
...HE SWERVES...
...AND SCORES!
OH NO! SUPPORTERS HAVE RUN ONTO THE PITCH!
THEY SEEM TO BE... PUNCHING BECKHAM!
HA! HA! GET OFF ME, CRAIG!
AAAIIIIIEEEE
...WAYNE?
WAYNE!

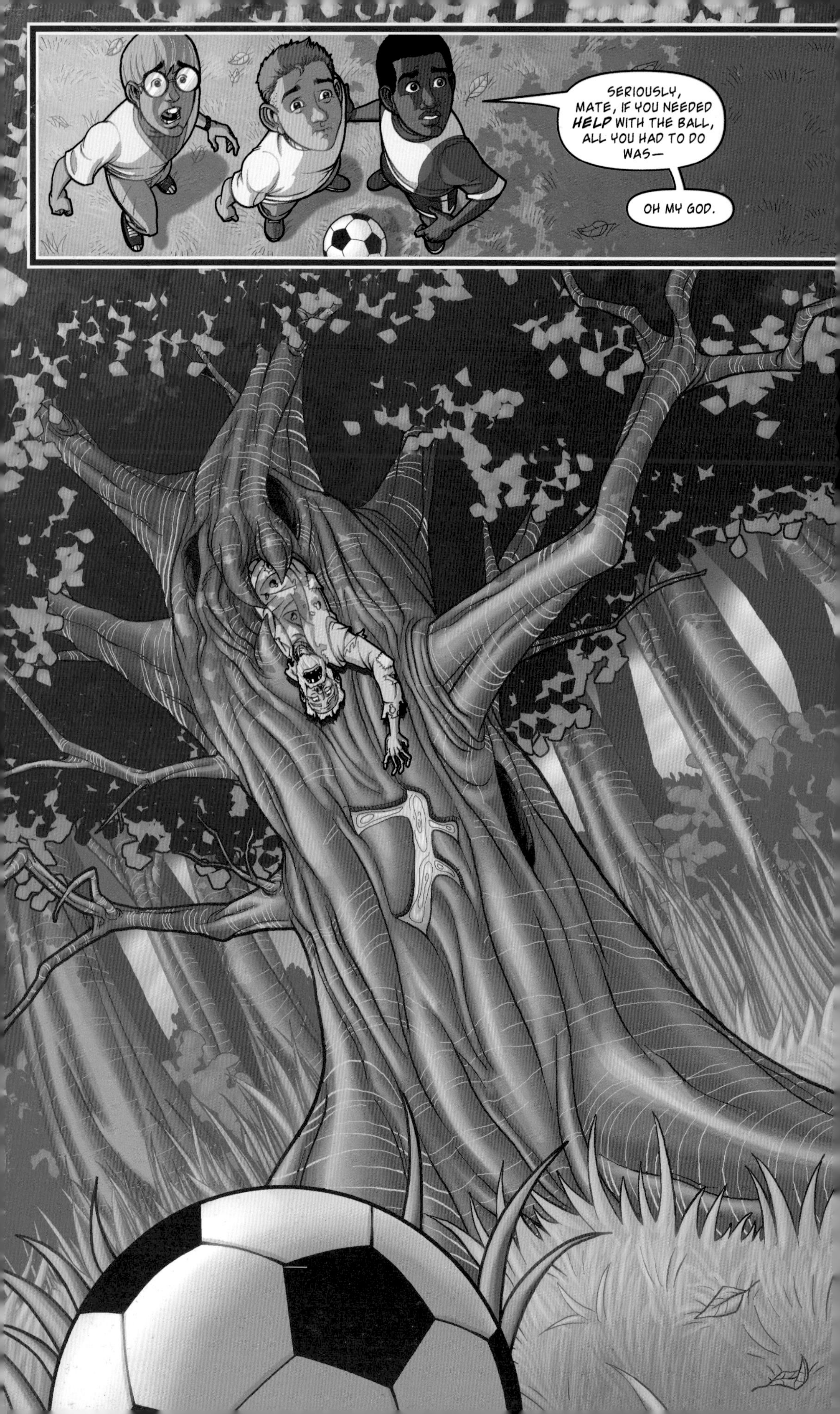
SERIOUSLY, MATE, IF YOU NEEDED **HELP** WITH THE BALL, ALL YOU HAD TO DO WAS—
OH MY GOD.

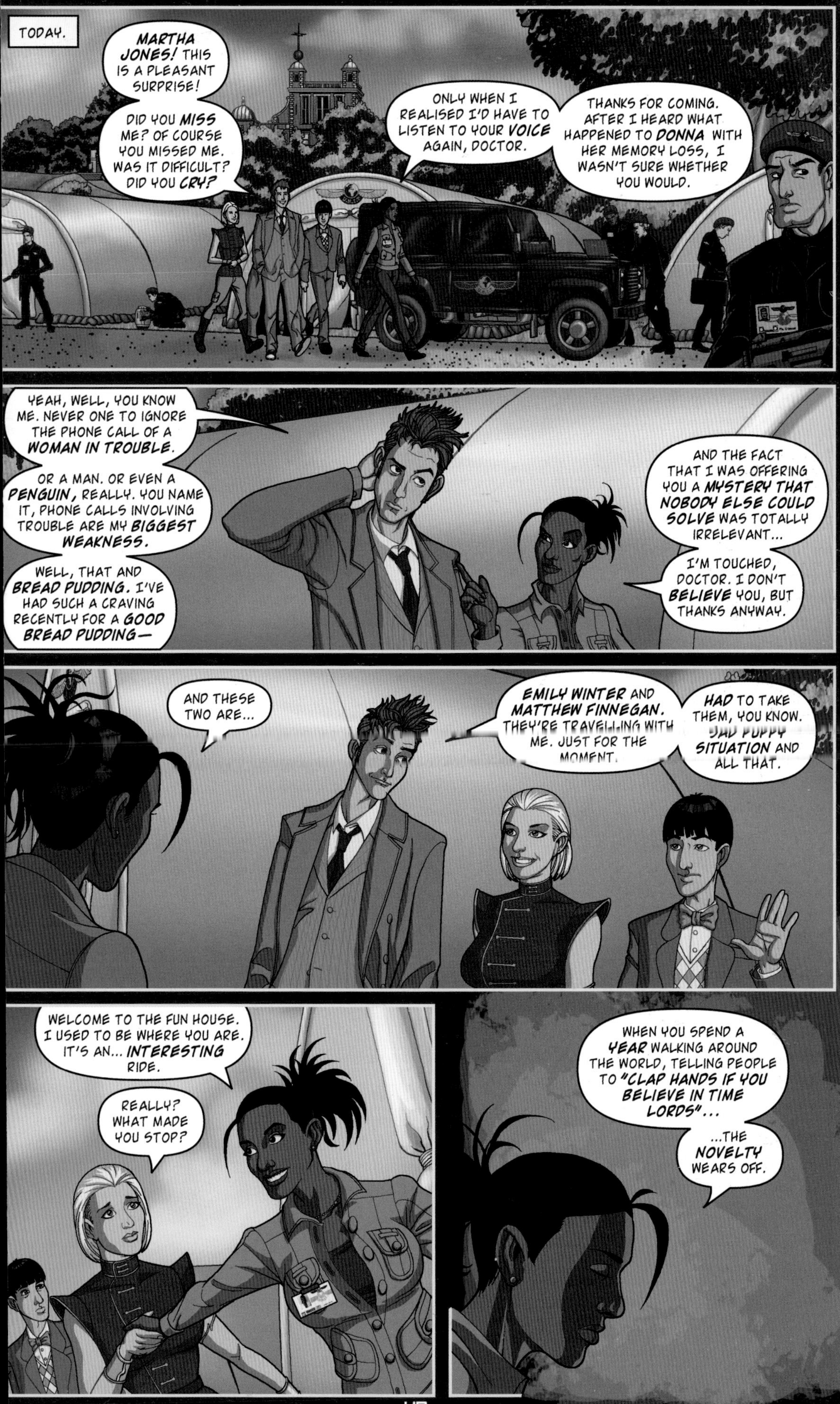

TODAY.
MARTHA JONES! THIS IS A PLEASANT SURPRISE!
DID YOU MISS ME? OF COURSE YOU MISSED ME. WAS IT DIFFICULT? DID YOU CRY?
ONLY WHEN I REALISED I'D HAVE TO LISTEN TO YOUR VOICE AGAIN, DOCTOR.
THANKS FOR COMING. AFTER I HEARD WHAT HAPPENED TO DONNA WITH HER MEMORY LOSS, I WASN'T SURE WHETHER YOU WOULD.
YEAH, WELL, YOU KNOW ME. NEVER ONE TO IGNORE THE PHONE CALL OF A WOMAN IN TROUBLE.
OR A MAN. OR EVEN A PENGUIN, REALLY. YOU NAME IT, PHONE CALLS INVOLVING TROUBLE ARE MY BIGGEST WEAKNESS.
WELL, THAT AND BREAD PUDDING. I'VE HAD SUCH A CRAVING RECENTLY FOR A GOOD BREAD PUDDING—
AND THE FACT THAT I WAS OFFERING YOU A MYSTERY THAT NOBODY ELSE COULD SOLVE WAS TOTALLY IRRELEVANT...
I'M TOUCHED, DOCTOR. I DON'T BELIEVE YOU, BUT THANKS ANYWAY.
AND THESE TWO ARE...
EMILY WINTER AND MATTHEW FINNEGAN. THEY'RE TRAVELLING WITH ME. JUST FOR THE MOMENT.
HAD TO TAKE THEM, YOU KNOW. SAD PUPPY SITUATION AND ALL THAT.
WELCOME TO THE FUN HOUSE. I USED TO BE WHERE YOU ARE. IT'S AN... INTERESTING RIDE.
REALLY? WHAT MADE YOU STOP?
WHEN YOU SPEND A YEAR WALKING AROUND THE WORLD, TELLING PEOPLE TO "CLAP HANDS IF YOU BELIEVE IN TIME LORDS"...
...THE NOVELTY WEARS OFF.

SO—SCIENTIFIC ADVISOR TO *UNIT*, EH? THOUGHT YOU'D WALKED AWAY FROM THEM AFTER THE *OSTERHAGEN* HEARINGS.

I DID. I'M PURELY FREELANCE, A SHORT-TERM THING. A FAVOUR TO *MALCOLM TAYLOR*.

HE'S IN *GENEVA* AT THE MOMENT— SOMETHING ABOUT PERU—SO I STEPPED IN WHEN THEY NEEDED ME.

MALCOLM'S SENT THREE TEXTS IN THE LAST *TEN MINUTES* ALONE. YOU HAVE NO IDEA HOW *FURIOUS* HE IS FOR MISSING YOU.

YOU'VE MADE MY *WEEK*, DOCTOR.

CAPTAIN MAGAMBO! NO SALUTE? YOU'RE LEARNING!

SO WHAT'S SO IMPORTANT THAT YOU JUST *HAD* TO INTERRUPT MY DAY? I WAS *THIS CLOSE* TO A CURE TO *BOLONIAN BOAR FLU!*

TEN QUID SAYS HE WAS READING A BOOK, HAVING A CUP OF TEA, OR SLEEPING.

I'M AFRAID I CAN'T SAY.

BUT I *WON'T* BE TAKING THAT BET, IF YOU KNOW WHAT I MEAN.

DON'T BE ANNOYED AT MARTHA FOR CALLING YOU, DOCTOR, SHE DIDN'T *WANT* TO. SHE FELT THIS WAS SOMETHING UNIT COULD FINISH ON OUR OWN.

IT WAS I WHO INVOKED THE *CODE NINE.*

SO—IT'S EITHER *REALLY BAD*, OR YOU HAVE A LACK OF *FAITH* IN ANYONE ELSE SOLVING THIS.

WHICH IS IT, MAGAMBO?

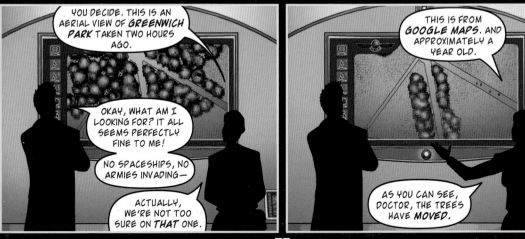

YOU DECIDE. THIS IS AN AERIAL VIEW OF *GREENWICH PARK* TAKEN TWO HOURS AGO.

OKAY, WHAT AM I LOOKING FOR? IT ALL SEEMS PERFECTLY FINE TO ME!

NO SPACESHIPS, NO ARMIES INVADING—

ACTUALLY, WE'RE NOT TOO SURE ON *THAT* ONE.

THIS IS FROM *GOOGLE MAPS*. AND APPROXIMATELY A YEAR OLD.

AS YOU CAN SEE, DOCTOR, THE TREES HAVE *MOVED.*

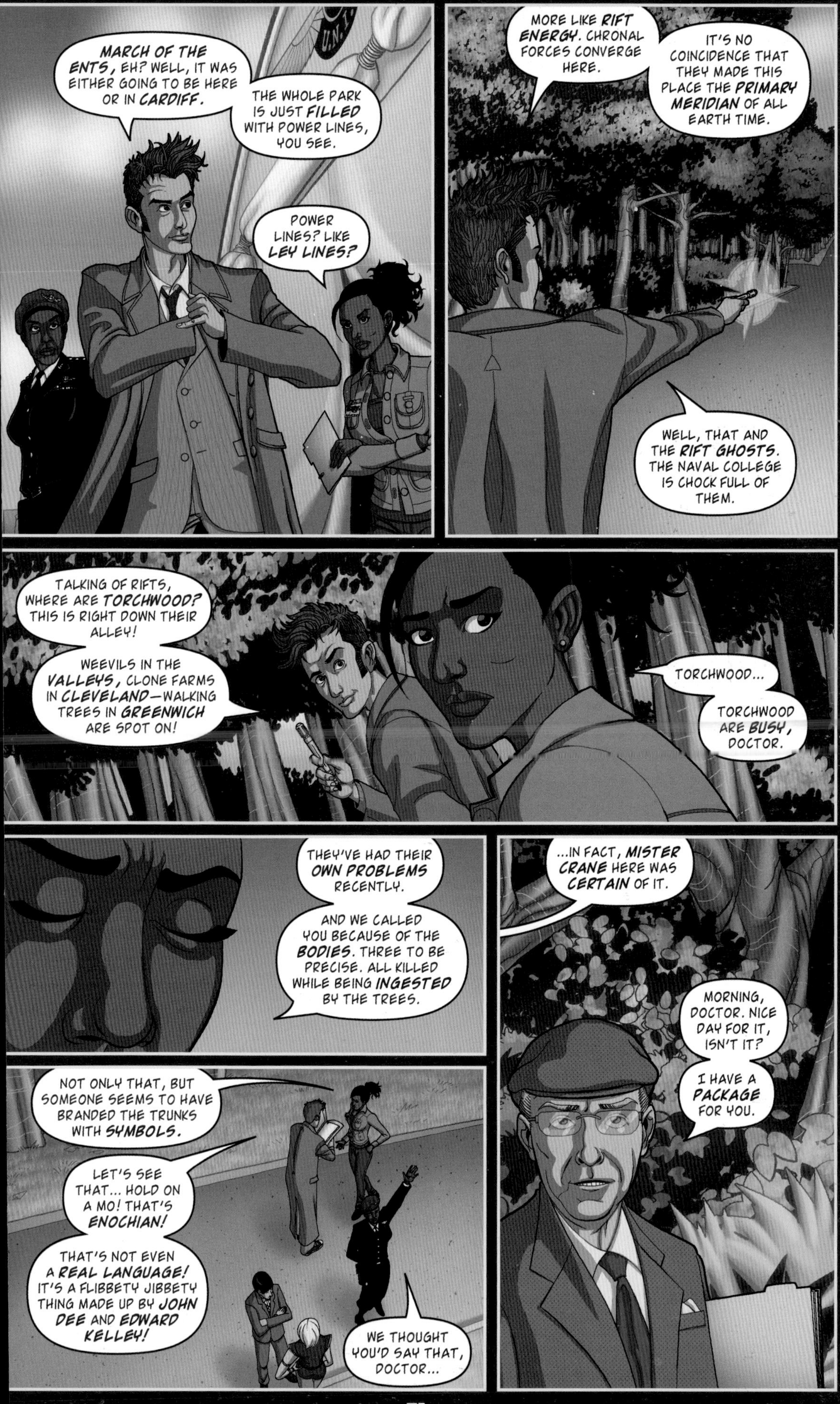
MARCH OF THE ENTS, EH? WELL, IT WAS EITHER GOING TO BE HERE OR IN CARDIFF.
THE WHOLE PARK IS JUST FILLED WITH POWER LINES, YOU SEE.
POWER LINES? LIKE LEY LINES?
MORE LIKE RIFT ENERGY. CHRONAL FORCES CONVERGE HERE.
IT'S NO COINCIDENCE THAT THEY MADE THIS PLACE THE PRIMARY MERIDIAN OF ALL EARTH TIME.
WELL, THAT AND THE RIFT GHOSTS. THE NAVAL COLLEGE IS CHOCK FULL OF THEM.
TALKING OF RIFTS, WHERE ARE TORCHWOOD? THIS IS RIGHT DOWN THEIR ALLEY!
WEEVILS IN THE VALLEYS, CLONE FARMS IN CLEVELAND—WALKING TREES IN GREENWICH ARE SPOT ON!
TORCHWOOD...
TORCHWOOD ARE BUSY, DOCTOR.
THEY'VE HAD THEIR OWN PROBLEMS RECENTLY.
AND WE CALLED YOU BECAUSE OF THE BODIES. THREE TO BE PRECISE. ALL KILLED WHILE BEING INGESTED BY THE TREES.
NOT ONLY THAT, BUT SOMEONE SEEMS TO HAVE BRANDED THE TRUNKS WITH SYMBOLS.
LET'S SEE THAT... HOLD ON A MO! THAT'S ENOCHIAN!
THAT'S NOT EVEN A REAL LANGUAGE! IT'S A FLIBBETY JIBBETY THING MADE UP BY JOHN DEE AND EDWARD KELLEY!
WE THOUGHT YOU'D SAY THAT, DOCTOR...
...IN FACT, MISTER CRANE HERE WAS CERTAIN OF IT.
MORNING, DOCTOR. NICE DAY FOR IT, ISN'T IT?
I HAVE A PACKAGE FOR YOU.

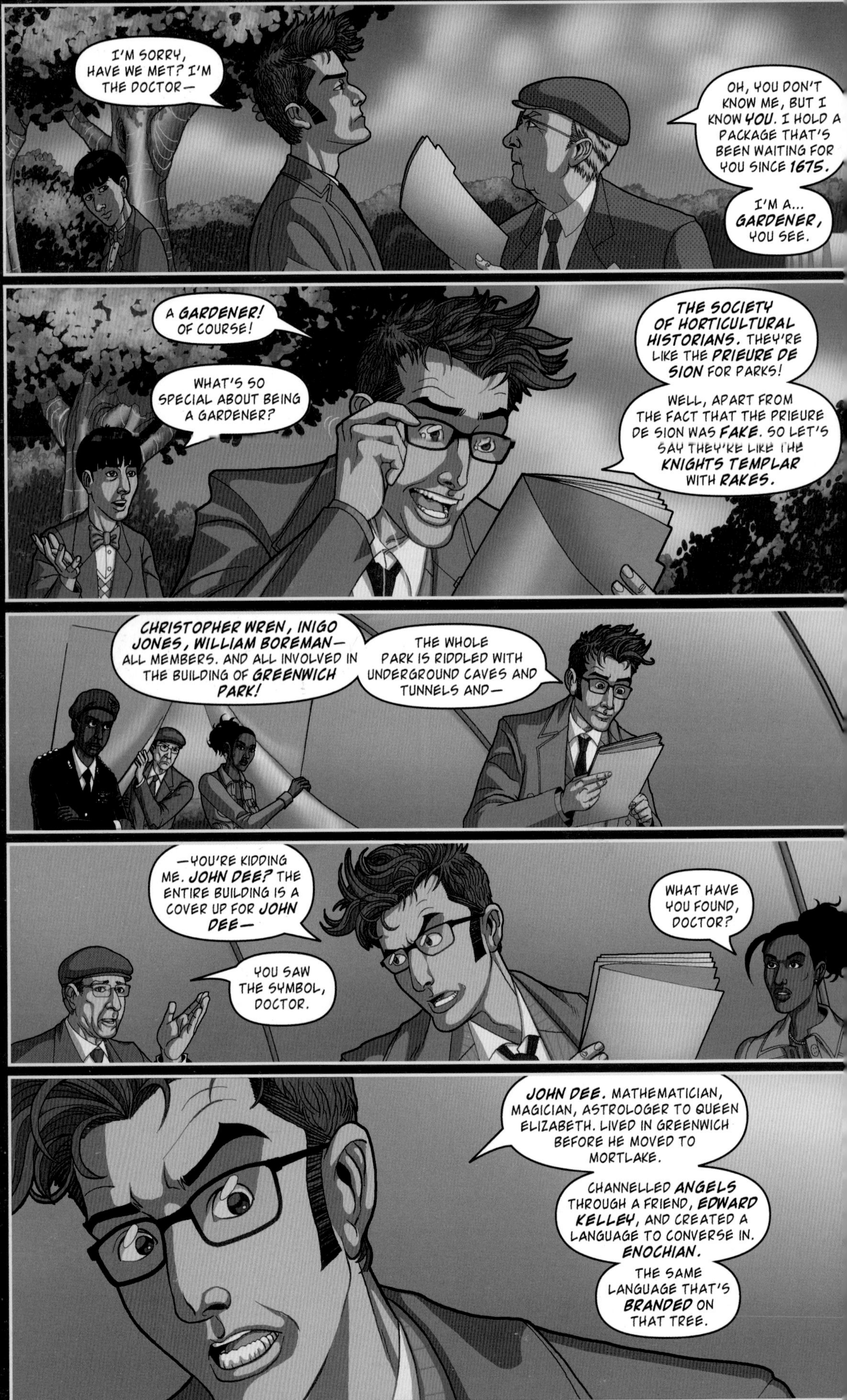
I'M SORRY, HAVE WE MET? I'M THE DOCTOR—
OH, YOU DON'T KNOW ME, BUT I KNOW YOU. I HOLD A PACKAGE THAT'S BEEN WAITING FOR YOU SINCE 1675.
I'M A... GARDENER, YOU SEE.
A GARDENER! OF COURSE!
WHAT'S SO SPECIAL ABOUT BEING A GARDENER?
THE SOCIETY OF HORTICULTURAL HISTORIANS. THEY'RE LIKE THE PRIEURE DE SION FOR PARKS!
WELL, APART FROM THE FACT THAT THE PRIEURE DE SION WAS FAKE. SO LET'S SAY THEY'RE LIKE THE KNIGHTS TEMPLAR WITH RAKES.
CHRISTOPHER WREN, INIGO JONES, WILLIAM BOREMAN— ALL MEMBERS. AND ALL INVOLVED IN THE BUILDING OF GREENWICH PARK!
THE WHOLE PARK IS RIDDLED WITH UNDERGROUND CAVES AND TUNNELS AND—
—YOU'RE KIDDING ME. JOHN DEE? THE ENTIRE BUILDING IS A COVER UP FOR JOHN DEE—
WHAT HAVE YOU FOUND, DOCTOR?
YOU SAW THE SYMBOL, DOCTOR.
JOHN DEE. MATHEMATICIAN, MAGICIAN, ASTROLOGER TO QUEEN ELIZABETH. LIVED IN GREENWICH BEFORE HE MOVED TO MORTLAKE.
CHANNELLED ANGELS THROUGH A FRIEND, EDWARD KELLEY, AND CREATED A LANGUAGE TO CONVERSE IN. ENOCHIAN.
THE SAME LANGUAGE THAT'S BRANDED ON THAT TREE.

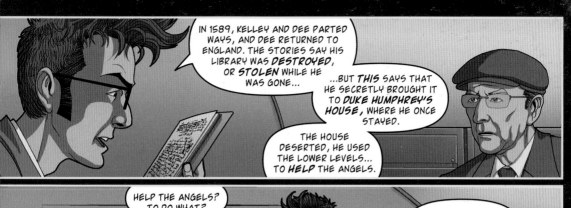

IN 1589, KELLEY AND DEE PARTED WAYS, AND DEE RETURNED TO ENGLAND. THE STORIES SAY HIS LIBRARY WAS **DESTROYED**, OR **STOLEN** WHILE HE WAS GONE...

...BUT **THIS** SAYS THAT HE SECRETLY BROUGHT IT TO **DUKE HUMPHREY'S HOUSE**, WHERE HE ONCE STAYED.

THE HOUSE DESERTED, HE USED THE LOWER LEVELS... TO **HELP** THE ANGELS.

HELP THE ANGELS? TO DO WHAT?

IT DOESN'T SAY. IT SIMPLY STATES THAT HE TRIED TO **DESTROY** THEM, BUT THEN CHANGED HIS MIND.

HE SEALED THEM DEEP IN THE CELLARS AND GAVE HIS SERVANTS STRICT INSTRUCTIONS TO **NEVER** OPEN THE DOORS... UNLESS **"THE DOCTOR"** WAS THERE.

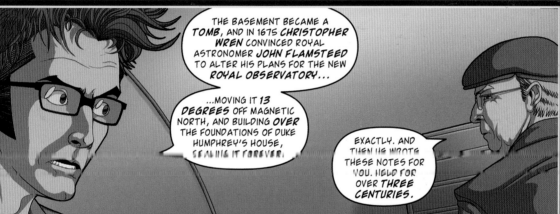

THE BASEMENT BECAME A **TOMB**, AND IN 1675 **CHRISTOPHER WREN** CONVINCED ROYAL ASTRONOMER **JOHN FLAMSTEED** TO ALTER HIS PLANS FOR THE NEW **ROYAL OBSERVATORY...**

...MOVING IT **13 DEGREES** OFF MAGNETIC NORTH, AND BUILDING **OVER** THE FOUNDATIONS OF DUKE HUMPHREY'S HOUSE, SEALING IT FOREVER.

EXACTLY. AND THEN HE WROTE THESE NOTES FOR YOU. HELD FOR OVER **THREE CENTURIES**.

ANGELS? HIDDEN ROOMS? WHAT DOES THIS HAVE TO DO WITH THE TREES?

EVERYTHING. IF I'M RIGHT, THEN THE "ANGELS" THAT DEE SPOKE TO HAVE BEEN TRAPPED UNDER THE OBSERVATORY FOR OVER **400 YEARS**—

—AND NOW THEY'RE **SICK** OF WAITING. THEY'VE FOUND A WAY OUT... THROUGH THE **PARK** ITSELF.

THE TREES AREN'T **BRANDED** WITH ENOCHIAN. THEY **ARE** ENOCHIAN. SENTIENT AND VERY, VERY **ANGRY**.

SO THIS TREE—IT'S ALIVE? I MEAN IT'S **EVIL** AND ALIVE?

WELL, EVIL ENOUGH TO THINK THAT AN **OLD MAN** IS A NOMMY SNACK.

BUT NOT ALIVE ENOUGH TO MARCH ACROSS A PARK GOING "HROOM HROOM, LITTLE HOBBIT."

REALLY? YOU'VE NEVER READ **LORD OF THE RINGS?**

I WAS A STUDIO RUNNER FROM THE AGE OF **FOURTEEN,** DOCTOR.

OBVIOUSLY A BOOK ABOUT TALKING TREES **WASN'T** TOP OF MY LIST.

IT'S NOT A BRAND. THAT SYMBOL WAS, WELL, **GROWN** THERE—WHICH MEANS THE TREE IS PROBABLY **CONTROLLED.**

MY MONEY'S ON WHATEVER'S UNDER THE OBSERVATORY.

WHY DID THE **GARDENERS** SEND THE LETTER TO **YOU?** HOW DID THEY **KNOW** ABOUT YOU?

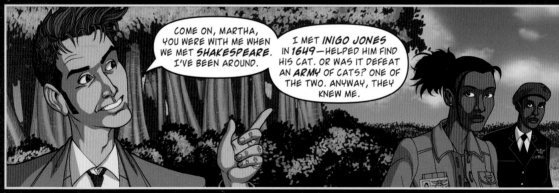

COME ON, MARTHA, YOU WERE WITH ME WHEN WE MET **SHAKESPEARE.** I'VE BEEN AROUND.

I MET **INIGO JONES** IN **1649**—HELPED HIM FIND HIS CAT. OR WAS IT DEFEAT AN **ARMY** OF CATS? ONE OF THE TWO. ANYWAY, THEY KNEW ME.

YOU... YOU MET **WILLIAM SHAKESPEARE?**

IT'S INERT AT THE MOMENT, WHICH MEANS THAT WHATEVER'S CONTROLLING IT HAS GOT **BORED.** WHICH MEANS THAT IF I WANT TO **TALK** TO IT, I HAVE TO FIND IT **FIRST.**

I'LL GO WITH EMILY AND OL' CRANEY TO SEE IF WE CAN USE ONE OF THE **TUNNELS** TO REACH IT.

AND US? WHILE YOU'RE OFF HAVING FUN, WHAT DO **WE** DO?

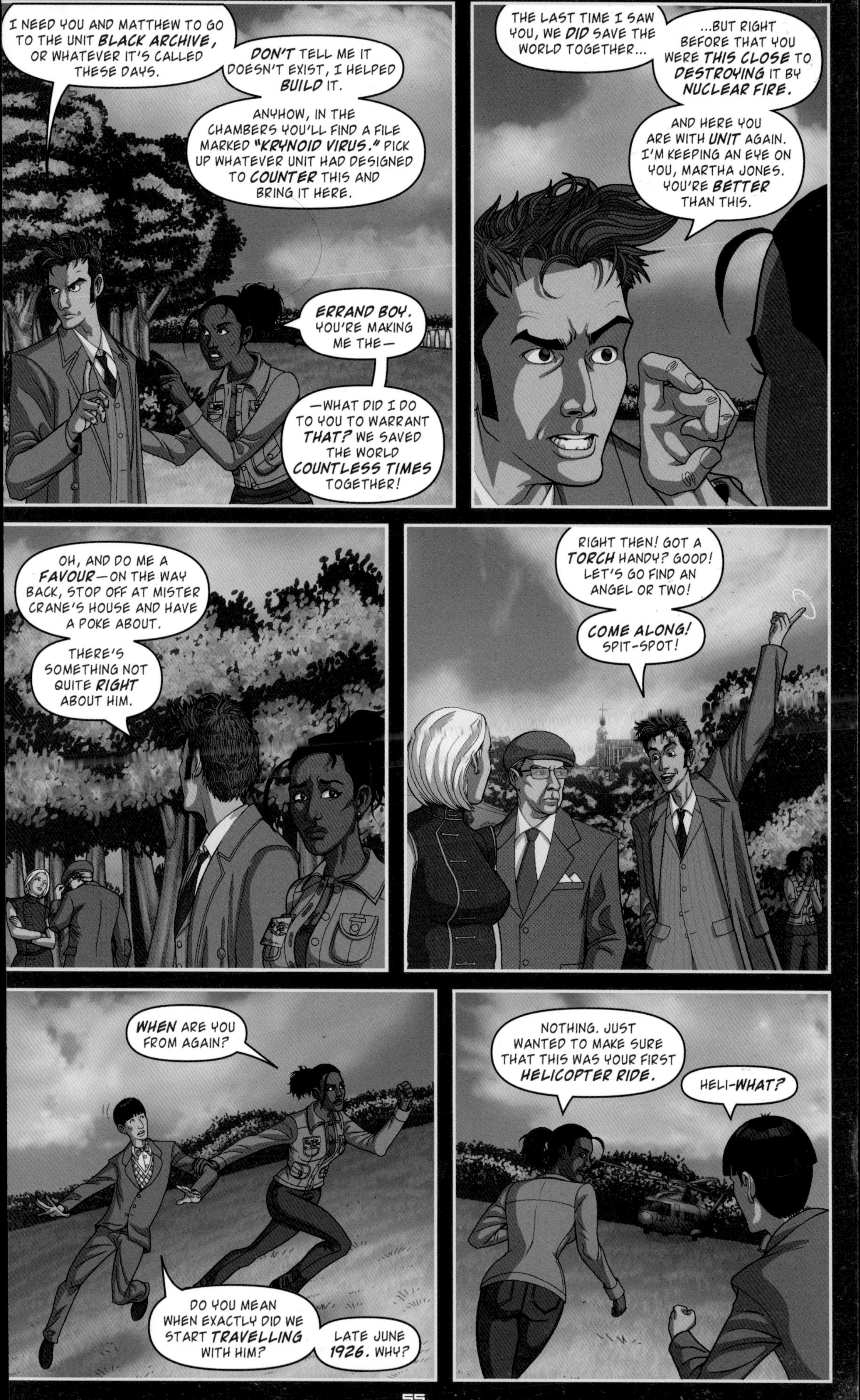

I NEED YOU AND MATTHEW TO GO TO THE UNIT BLACK ARCHIVE, OR WHATEVER IT'S CALLED THESE DAYS.
DON'T TELL ME IT DOESN'T EXIST, I HELPED BUILD IT.
ANYHOW, IN THE CHAMBERS YOU'LL FIND A FILE MARKED "KRYNOID VIRUS." PICK UP WHATEVER UNIT HAD DESIGNED TO COUNTER THIS AND BRING IT HERE.
ERRAND BOY. YOU'RE MAKING ME THE—
—WHAT DID I DO TO YOU TO WARRANT THAT? WE SAVED THE WORLD COUNTLESS TIMES TOGETHER!
THE LAST TIME I SAW YOU, WE DID SAVE THE WORLD TOGETHER...
...BUT RIGHT BEFORE THAT YOU WERE THIS CLOSE TO DESTROYING IT BY NUCLEAR FIRE.
AND HERE YOU ARE WITH UNIT AGAIN. I'M KEEPING AN EYE ON YOU, MARTHA JONES. YOU'RE BETTER THAN THIS.
OH, AND DO ME A FAVOUR—ON THE WAY BACK, STOP OFF AT MISTER CRANE'S HOUSE AND HAVE A POKE ABOUT.
THERE'S SOMETHING NOT QUITE RIGHT ABOUT HIM.
RIGHT THEN! GOT A TORCH HANDY? GOOD! LET'S GO FIND AN ANGEL OR TWO!
COME ALONG! SPIT-SPOT!
WHEN ARE YOU FROM AGAIN?
DO YOU MEAN WHEN EXACTLY DID WE START TRAVELLING WITH HIM?
LATE JUNE 1926. WHY?
NOTHING. JUST WANTED TO MAKE SURE THAT THIS WAS YOUR FIRST HELICOPTER RIDE.
HELI-WHAT?

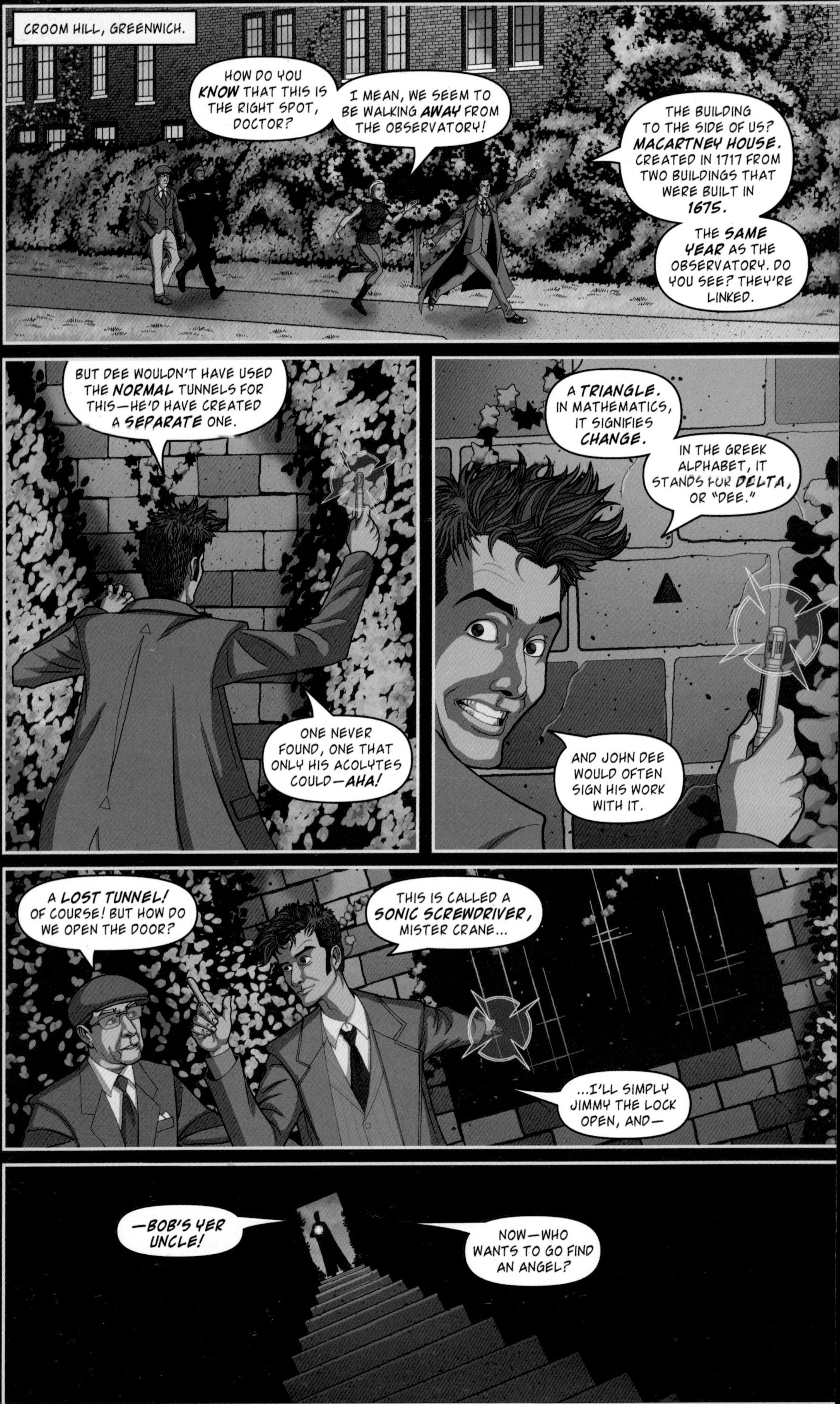
CROOM HILL, GREENWICH.
HOW DO YOU KNOW THAT THIS IS THE RIGHT SPOT, DOCTOR?
I MEAN, WE SEEM TO BE WALKING AWAY FROM THE OBSERVATORY!
THE BUILDING TO THE SIDE OF US? MACARTNEY HOUSE. CREATED IN 1717 FROM TWO BUILDINGS THAT WERE BUILT IN 1675.
THE SAME YEAR AS THE OBSERVATORY. DO YOU SEE? THEY'RE LINKED.
BUT DEE WOULDN'T HAVE USED THE NORMAL TUNNELS FOR THIS—HE'D HAVE CREATED A SEPARATE ONE.
ONE NEVER FOUND, ONE THAT ONLY HIS ACOLYTES COULD—AHA!
A TRIANGLE. IN MATHEMATICS, IT SIGNIFIES CHANGE.
IN THE GREEK ALPHABET, IT STANDS FOR DELTA, OR "DEE."
AND JOHN DEE WOULD OFTEN SIGN HIS WORK WITH IT.
A LOST TUNNEL! OF COURSE! BUT HOW DO WE OPEN THE DOOR?
THIS IS CALLED A SONIC SCREWDRIVER, MISTER CRANE...
...I'LL SIMPLY JIMMY THE LOCK OPEN, AND—
—BOB'S YER UNCLE!
NOW—WHO WANTS TO GO FIND AN ANGEL?

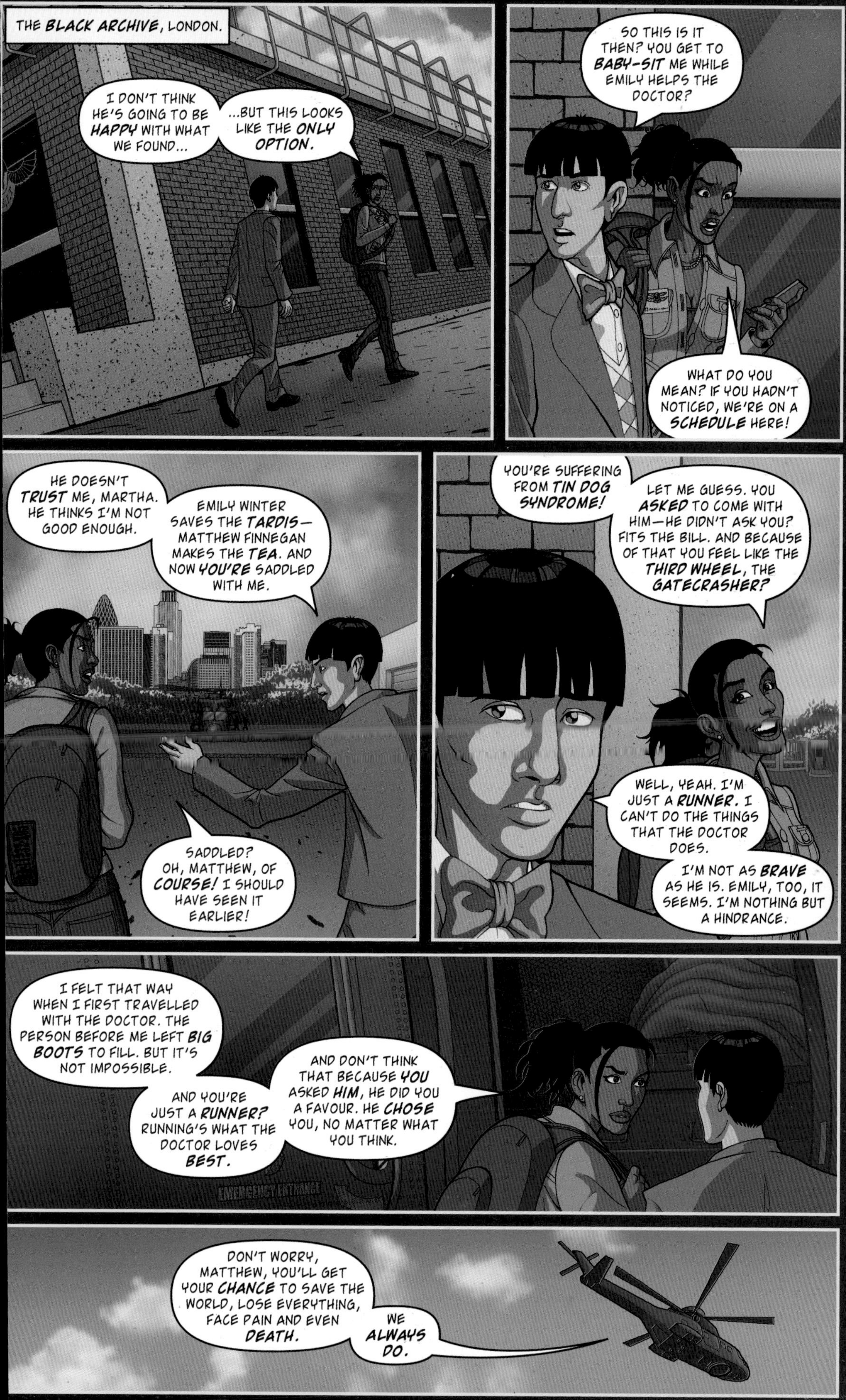
THE BLACK ARCHIVE, LONDON.
I DON'T THINK HE'S GOING TO BE HAPPY WITH WHAT WE FOUND...
...BUT THIS LOOKS LIKE THE ONLY OPTION.
SO THIS IS IT THEN? YOU GET TO BABY-SIT ME WHILE EMILY HELPS THE DOCTOR?
WHAT DO YOU MEAN? IF YOU HADN'T NOTICED, WE'RE ON A SCHEDULE HERE!
HE DOESN'T TRUST ME, MARTHA. HE THINKS I'M NOT GOOD ENOUGH.
EMILY WINTER SAVES THE TARDIS— MATTHEW FINNEGAN MAKES THE TEA. AND NOW YOU'RE SADDLED WITH ME.
SADDLED? OH, MATTHEW, OF COURSE! I SHOULD HAVE SEEN IT EARLIER!
YOU'RE SUFFERING FROM TIN DOG SYNDROME!
LET ME GUESS. YOU ASKED TO COME WITH HIM—HE DIDN'T ASK YOU? FITS THE BILL. AND BECAUSE OF THAT YOU FEEL LIKE THE THIRD WHEEL, THE GATECRASHER?
WELL, YEAH. I'M JUST A RUNNER. I CAN'T DO THE THINGS THAT THE DOCTOR DOES.
I'M NOT AS BRAVE AS HE IS. EMILY, TOO, IT SEEMS. I'M NOTHING BUT A HINDRANCE.
I FELT THAT WAY WHEN I FIRST TRAVELLED WITH THE DOCTOR. THE PERSON BEFORE ME LEFT BIG BOOTS TO FILL. BUT IT'S NOT IMPOSSIBLE.
AND YOU'RE JUST A RUNNER? RUNNING'S WHAT THE DOCTOR LOVES BEST.
AND DON'T THINK THAT BECAUSE YOU ASKED HIM, HE DID YOU A FAVOUR. HE CHOSE YOU, NO MATTER WHAT YOU THINK.
EMERGENCY ENTRANCE
DON'T WORRY, MATTHEW, YOU'LL GET YOUR CHANCE TO SAVE THE WORLD, LOSE EVERYTHING, FACE PAIN AND EVEN DEATH.
WE ALWAYS DO.

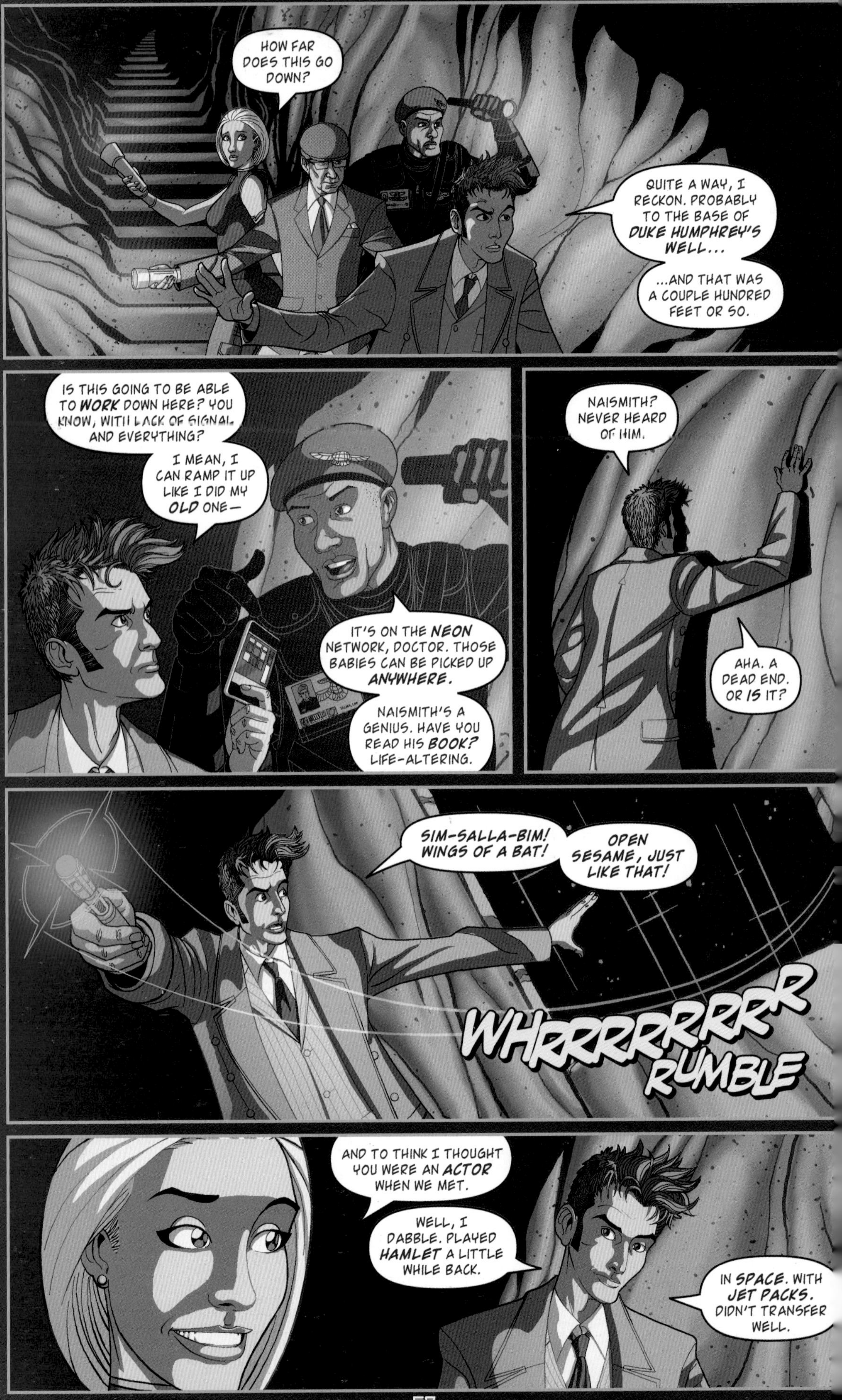

HOW FAR DOES THIS GO DOWN?
QUITE A WAY, I RECKON. PROBABLY TO THE BASE OF DUKE HUMPHREY'S WELL...
...AND THAT WAS A COUPLE HUNDRED FEET OR SO.
IS THIS GOING TO BE ABLE TO WORK DOWN HERE? YOU KNOW, WITH LACK OF SIGNAL AND EVERYTHING?
I MEAN, I CAN RAMP IT UP LIKE I DID MY OLD ONE—
IT'S ON THE NEON NETWORK, DOCTOR. THOSE BABIES CAN BE PICKED UP ANYWHERE.
NAISMITH'S A GENIUS. HAVE YOU READ HIS BOOK? LIFE-ALTERING.
NAISMITH? NEVER HEARD OF HIM.
AHA. A DEAD END. OR IS IT?
SIM-SALLA-BIM! WINGS OF A BAT!
OPEN SESAME, JUST LIKE THAT!
WHRRRRRRRR
RUMBLE
AND TO THINK I THOUGHT YOU WERE AN ACTOR WHEN WE MET.
WELL, I DABBLE. PLAYED HAMLET A LITTLE WHILE BACK.
IN SPACE. WITH JET PACKS. DIDN'T TRANSFER WELL.

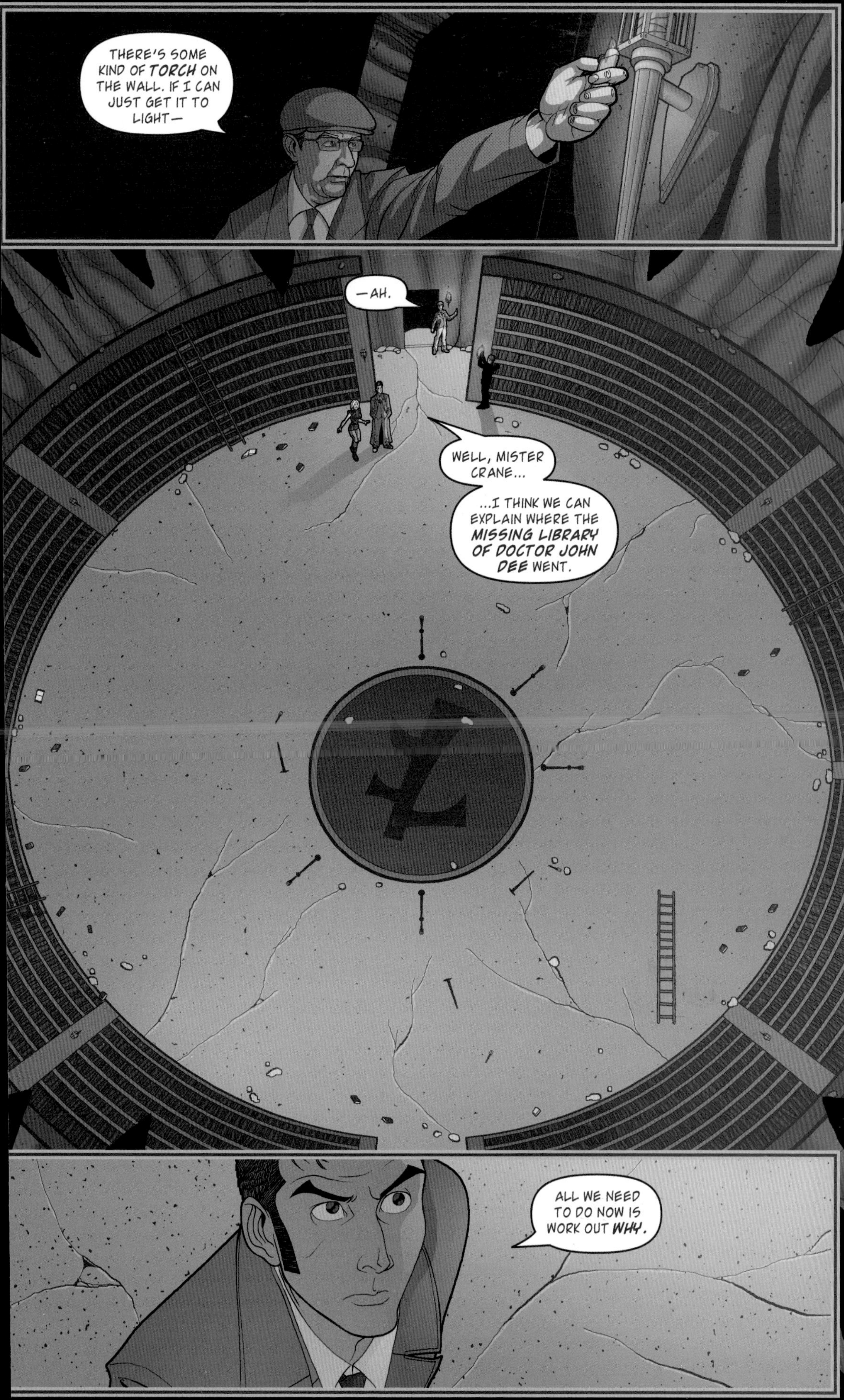
THERE'S SOME KIND OF TORCH ON THE WALL. IF I CAN JUST GET IT TO LIGHT—
—AH.
WELL, MISTER CRANE...
...I THINK WE CAN EXPLAIN WHERE THE MISSING LIBRARY OF DOCTOR JOHN DEE WENT.
ALL WE NEED TO DO NOW IS WORK OUT WHY.

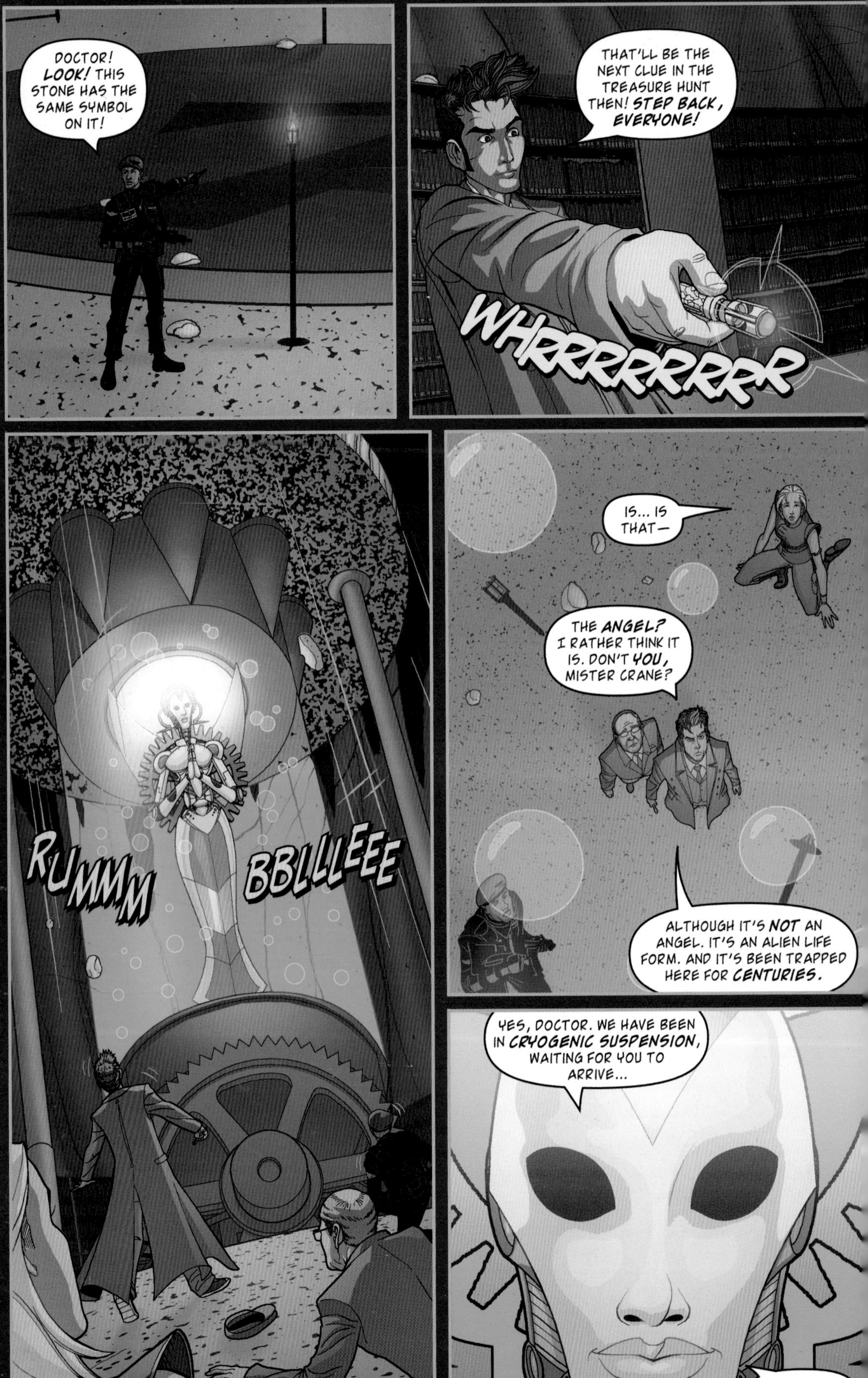
DOCTOR! LOOK! THIS STONE HAS THE SAME SYMBOL ON IT!
THAT'LL BE THE NEXT CLUE IN THE TREASURE HUNT THEN! STEP BACK, EVERYONE!
WHRRRRRRRRR
RUMMM BBLLLEEE
IS... IS THAT—
THE ANGEL? I RATHER THINK IT IS. DON'T YOU, MISTER CRANE?
ALTHOUGH IT'S NOT AN ANGEL. IT'S AN ALIEN LIFE FORM. AND IT'S BEEN TRAPPED HERE FOR CENTURIES.
YES, DOCTOR. WE HAVE BEEN IN CRYOGENIC SUSPENSION, WAITING FOR YOU TO ARRIVE...
...AND TAKE US HOME.

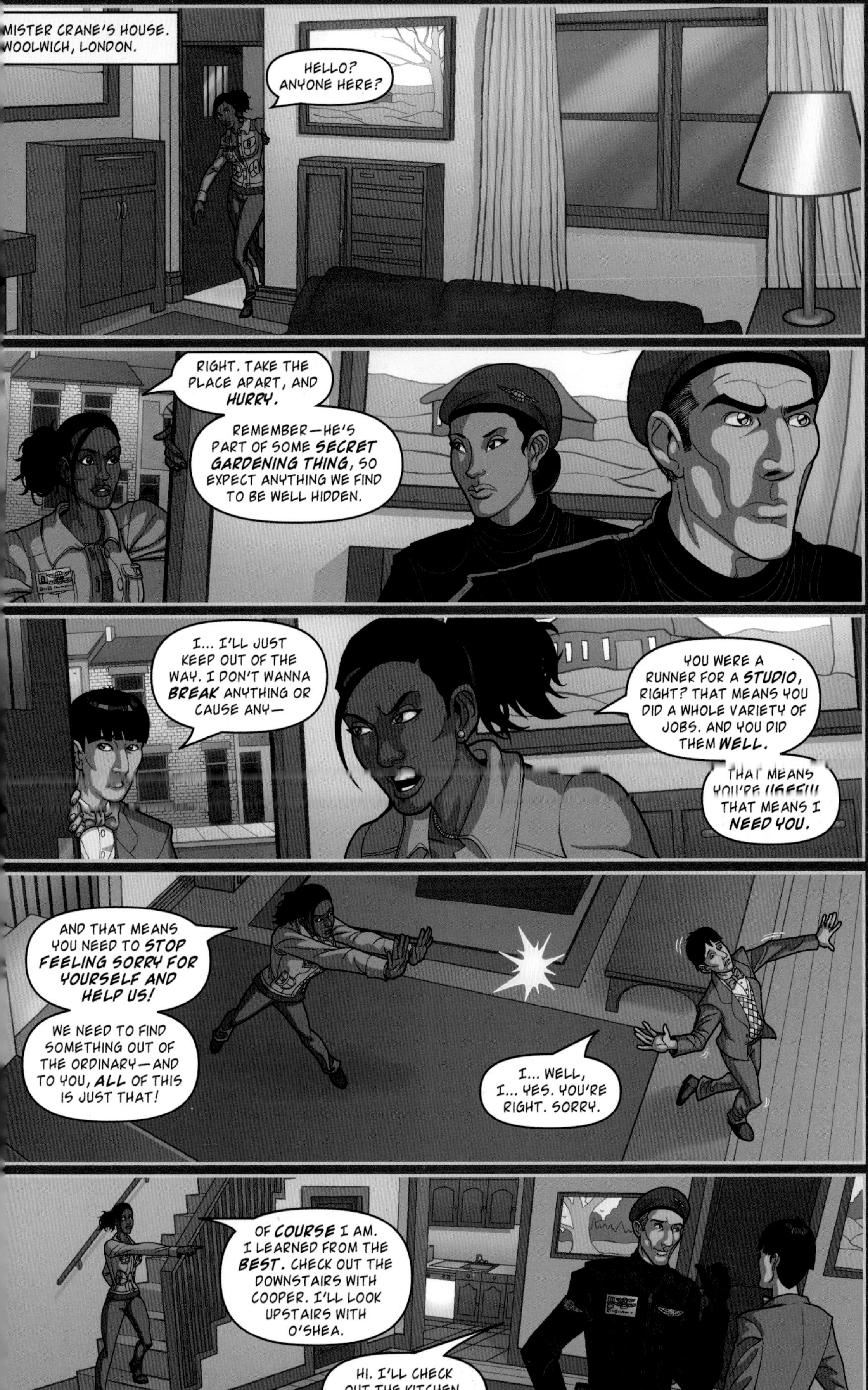
MISTER CRANE'S HOUSE. WOOLWICH, LONDON.
HELLO? ANYONE HERE?
RIGHT. TAKE THE PLACE APART, AND HURRY.
REMEMBER—HE'S PART OF SOME SECRET GARDENING THING, SO EXPECT ANYTHING WE FIND TO BE WELL HIDDEN.
I... I'LL JUST KEEP OUT OF THE WAY. I DON'T WANNA BREAK ANYTHING OR CAUSE ANY—
YOU WERE A RUNNER FOR A STUDIO, RIGHT? THAT MEANS YOU DID A WHOLE VARIETY OF JOBS. AND YOU DID THEM WELL.
THAT MEANS YOU'RE USEFUL! THAT MEANS I NEED YOU.
AND THAT MEANS YOU NEED TO STOP FEELING SORRY FOR YOURSELF AND HELP US!
WE NEED TO FIND SOMETHING OUT OF THE ORDINARY—AND TO YOU, ALL OF THIS IS JUST THAT!
I... WELL, I... YES. YOU'RE RIGHT. SORRY.
OF COURSE I AM. I LEARNED FROM THE BEST. CHECK OUT THE DOWNSTAIRS WITH COOPER. I'LL LOOK UPSTAIRS WITH O'SHEA.
HI. I'LL CHECK OUT THE KITCHEN, YOU CHECK THE SIDE CABINET.

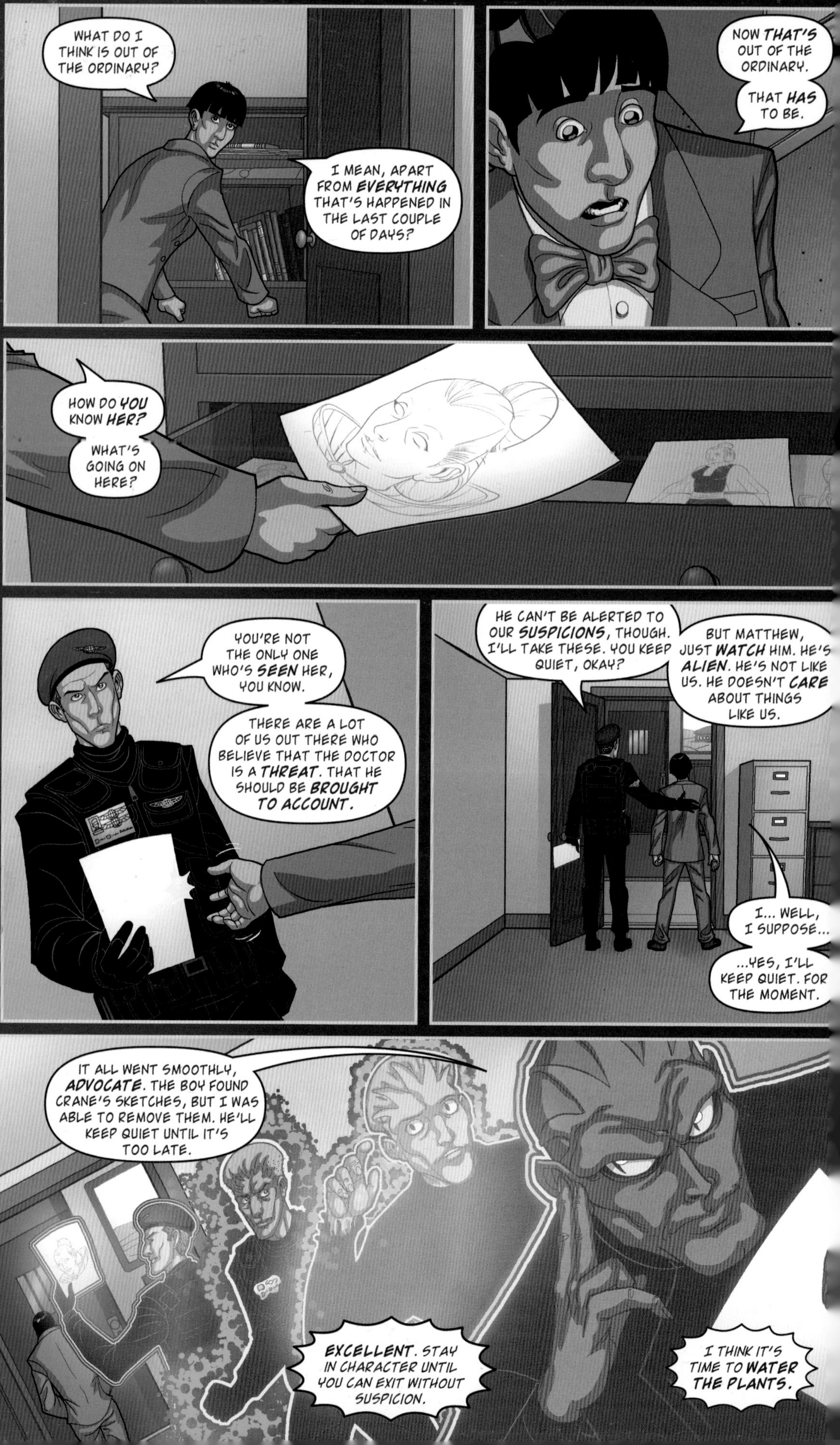
WHAT DO I THINK IS OUT OF THE ORDINARY?
I MEAN, APART FROM EVERYTHING THAT'S HAPPENED IN THE LAST COUPLE OF DAYS?
NOW THAT'S OUT OF THE ORDINARY.
THAT HAS TO BE.
HOW DO YOU KNOW HER?
WHAT'S GOING ON HERE?
YOU'RE NOT THE ONLY ONE WHO'S SEEN HER, YOU KNOW.
THERE ARE A LOT OF US OUT THERE WHO BELIEVE THAT THE DOCTOR IS A THREAT. THAT HE SHOULD BE BROUGHT TO ACCOUNT.
HE CAN'T BE ALERTED TO OUR SUSPICIONS, THOUGH. I'LL TAKE THESE. YOU KEEP QUIET, OKAY?
BUT MATTHEW, JUST WATCH HIM. HE'S ALIEN. HE'S NOT LIKE US. HE DOESN'T CARE ABOUT THINGS LIKE US.
I... WELL, I SUPPOSE...
...YES, I'LL KEEP QUIET. FOR THE MOMENT.
IT ALL WENT SMOOTHLY, ADVOCATE. THE BOY FOUND CRANE'S SKETCHES, BUT I WAS ABLE TO REMOVE THEM. HE'LL KEEP QUIET UNTIL IT'S TOO LATE.
EXCELLENT. STAY IN CHARACTER UNTIL YOU CAN EXIT WITHOUT SUSPICION.
I THINK IT'S TIME TO WATER THE PLANTS.

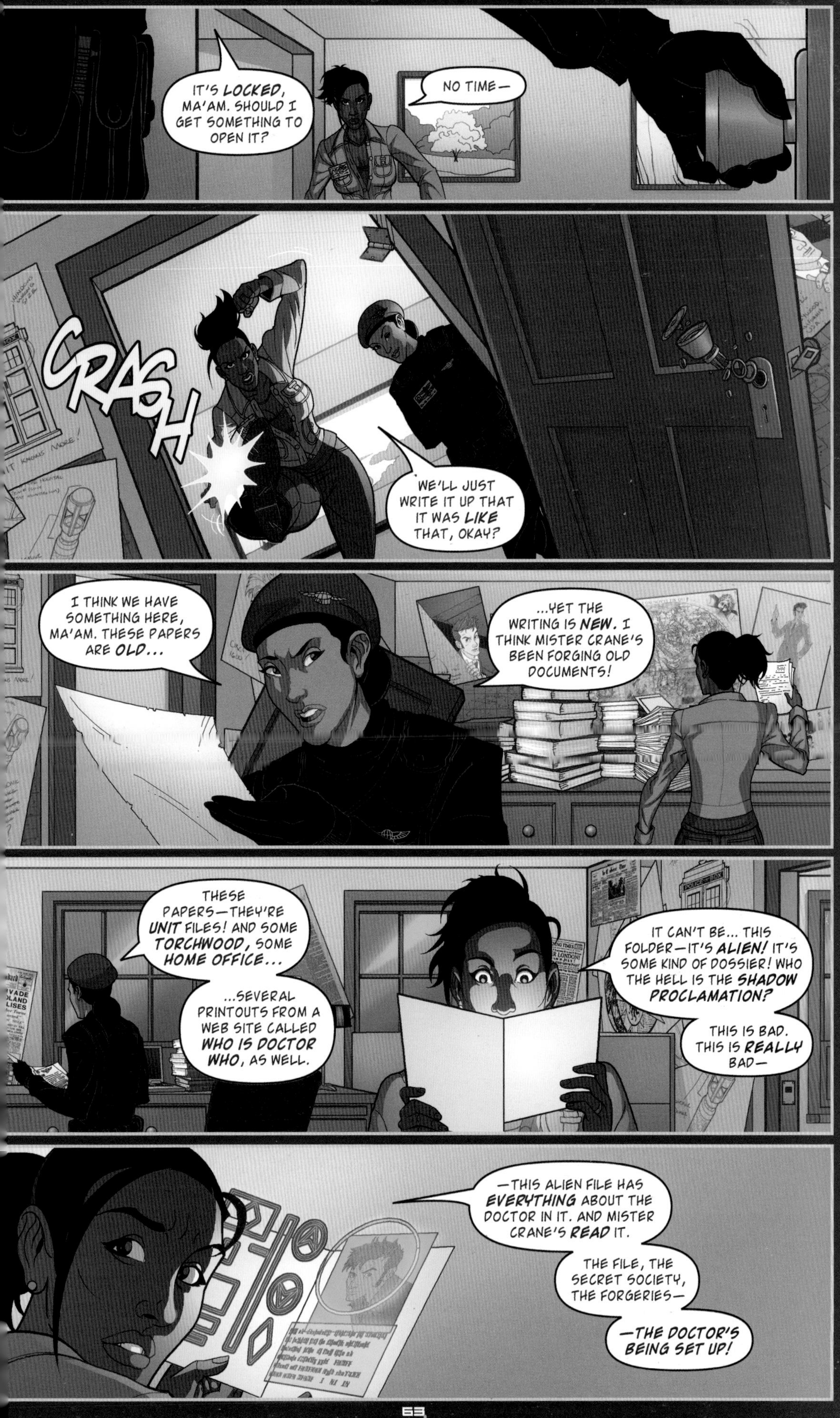
IT'S LOCKED, MA'AM. SHOULD I GET SOMETHING TO OPEN IT?
NO TIME—
CRASH
WE'LL JUST WRITE IT UP THAT IT WAS LIKE THAT, OKAY?
I THINK WE HAVE SOMETHING HERE, MA'AM. THESE PAPERS ARE OLD...
...YET THE WRITING IS NEW. I THINK MISTER CRANE'S BEEN FORGING OLD DOCUMENTS!
THESE PAPERS—THEY'RE UNIT FILES! AND SOME TORCHWOOD, SOME HOME OFFICE...
...SEVERAL PRINTOUTS FROM A WEB SITE CALLED WHO IS DOCTOR WHO, AS WELL.
IT CAN'T BE... THIS FOLDER—IT'S ALIEN! IT'S SOME KIND OF DOSSIER! WHO THE HELL IS THE SHADOW PROCLAMATION?
THIS IS BAD. THIS IS REALLY BAD—
—THIS ALIEN FILE HAS EVERYTHING ABOUT THE DOCTOR IN IT. AND MISTER CRANE'S READ IT.
THE FILE, THE SECRET SOCIETY, THE FORGERIES—
—THE DOCTOR'S BEING SET UP!

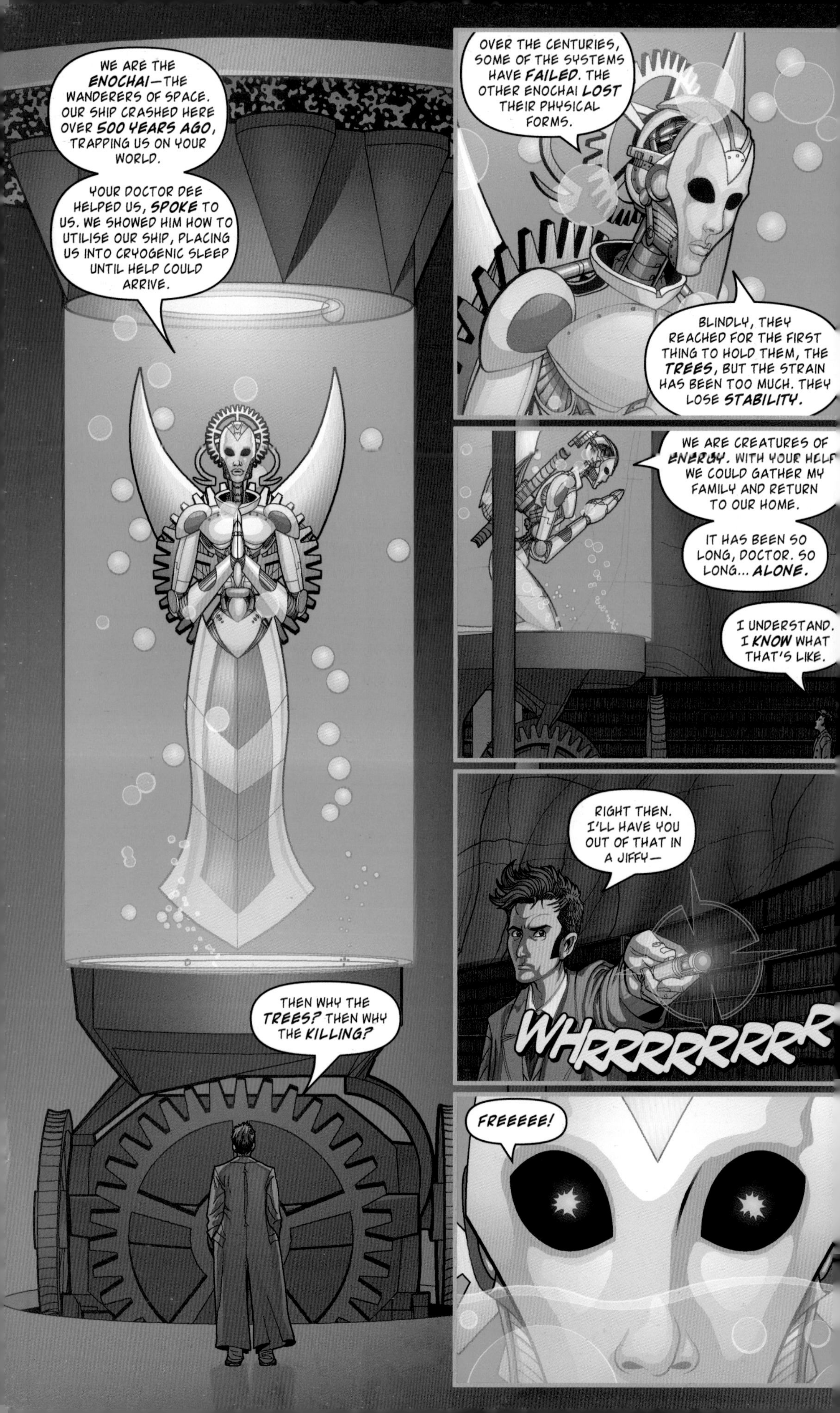
WE ARE THE ENOCHAI—THE WANDERERS OF SPACE. OUR SHIP CRASHED HERE OVER 500 YEARS AGO, TRAPPING US ON YOUR WORLD.
YOUR DOCTOR DEE HELPED US, SPOKE TO US. WE SHOWED HIM HOW TO UTILISE OUR SHIP, PLACING US INTO CRYOGENIC SLEEP UNTIL HELP COULD ARRIVE.
THEN WHY THE TREES? THEN WHY THE KILLING?
OVER THE CENTURIES, SOME OF THE SYSTEMS HAVE FAILED. THE OTHER ENOCHAI LOST THEIR PHYSICAL FORMS.
BLINDLY, THEY REACHED FOR THE FIRST THING TO HOLD THEM, THE TREES, BUT THE STRAIN HAS BEEN TOO MUCH. THEY LOSE STABILITY.
WE ARE CREATURES OF ENERGY. WITH YOUR HELP WE COULD GATHER MY FAMILY AND RETURN TO OUR HOME.
IT HAS BEEN SO LONG, DOCTOR. SO LONG... ALONE.
I UNDERSTAND. I KNOW WHAT THAT'S LIKE.
RIGHT THEN. I'LL HAVE YOU OUT OF THAT IN A JIFFY—
WHRRRRRRRR
FREEEEE!

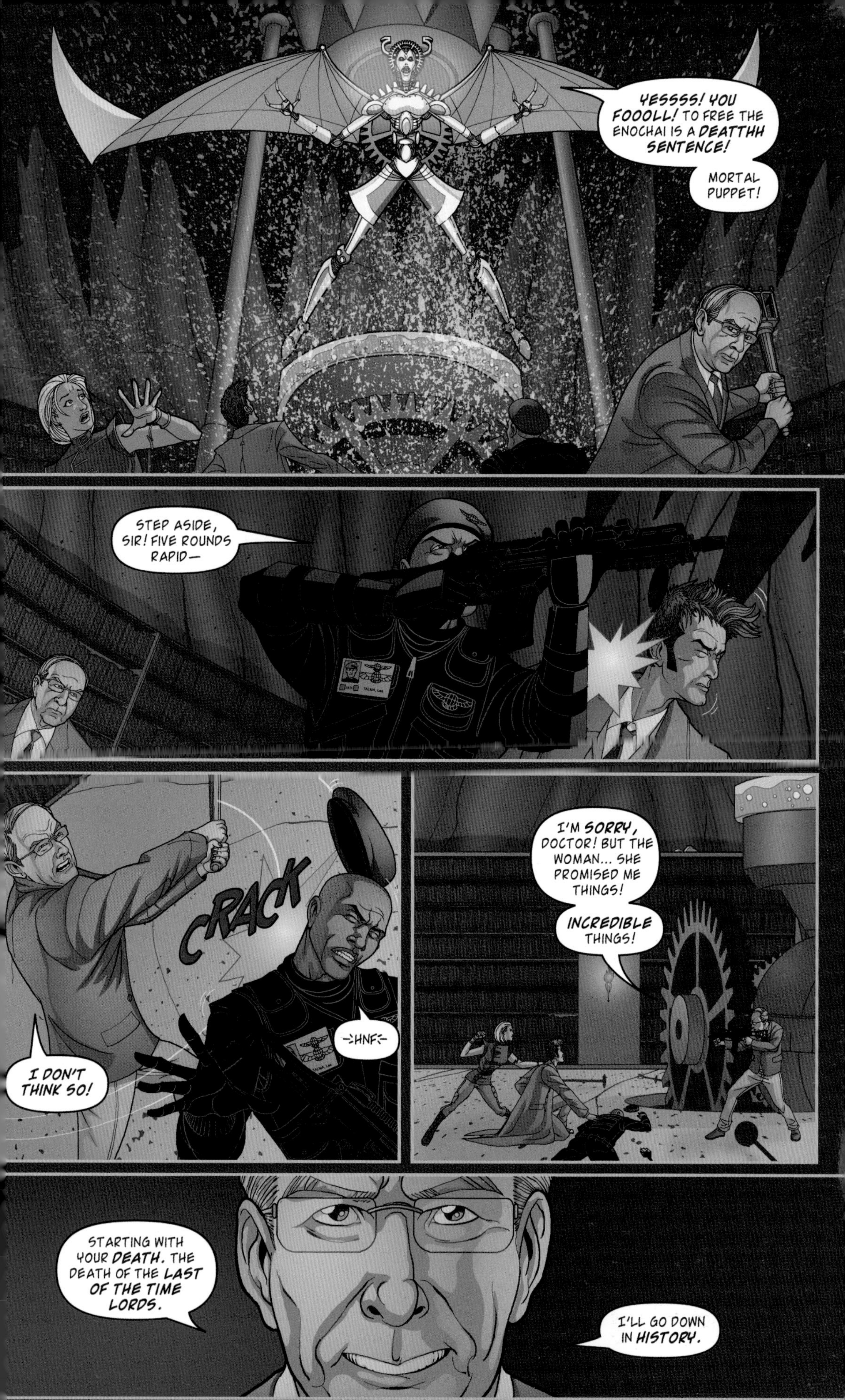
YESSSS! YOU FOOOLL! TO FREE THE ENOCHAI IS A DEATTHH SENTENCE!
MORTAL PUPPET!
STEP ASIDE, SIR! FIVE ROUNDS RAPID—
CRACK
-HNF-
I DON'T THINK SO!
I'M SORRY, DOCTOR! BUT THE WOMAN... SHE PROMISED ME THINGS!
INCREDIBLE THINGS!
STARTING WITH YOUR DEATH. THE DEATH OF THE LAST OF THE TIME LORDS.
I'LL GO DOWN IN HISTORY.

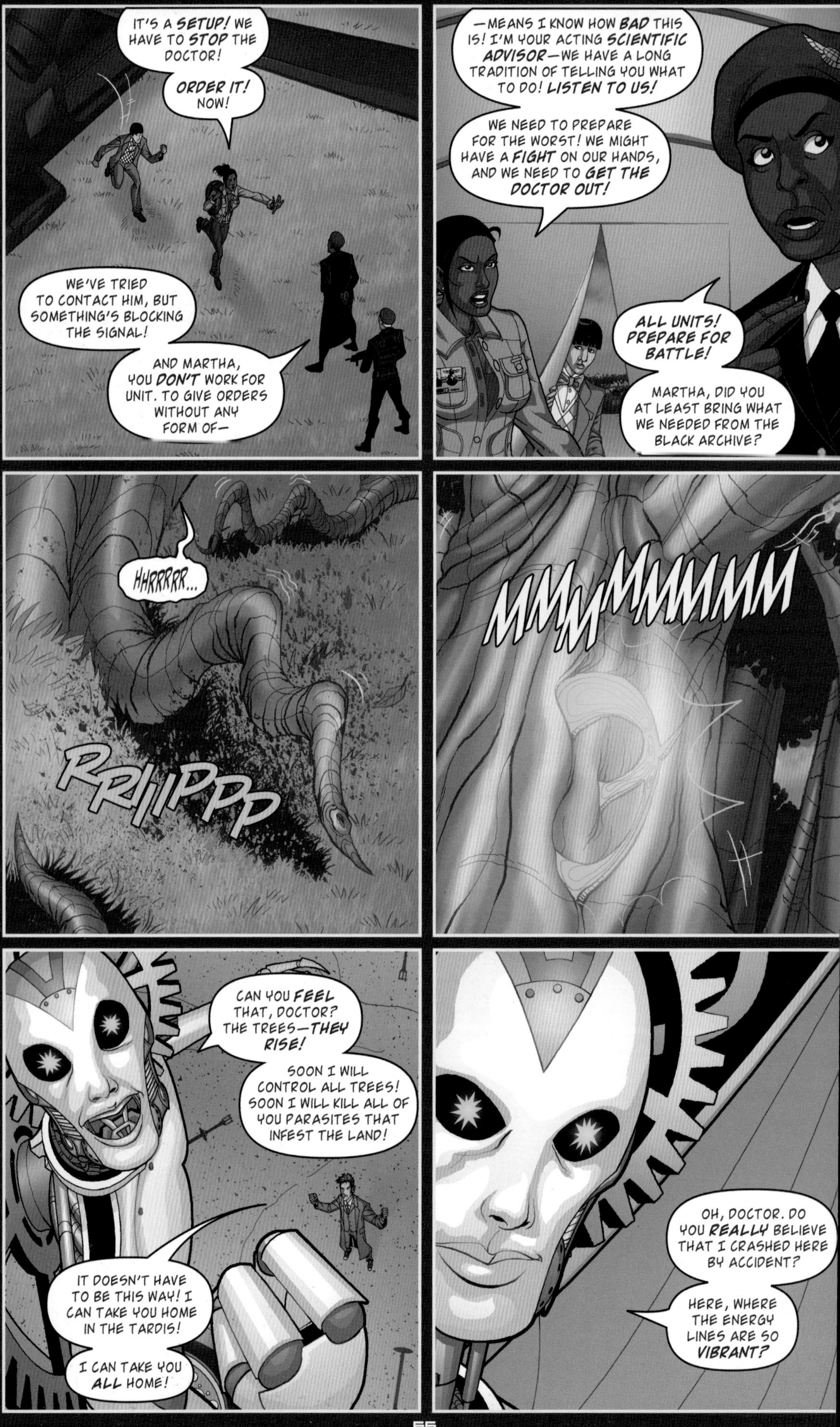
IT'S A SETUP! WE HAVE TO STOP THE DOCTOR!
ORDER IT! NOW!
WE'VE TRIED TO CONTACT HIM, BUT SOMETHING'S BLOCKING THE SIGNAL!
AND MARTHA, YOU DON'T WORK FOR UNIT. TO GIVE ORDERS WITHOUT ANY FORM OF—
—MEANS I KNOW HOW BAD THIS IS! I'M YOUR ACTING SCIENTIFIC ADVISOR—WE HAVE A LONG TRADITION OF TELLING YOU WHAT TO DO! LISTEN TO US!
WE NEED TO PREPARE FOR THE WORST! WE MIGHT HAVE A FIGHT ON OUR HANDS, AND WE NEED TO GET THE DOCTOR OUT!
ALL UNITS! PREPARE FOR BATTLE!
MARTHA, DID YOU AT LEAST BRING WHAT WE NEEDED FROM THE BLACK ARCHIVE?
HHRRRRR...
RRIIIPPP
MMMMMMMMM
CAN YOU FEEL THAT, DOCTOR? THE TREES—THEY RISE!
SOON I WILL CONTROL ALL TREES! SOON I WILL KILL ALL OF YOU PARASITES THAT INFEST THE LAND!
IT DOESN'T HAVE TO BE THIS WAY! I CAN TAKE YOU HOME IN THE TARDIS!
I CAN TAKE YOU ALL HOME!
OH, DOCTOR. DO YOU REALLY BELIEVE THAT I CRASHED HERE BY ACCIDENT?
HERE, WHERE THE ENERGY LINES ARE SO VIBRANT?

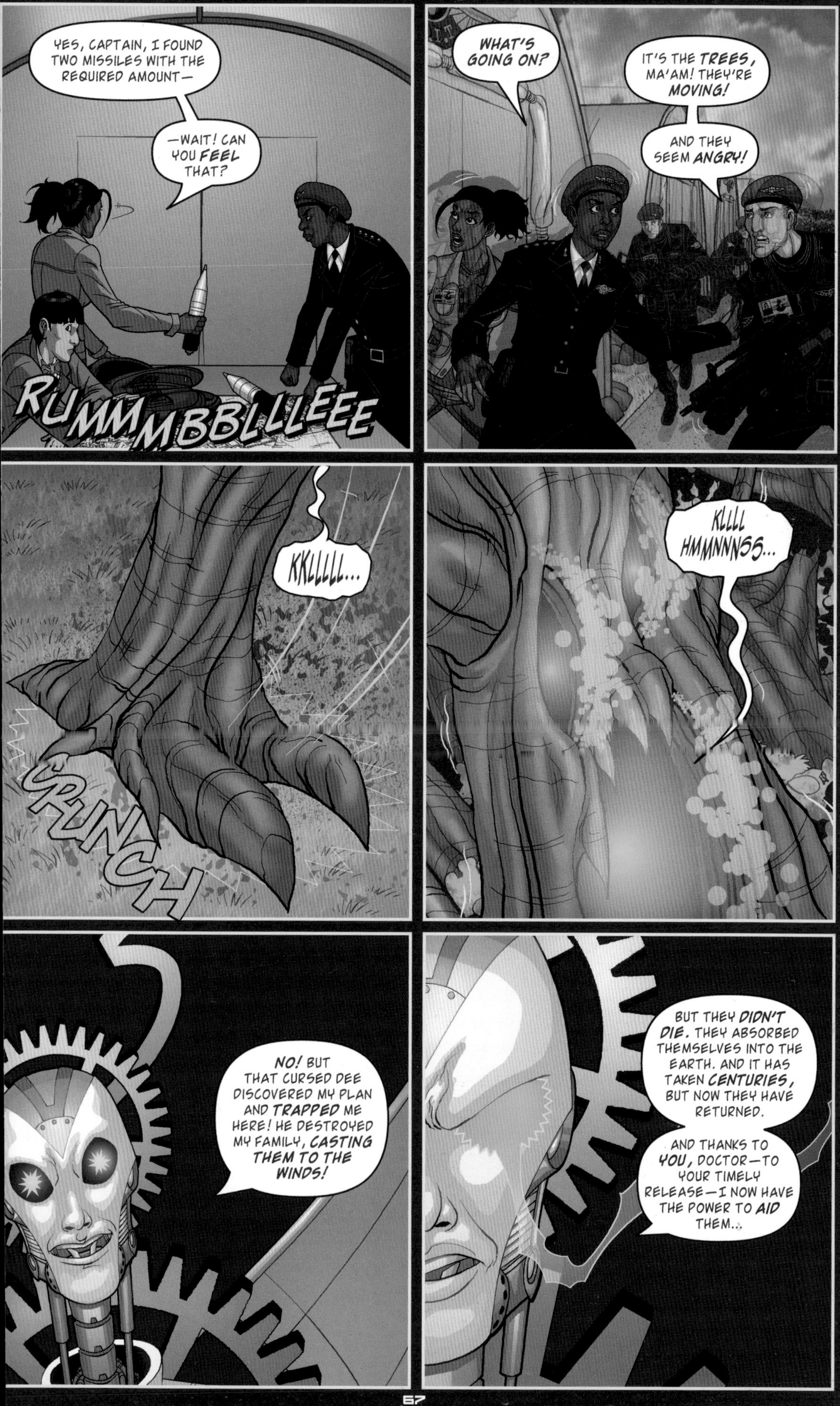

YES, CAPTAIN, I FOUND TWO MISSILES WITH THE REQUIRED AMOUNT—
—WAIT! CAN YOU FEEL THAT?
RUMMMBBLLLEEE
WHAT'S GOING ON?
IT'S THE TREES, MA'AM! THEY'RE MOVING!
AND THEY SEEM ANGRY!
KKLLLLL...
CRUNCH
KLLLL HMMNNNSS...
NO! BUT THAT CURSED DEE DISCOVERED MY PLAN AND TRAPPED ME HERE! HE DESTROYED MY FAMILY, CASTING THEM TO THE WINDS!
BUT THEY DIDN'T DIE. THEY ABSORBED THEMSELVES INTO THE EARTH. AND IT HAS TAKEN CENTURIES, BUT NOW THEY HAVE RETURNED.
AND THANKS TO YOU, DOCTOR—TO YOUR TIMELY RELEASE—I NOW HAVE THE POWER TO AID THEM...

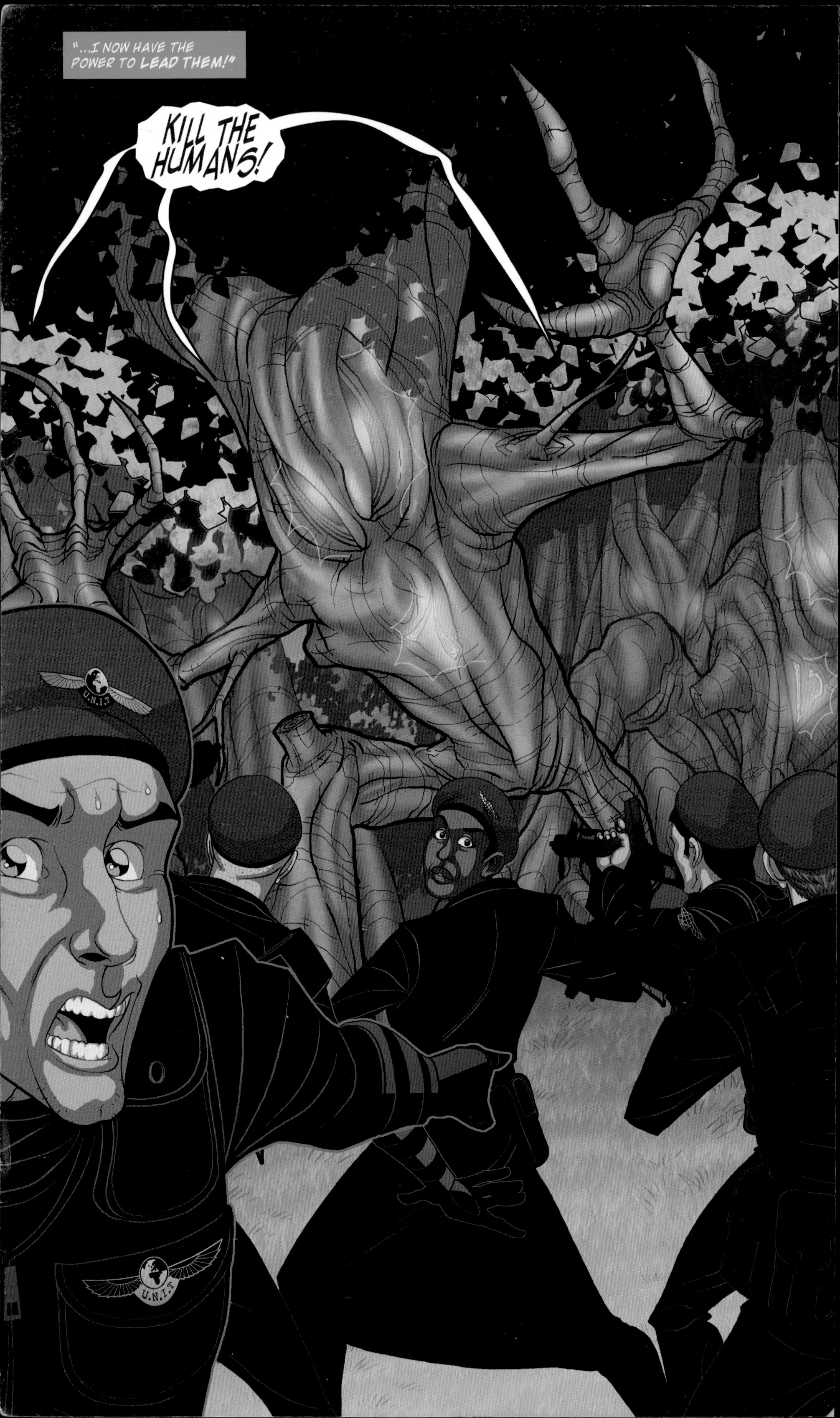
"...I NOW HAVE THE POWER TO LEAD THEM!"
KILL THE HUMANS!
U.N.I.T
U.N.I.T

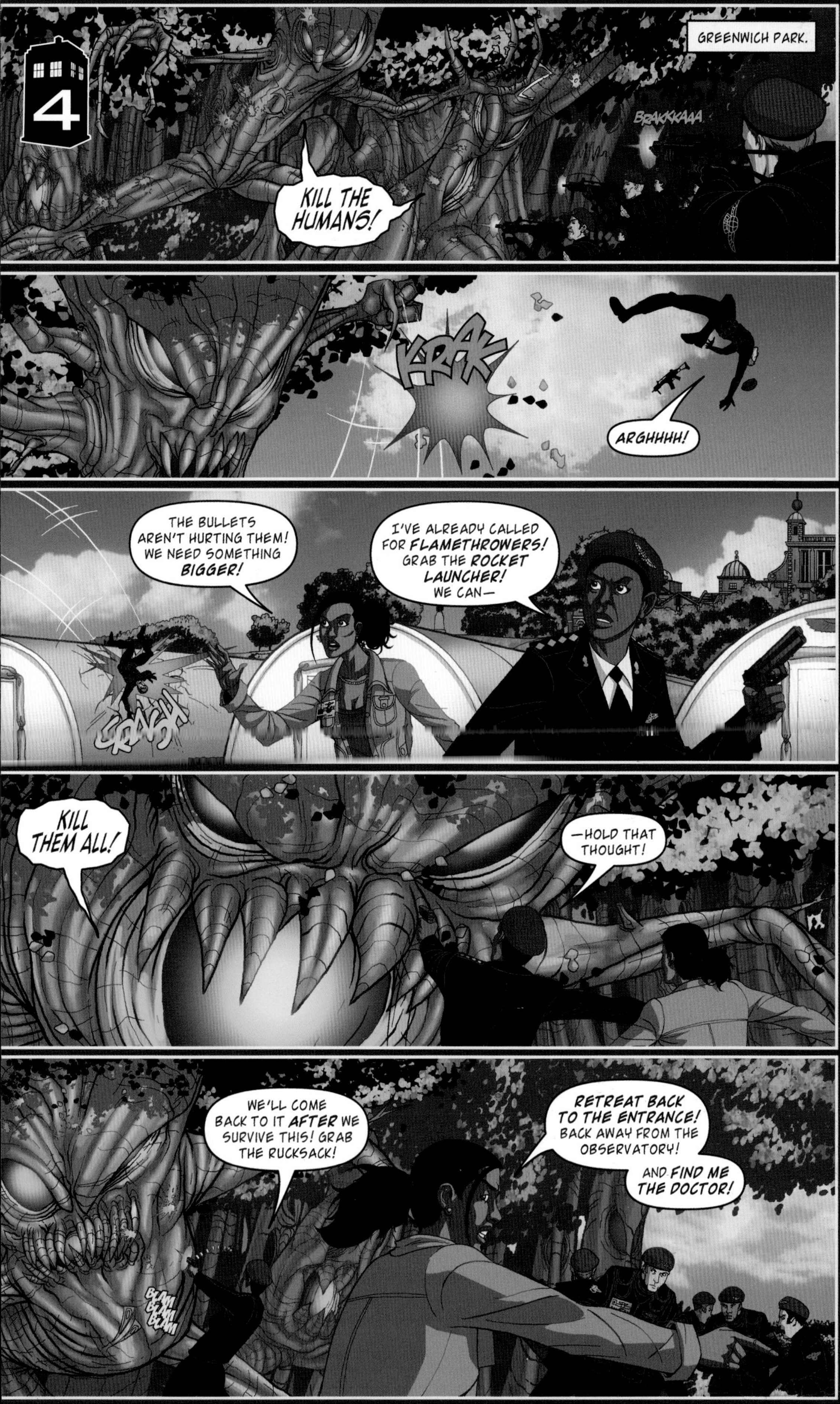
4
GREENWICH PARK.
BRAKKKAAA
KILL THE HUMANS!
KRAK
ARGHHHH!
THE BULLETS AREN'T HURTING THEM! WE NEED SOMETHING BIGGER!
I'VE ALREADY CALLED FOR FLAMETHROWERS! GRAB THE ROCKET LAUNCHER! WE CAN—
KILL THEM ALL!
—HOLD THAT THOUGHT!
WE'LL COME BACK TO IT AFTER WE SURVIVE THIS! GRAB THE RUCKSACK!
RETREAT BACK TO THE ENTRANCE! BACK AWAY FROM THE OBSERVATORY!
AND FIND ME THE DOCTOR!
BLAM BLAM BLAM

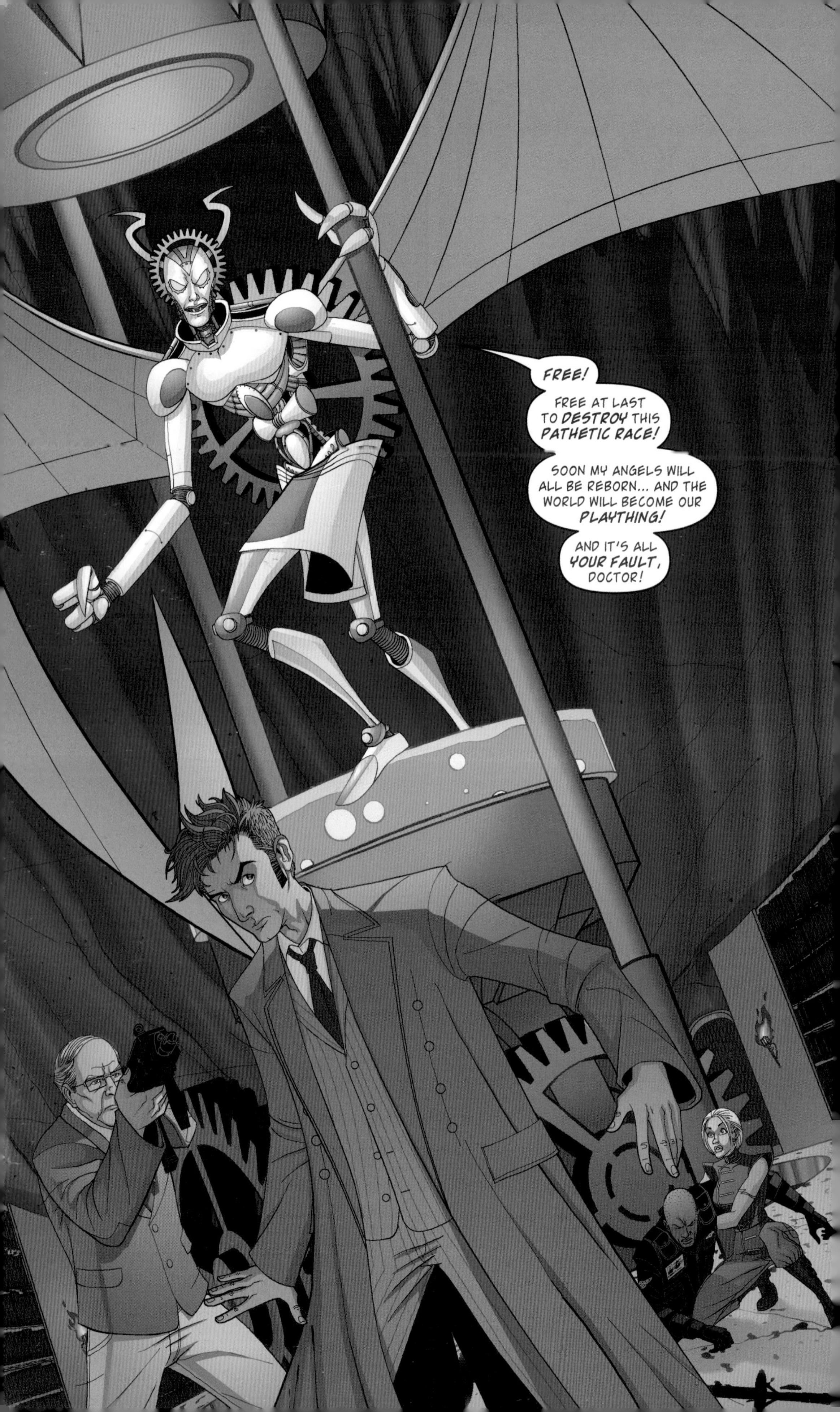
FREE!
FREE AT LAST TO DESTROY THIS PATHETIC RACE!
SOON MY ANGELS WILL ALL BE REBORN... AND THE WORLD WILL BECOME OUR PLAYTHING!
AND IT'S ALL YOUR FAULT, DOCTOR!

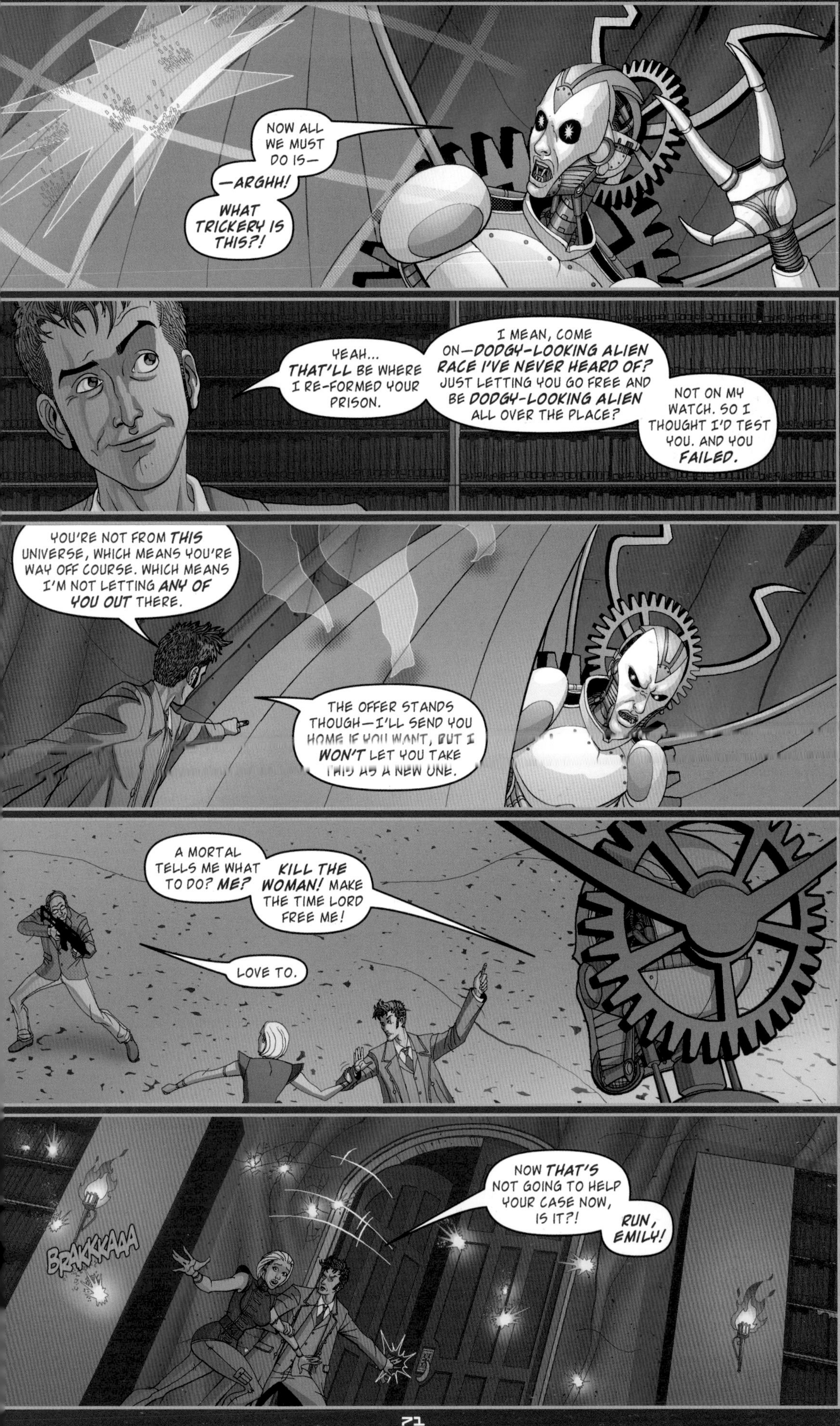
NOW ALL WE MUST DO IS—
—ARGHH!
WHAT TRICKERY IS THIS?!
YEAH... THAT'LL BE WHERE I RE-FORMED YOUR PRISON.
I MEAN, COME ON—DODGY-LOOKING ALIEN RACE I'VE NEVER HEARD OF? JUST LETTING YOU GO FREE AND BE DODGY-LOOKING ALIEN ALL OVER THE PLACE?
NOT ON MY WATCH. SO I THOUGHT I'D TEST YOU. AND YOU FAILED.
YOU'RE NOT FROM THIS UNIVERSE, WHICH MEANS YOU'RE WAY OFF COURSE. WHICH MEANS I'M NOT LETTING ANY OF YOU OUT THERE.
THE OFFER STANDS THOUGH—I'LL SEND YOU HOME IF YOU WANT, BUT I WON'T LET YOU TAKE THIS AS A NEW ONE.
A MORTAL TELLS ME WHAT TO DO? ME?
KILL THE WOMAN! MAKE THE TIME LORD FREE ME!
LOVE TO.
BRAKKKAAA
NOW THAT'S NOT GOING TO HELP YOUR CASE NOW, IS IT?!
RUN, EMILY!

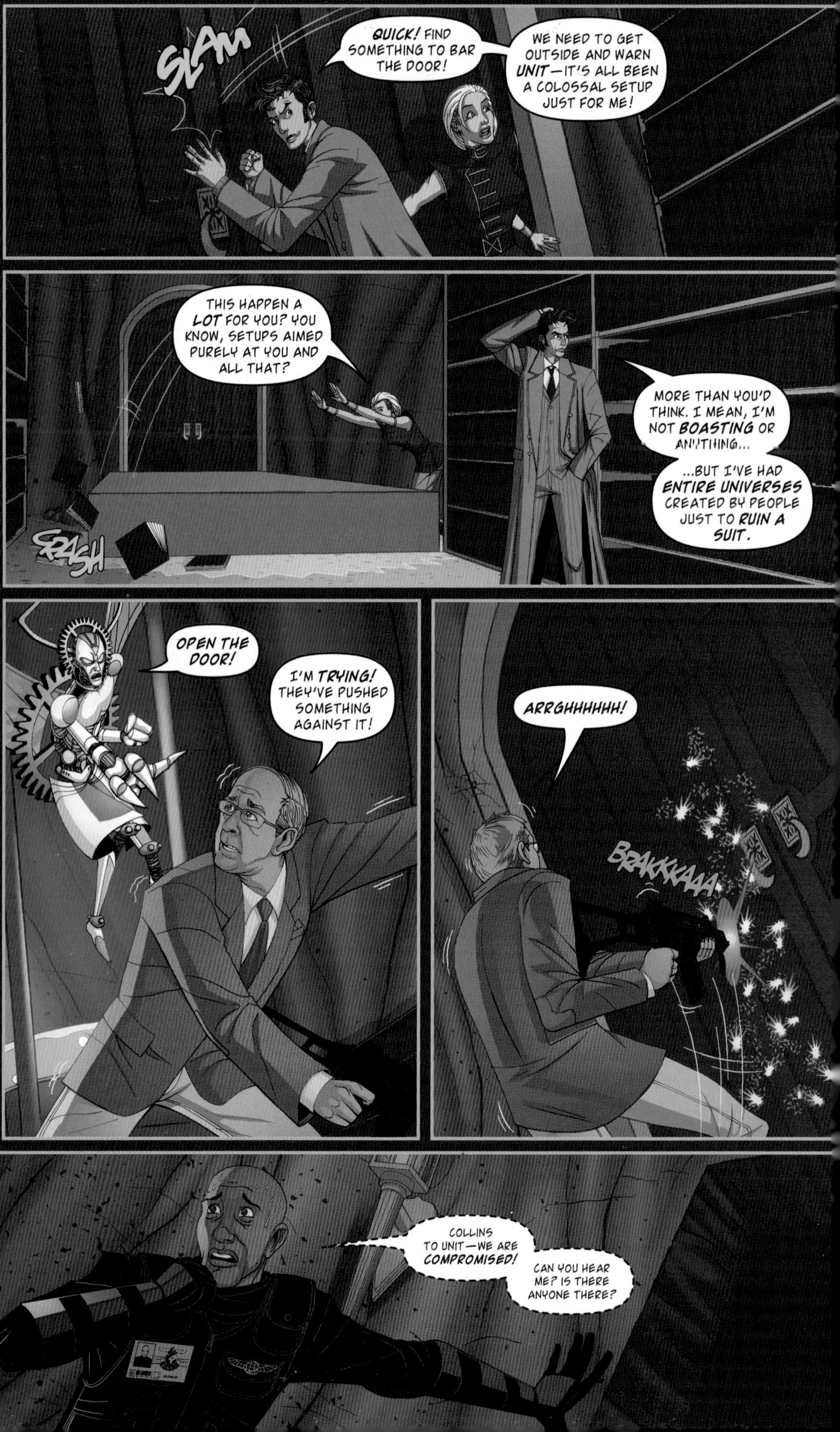
SLAM
QUICK! FIND SOMETHING TO BAR THE DOOR!
WE NEED TO GET OUTSIDE AND WARN UNIT—IT'S ALL BEEN A COLOSSAL SETUP JUST FOR ME!
THIS HAPPEN A LOT FOR YOU? YOU KNOW, SETUPS AIMED PURELY AT YOU AND ALL THAT?
CRASH
MORE THAN YOU'D THINK. I MEAN, I'M NOT BOASTING OR ANYTHING...
...BUT I'VE HAD ENTIRE UNIVERSES CREATED BY PEOPLE JUST TO RUIN A SUIT.
OPEN THE DOOR!
I'M TRYING! THEY'VE PUSHED SOMETHING AGAINST IT!
ARRGHHHHHH!
BRAKKKAAA
COLLINS TO UNIT—WE ARE COMPROMISED!
CAN YOU HEAR ME? IS THERE ANYONE THERE?

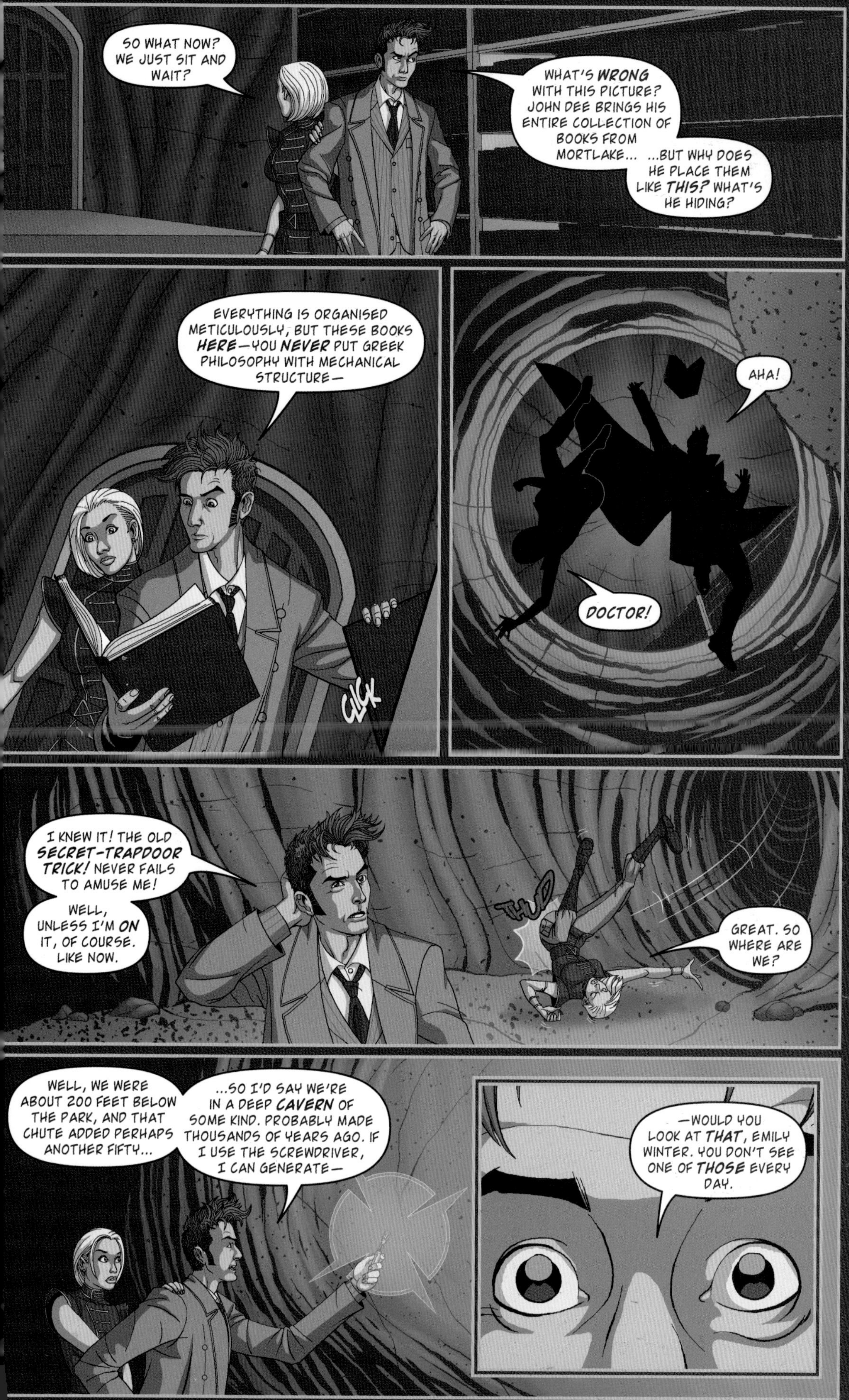
SO WHAT NOW? WE JUST SIT AND WAIT?
WHAT'S WRONG WITH THIS PICTURE? JOHN DEE BRINGS HIS ENTIRE COLLECTION OF BOOKS FROM MORTLAKE...
...BUT WHY DOES HE PLACE THEM LIKE THIS? WHAT'S HE HIDING?
EVERYTHING IS ORGANISED METICULOUSLY, BUT THESE BOOKS HERE—YOU NEVER PUT GREEK PHILOSOPHY WITH MECHANICAL STRUCTURE—
CLICK
AHA!
DOCTOR!
I KNEW IT! THE OLD SECRET-TRAPDOOR TRICK! NEVER FAILS TO AMUSE ME!
WELL, UNLESS I'M ON IT, OF COURSE. LIKE NOW.
THUD
GREAT. SO WHERE ARE WE?
WELL, WE WERE ABOUT 200 FEET BELOW THE PARK, AND THAT CHUTE ADDED PERHAPS ANOTHER FIFTY...
...SO I'D SAY WE'RE IN A DEEP CAVERN OF SOME KIND. PROBABLY MADE THOUSANDS OF YEARS AGO. IF I USE THE SCREWDRIVER, I CAN GENERATE—
—WOULD YOU LOOK AT THAT, EMILY WINTER. YOU DON'T SEE ONE OF THOSE EVERY DAY.

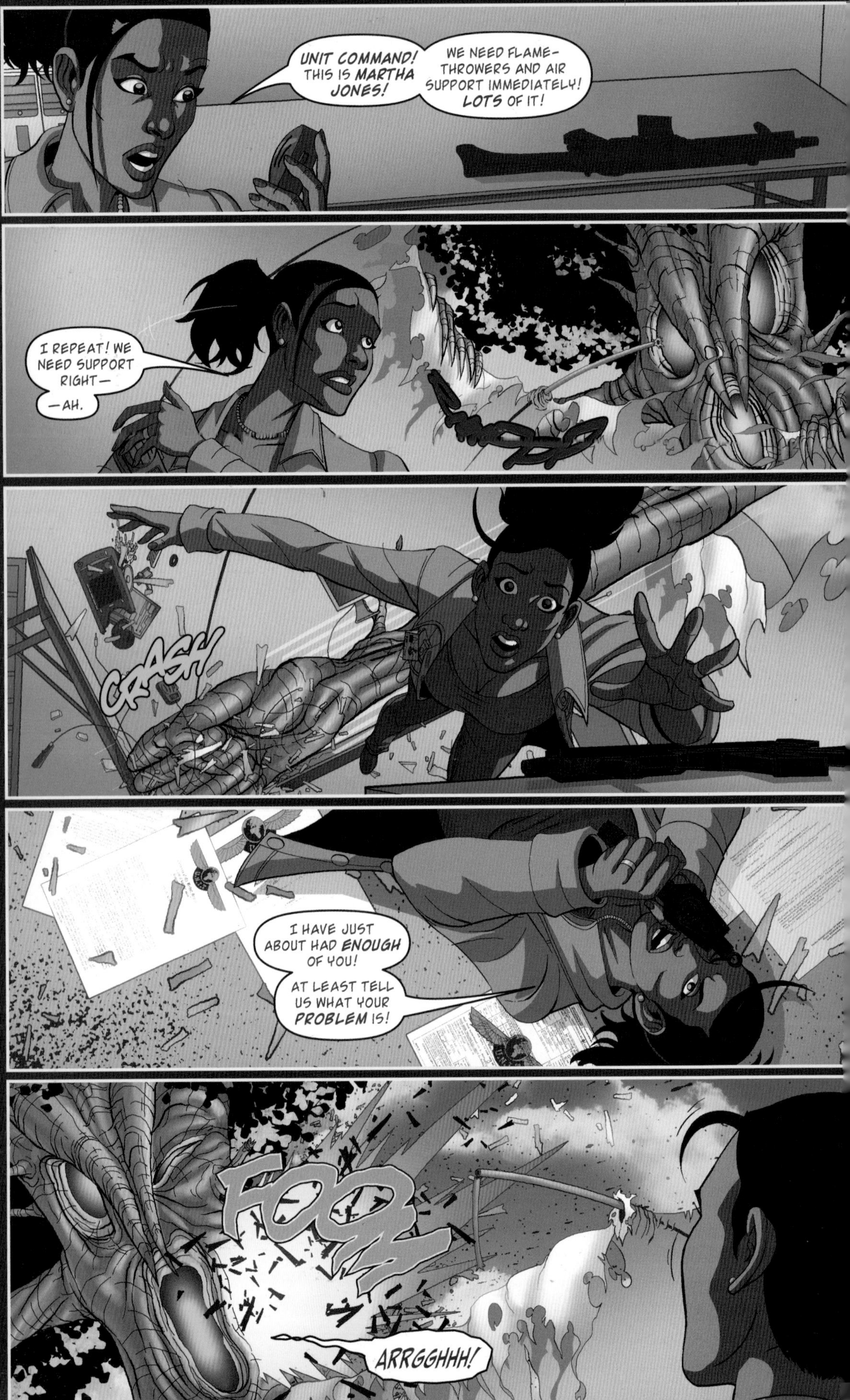
UNIT COMMAND! THIS IS MARTHA JONES!
WE NEED FLAME-THROWERS AND AIR SUPPORT IMMEDIATELY! LOTS OF IT!
I REPEAT! WE NEED SUPPORT RIGHT—
—AH.
CRASH
I HAVE JUST ABOUT HAD ENOUGH OF YOU!
AT LEAST TELL US WHAT YOUR PROBLEM IS!
FOOM
ARRGGHHH!

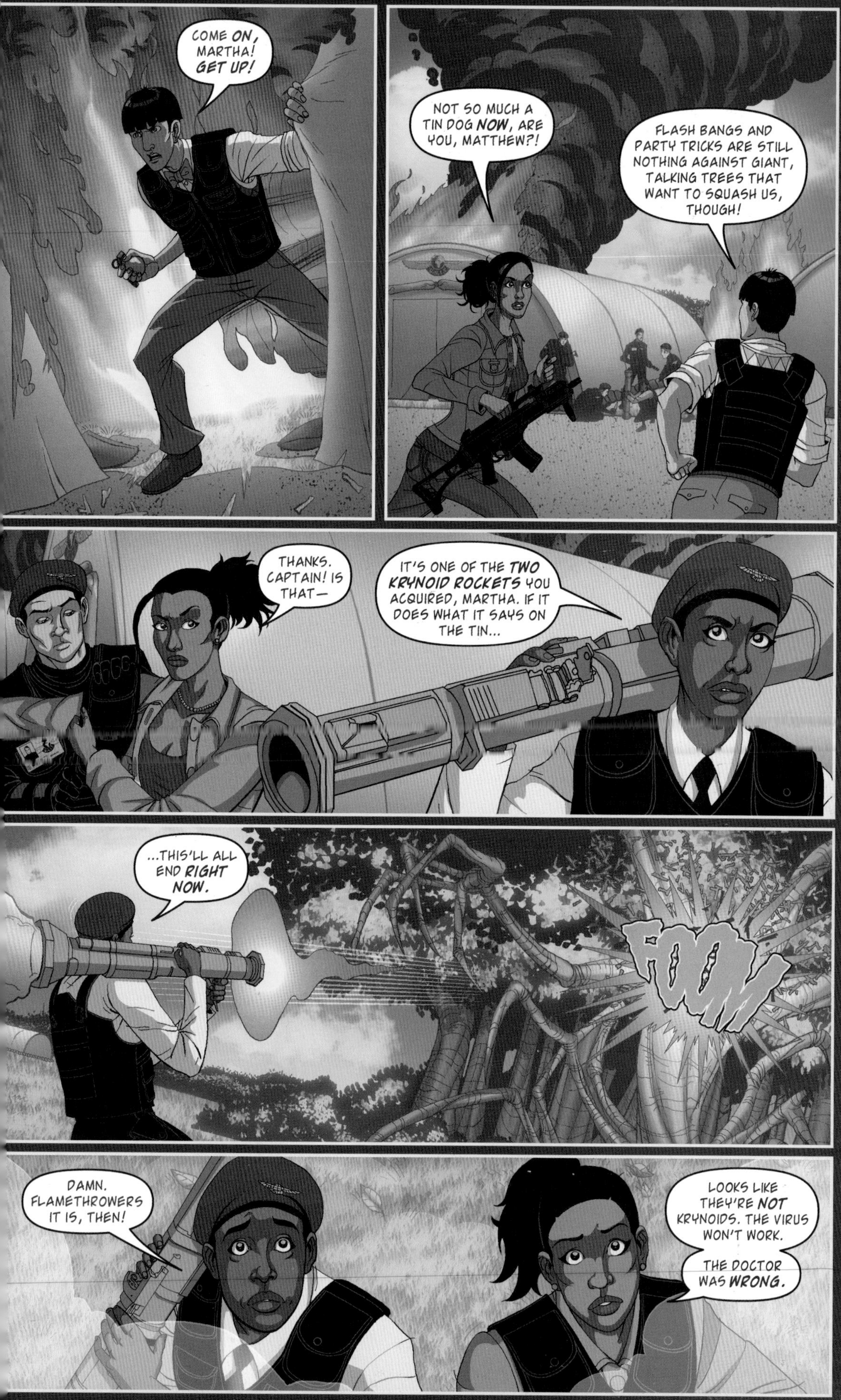
COME ON, MARTHA! GET UP!
NOT SO MUCH A TIN DOG NOW, ARE YOU, MATTHEW?!
FLASH BANGS AND PARTY TRICKS ARE STILL NOTHING AGAINST GIANT, TALKING TREES THAT WANT TO SQUASH US, THOUGH!
THANKS. CAPTAIN! IS THAT—
IT'S ONE OF THE TWO KRYNOID ROCKETS YOU ACQUIRED, MARTHA. IF IT DOES WHAT IT SAYS ON THE TIN...
...THIS'LL ALL END RIGHT NOW.
FOOM
DAMN. FLAMETHROWERS IT IS, THEN!
LOOKS LIKE THEY'RE NOT KRYNOIDS. THE VIRUS WON'T WORK.
THE DOCTOR WAS WRONG.

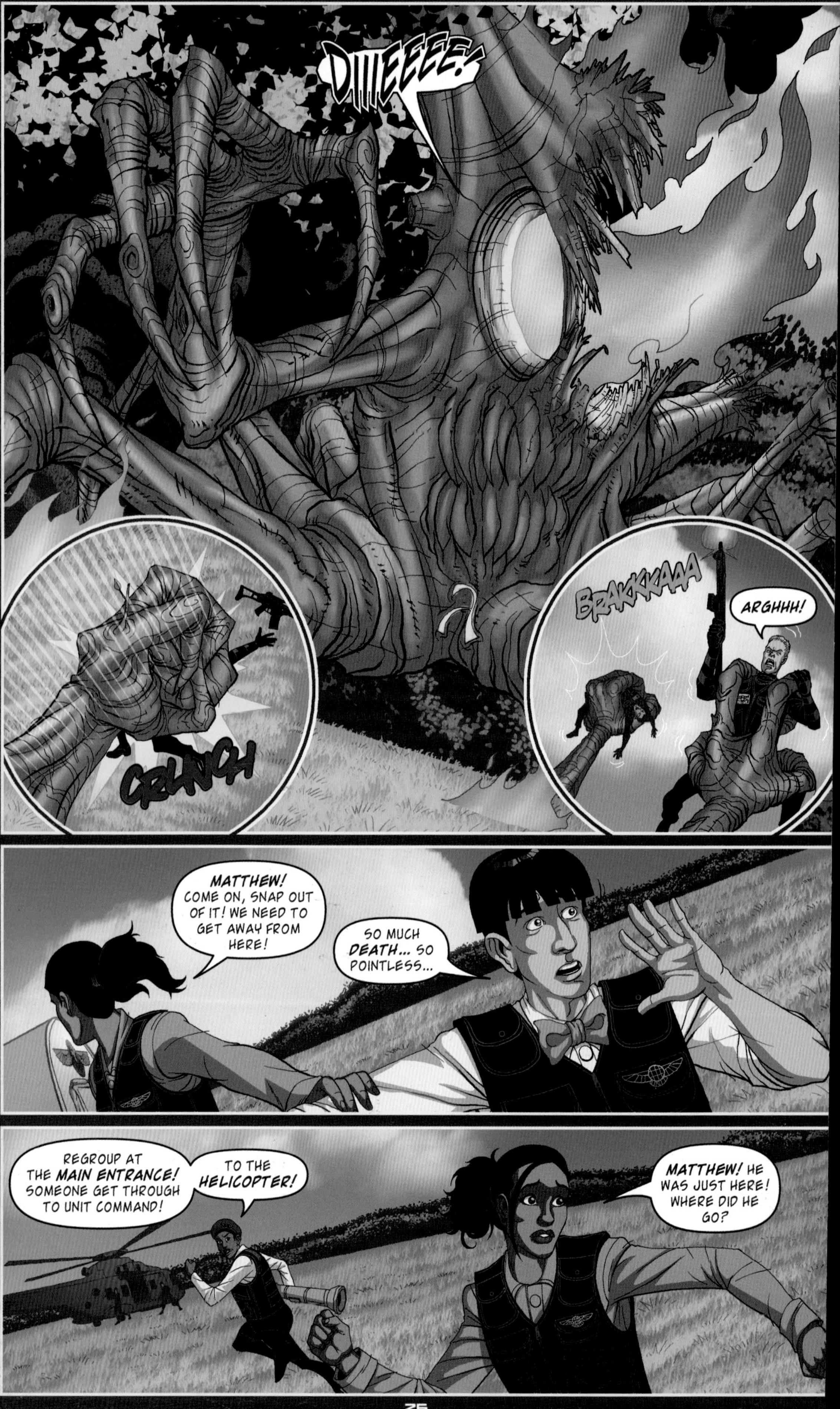
DIIIEEEE!
CRUNCH
BRAKKKAAA
ARGHHH!
MATTHEW! COME ON, SNAP OUT OF IT! WE NEED TO GET AWAY FROM HERE!
SO MUCH DEATH... SO POINTLESS...
REGROUP AT THE MAIN ENTRANCE! SOMEONE GET THROUGH TO UNIT COMMAND!
TO THE HELICOPTER!
MATTHEW! HE WAS JUST HERE! WHERE DID HE GO?

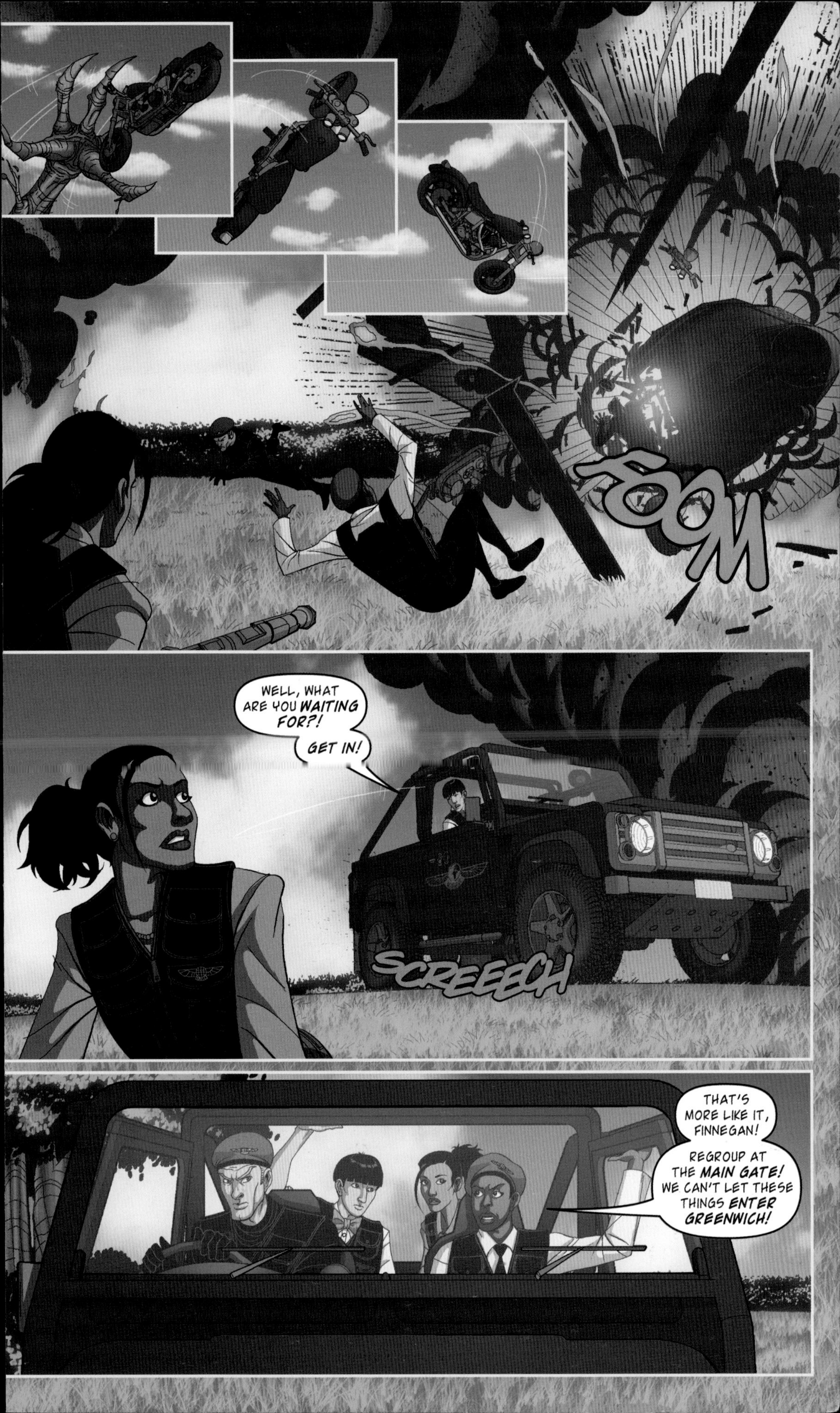
FOOM
WELL, WHAT ARE YOU WAITING FOR?!
GET IN!
SCREEEECH
THAT'S MORE LIKE IT, FINNEGAN!
REGROUP AT THE MAIN GATE! WE CAN'T LET THESE THINGS ENTER GREENWICH!

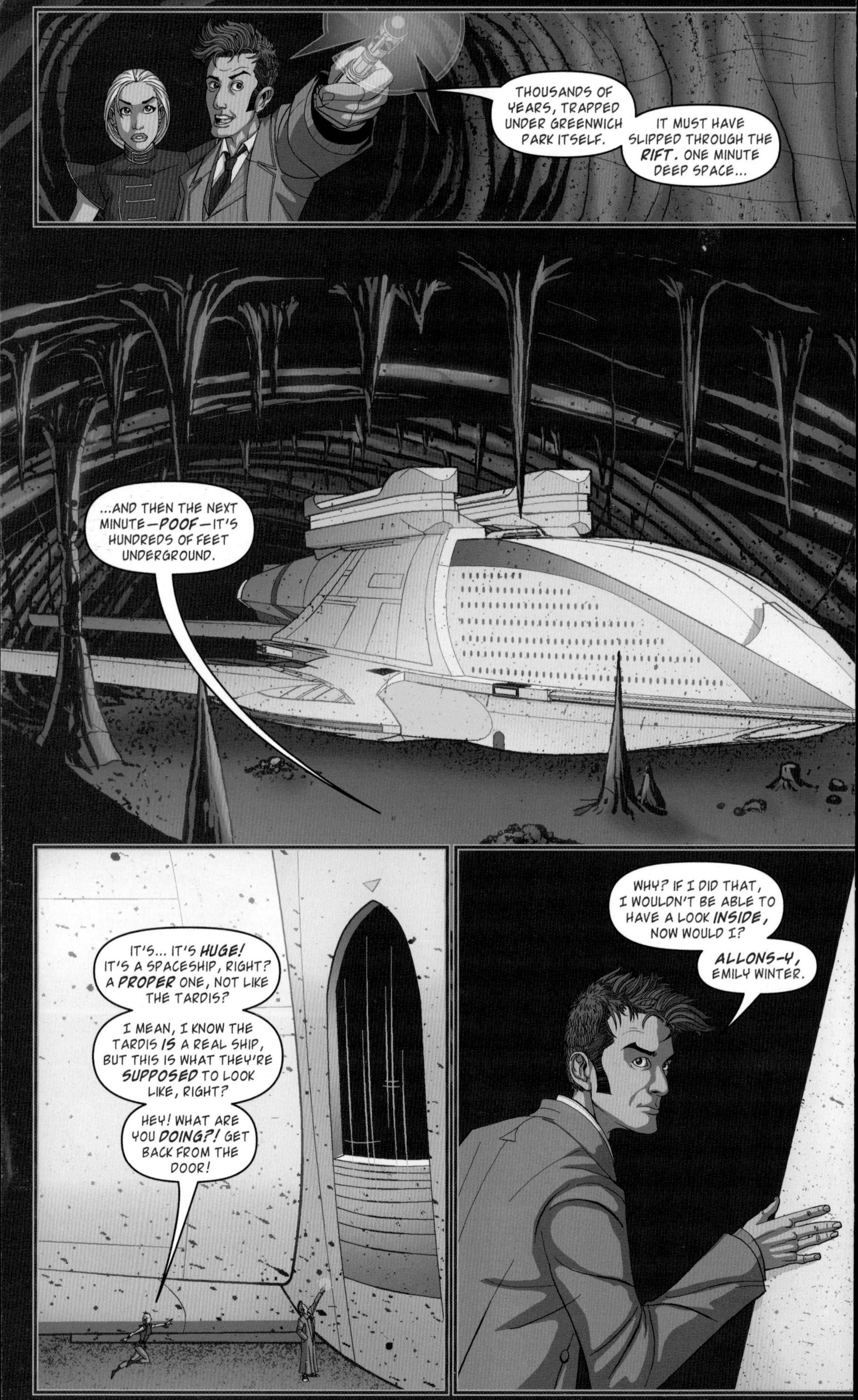
THOUSANDS OF YEARS, TRAPPED UNDER GREENWICH PARK ITSELF.
IT MUST HAVE SLIPPED THROUGH THE RIFT. ONE MINUTE DEEP SPACE...
...AND THEN THE NEXT MINUTE—POOF—IT'S HUNDREDS OF FEET UNDERGROUND.
IT'S... IT'S HUGE! IT'S A SPACESHIP, RIGHT? A PROPER ONE, NOT LIKE THE TARDIS?
I MEAN, I KNOW THE TARDIS IS A REAL SHIP, BUT THIS IS WHAT THEY'RE SUPPOSED TO LOOK LIKE, RIGHT?
HEY! WHAT ARE YOU DOING?! GET BACK FROM THE DOOR!
WHY? IF I DID THAT, I WOULDN'T BE ABLE TO HAVE A LOOK INSIDE, NOW WOULD I?
ALLONS-Y, EMILY WINTER.

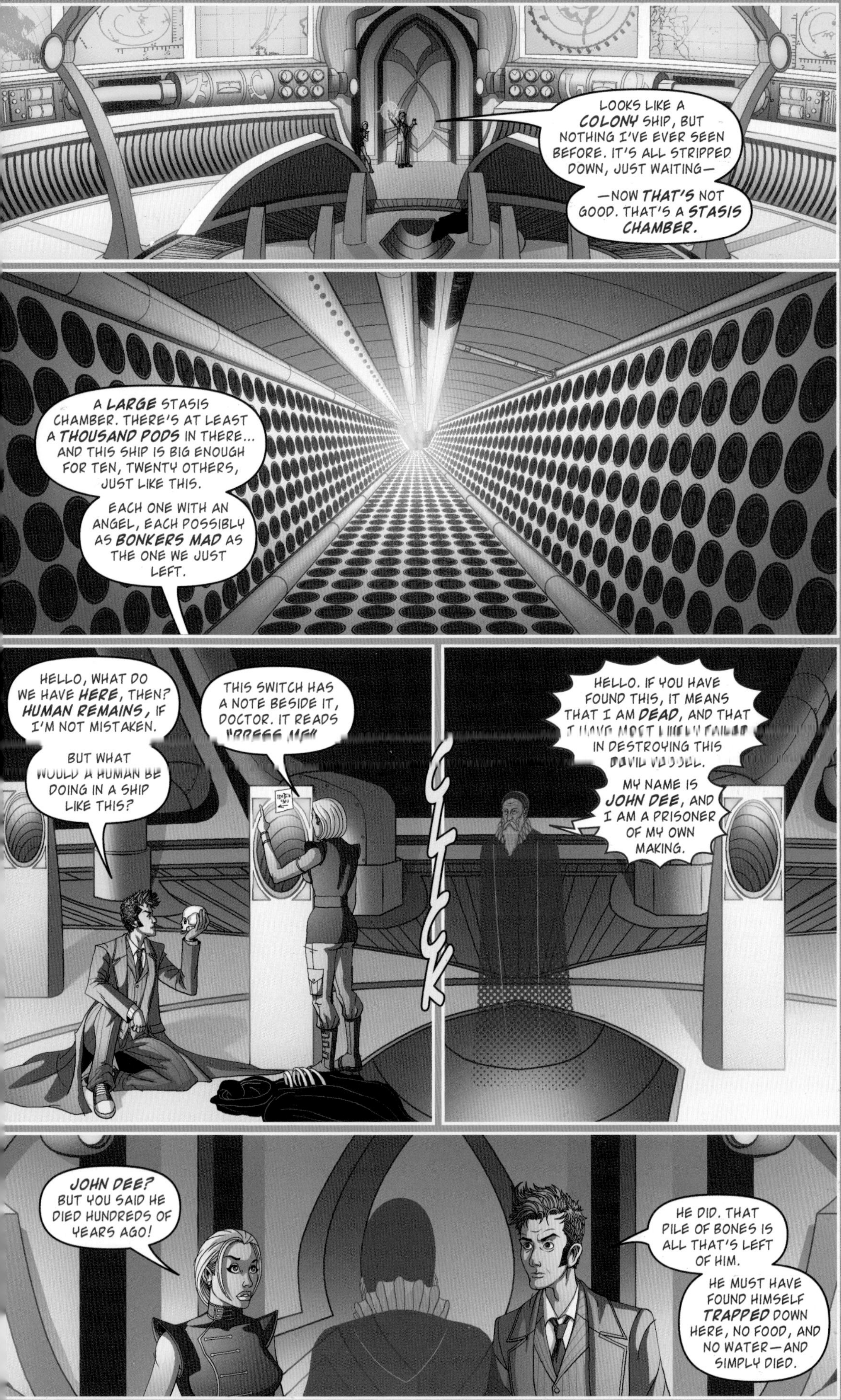

LOOKS LIKE A COLONY SHIP, BUT NOTHING I'VE EVER SEEN BEFORE. IT'S ALL STRIPPED DOWN, JUST WAITING—
—NOW THAT'S NOT GOOD. THAT'S A STASIS CHAMBER.
A LARGE STASIS CHAMBER. THERE'S AT LEAST A THOUSAND PODS IN THERE... AND THIS SHIP IS BIG ENOUGH FOR TEN, TWENTY OTHERS, JUST LIKE THIS.
EACH ONE WITH AN ANGEL, EACH POSSIBLY AS BONKERS MAD AS THE ONE WE JUST LEFT.
HELLO, WHAT DO WE HAVE HERE, THEN? HUMAN REMAINS, IF I'M NOT MISTAKEN.
BUT WHAT WOULD A HUMAN BE DOING IN A SHIP LIKE THIS?
THIS SWITCH HAS A NOTE BESIDE IT, DOCTOR. IT READS "PRESS ME"
CLICK
HELLO. IF YOU HAVE FOUND THIS, IT MEANS THAT I AM DEAD, AND THAT I HAVE MOST LIKELY FAILED IN DESTROYING THIS
MY NAME IS JOHN DEE, AND I AM A PRISONER OF MY OWN MAKING.
JOHN DEE? BUT YOU SAID HE DIED HUNDREDS OF YEARS AGO!
HE DID. THAT PILE OF BONES IS ALL THAT'S LEFT OF HIM.
HE MUST HAVE FOUND HIMSELF TRAPPED DOWN HERE, NO FOOD, AND NO WATER—AND SIMPLY DIED.

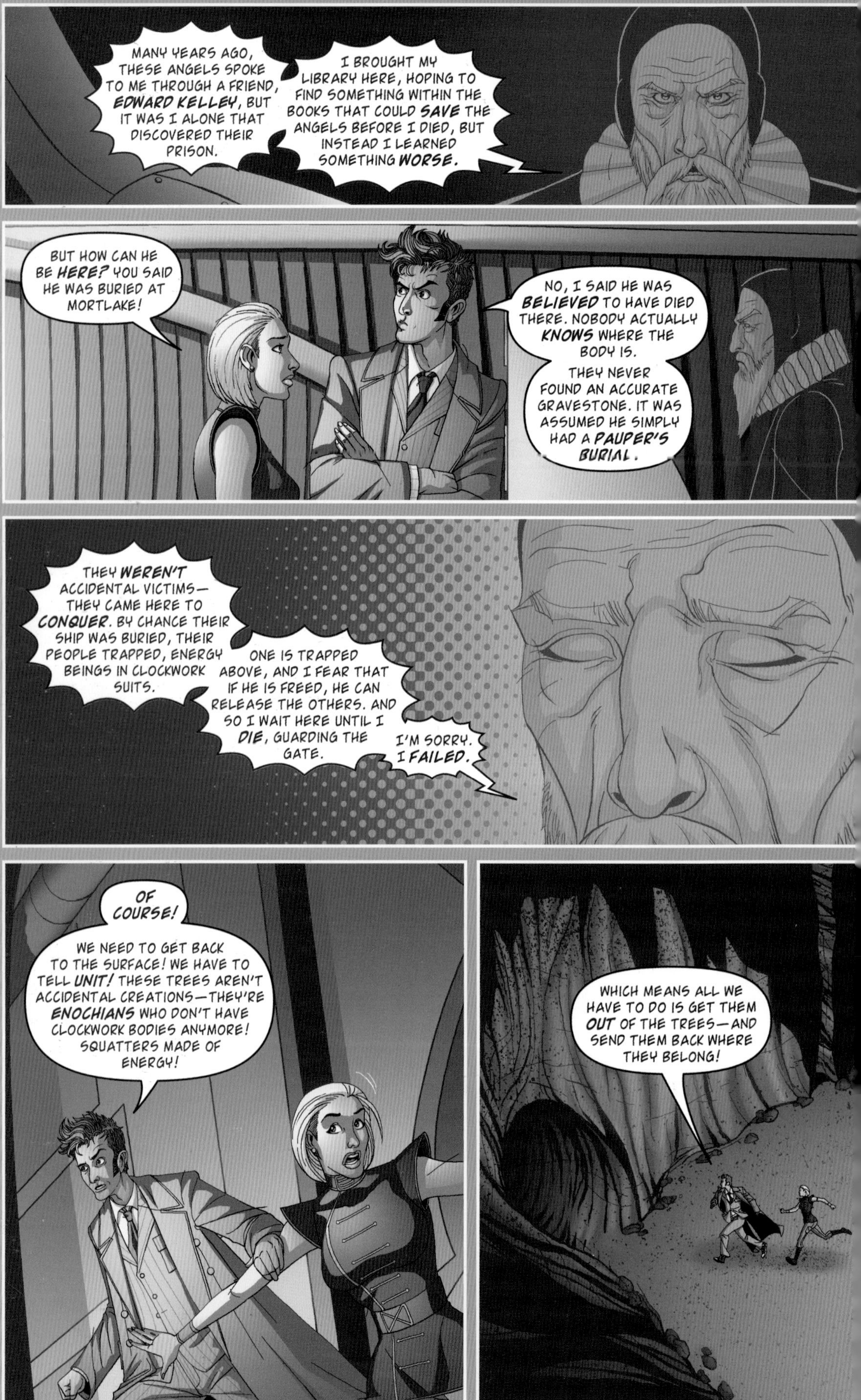
MANY YEARS AGO, THESE ANGELS SPOKE TO ME THROUGH A FRIEND, EDWARD KELLEY, BUT IT WAS I ALONE THAT DISCOVERED THEIR PRISON.
I BROUGHT MY LIBRARY HERE, HOPING TO FIND SOMETHING WITHIN THE BOOKS THAT COULD SAVE THE ANGELS BEFORE I DIED, BUT INSTEAD I LEARNED SOMETHING WORSE.
BUT HOW CAN HE BE HERE? YOU SAID HE WAS BURIED AT MORTLAKE!
NO, I SAID HE WAS BELIEVED TO HAVE DIED THERE. NOBODY ACTUALLY KNOWS WHERE THE BODY IS.
THEY NEVER FOUND AN ACCURATE GRAVESTONE. IT WAS ASSUMED HE SIMPLY HAD A PAUPER'S BURIAL.
THEY WEREN'T ACCIDENTAL VICTIMS—THEY CAME HERE TO CONQUER. BY CHANCE THEIR SHIP WAS BURIED, THEIR PEOPLE TRAPPED, ENERGY BEINGS IN CLOCKWORK SUITS.
ONE IS TRAPPED ABOVE, AND I FEAR THAT IF HE IS FREED, HE CAN RELEASE THE OTHERS. AND SO I WAIT HERE UNTIL I DIE, GUARDING THE GATE.
I'M SORRY. I FAILED.
OF COURSE!
WE NEED TO GET BACK TO THE SURFACE! WE HAVE TO TELL UNIT! THESE TREES AREN'T ACCIDENTAL CREATIONS—THEY'RE ENOCHIANS WHO DON'T HAVE CLOCKWORK BODIES ANYMORE! SQUATTERS MADE OF ENERGY!
WHICH MEANS ALL WE HAVE TO DO IS GET THEM OUT OF THE TREES—AND SEND THEM BACK WHERE THEY BELONG!

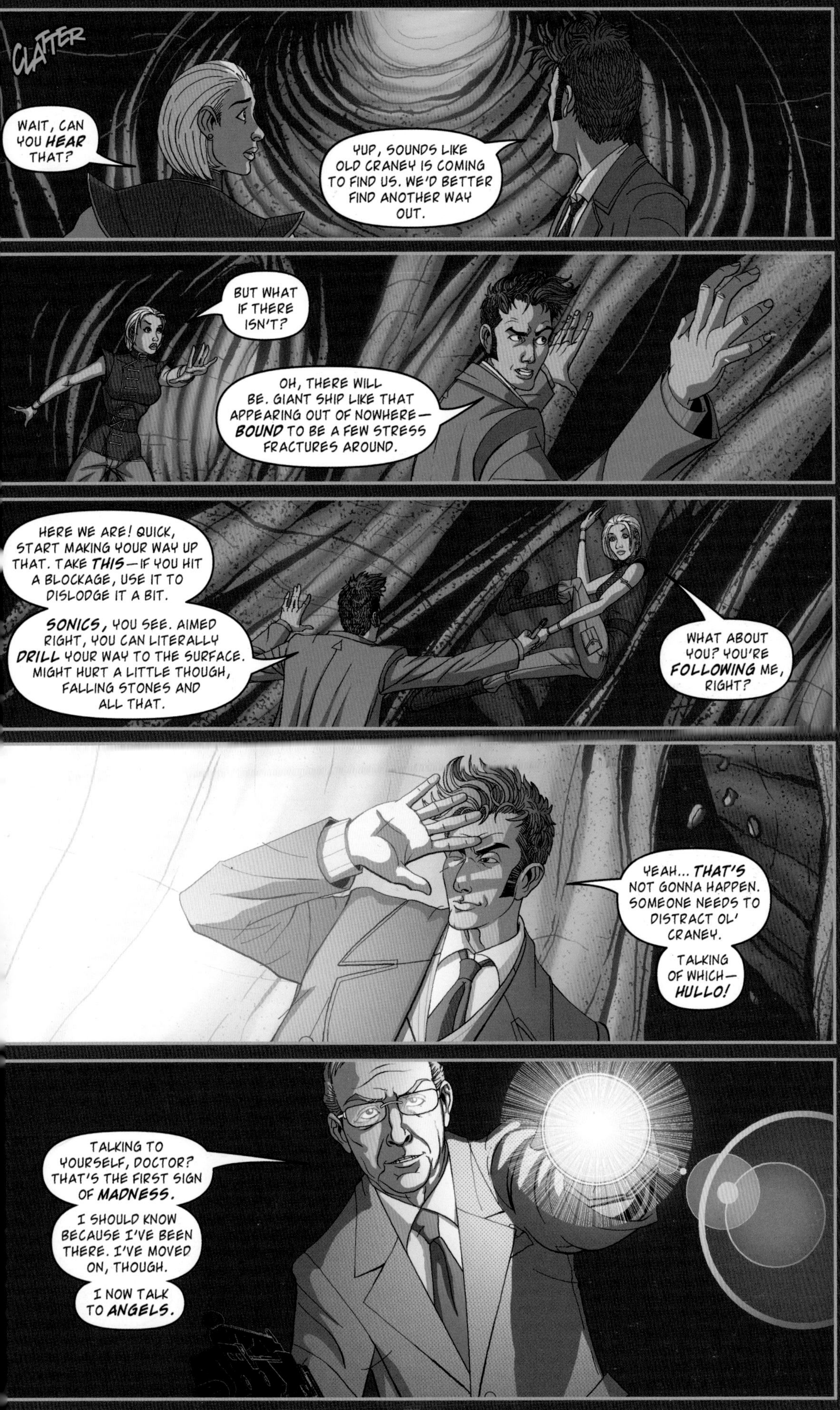
CLATTER
WAIT, CAN YOU HEAR THAT?
YUP, SOUNDS LIKE OLD CRANEY IS COMING TO FIND US. WE'D BETTER FIND ANOTHER WAY OUT.
BUT WHAT IF THERE ISN'T?
OH, THERE WILL BE. GIANT SHIP LIKE THAT APPEARING OUT OF NOWHERE— BOUND TO BE A FEW STRESS FRACTURES AROUND.
HERE WE ARE! QUICK, START MAKING YOUR WAY UP THAT. TAKE THIS—IF YOU HIT A BLOCKAGE, USE IT TO DISLODGE IT A BIT.
SONICS, YOU SEE. AIMED RIGHT, YOU CAN LITERALLY DRILL YOUR WAY TO THE SURFACE. MIGHT HURT A LITTLE THOUGH, FALLING STONES AND ALL THAT.
WHAT ABOUT YOU? YOU'RE FOLLOWING ME, RIGHT?
YEAH... THAT'S NOT GONNA HAPPEN. SOMEONE NEEDS TO DISTRACT OL' CRANEY.
TALKING OF WHICH— HULLO!
TALKING TO YOURSELF, DOCTOR? THAT'S THE FIRST SIGN OF MADNESS.
I SHOULD KNOW BECAUSE I'VE BEEN THERE. I'VE MOVED ON, THOUGH.
I NOW TALK TO ANGELS.

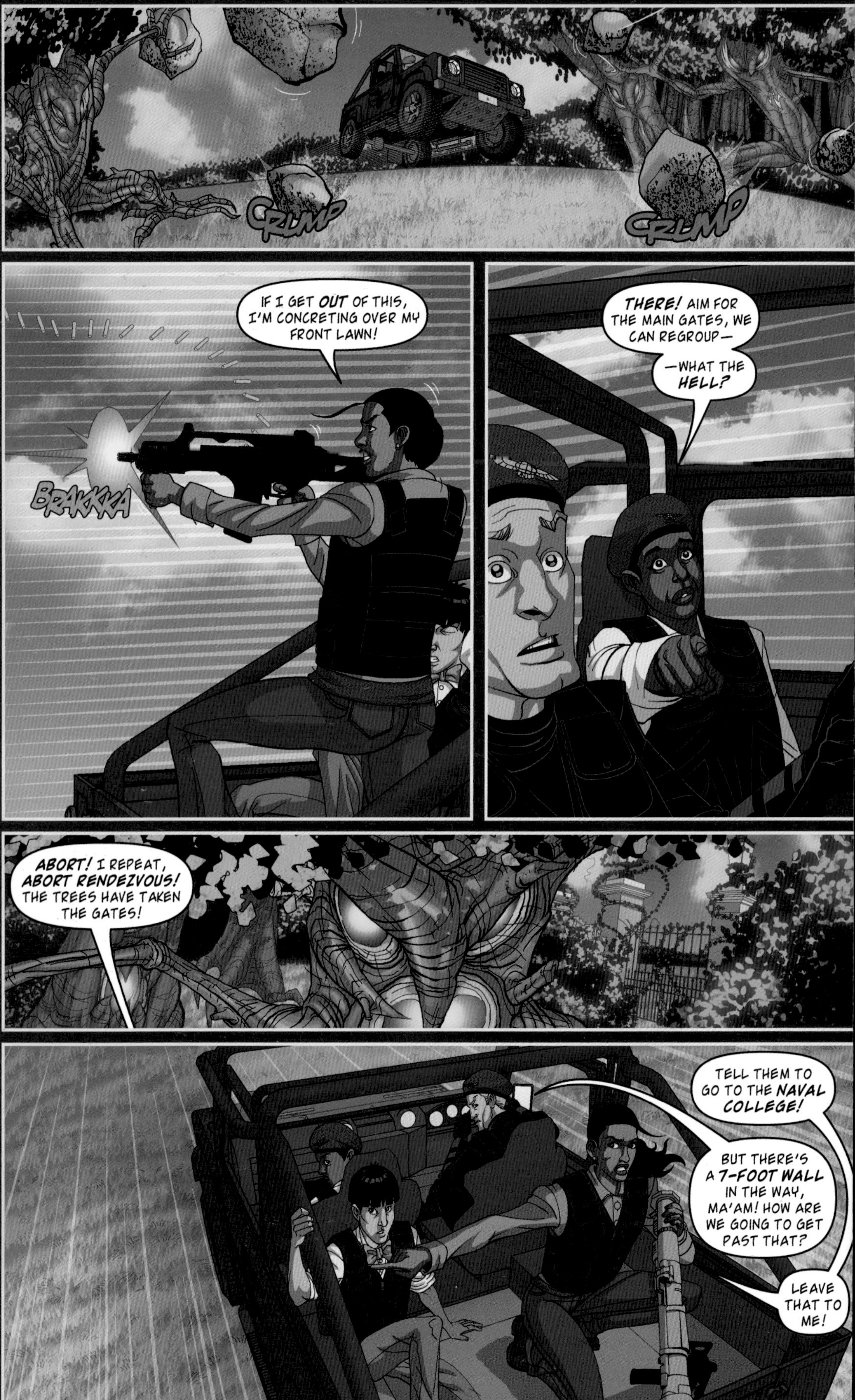
CRUMP
CRUMP
IF I GET OUT OF THIS, I'M CONCRETING OVER MY FRONT LAWN!
BRAKKKA
THERE! AIM FOR THE MAIN GATES, WE CAN REGROUP—
—WHAT THE HELL?
ABORT! I REPEAT, ABORT RENDEZVOUS! THE TREES HAVE TAKEN THE GATES!
TELL THEM TO GO TO THE NAVAL COLLEGE!
BUT THERE'S A 7-FOOT WALL IN THE WAY, MA'AM! HOW ARE WE GOING TO GET PAST THAT?
LEAVE THAT TO ME!

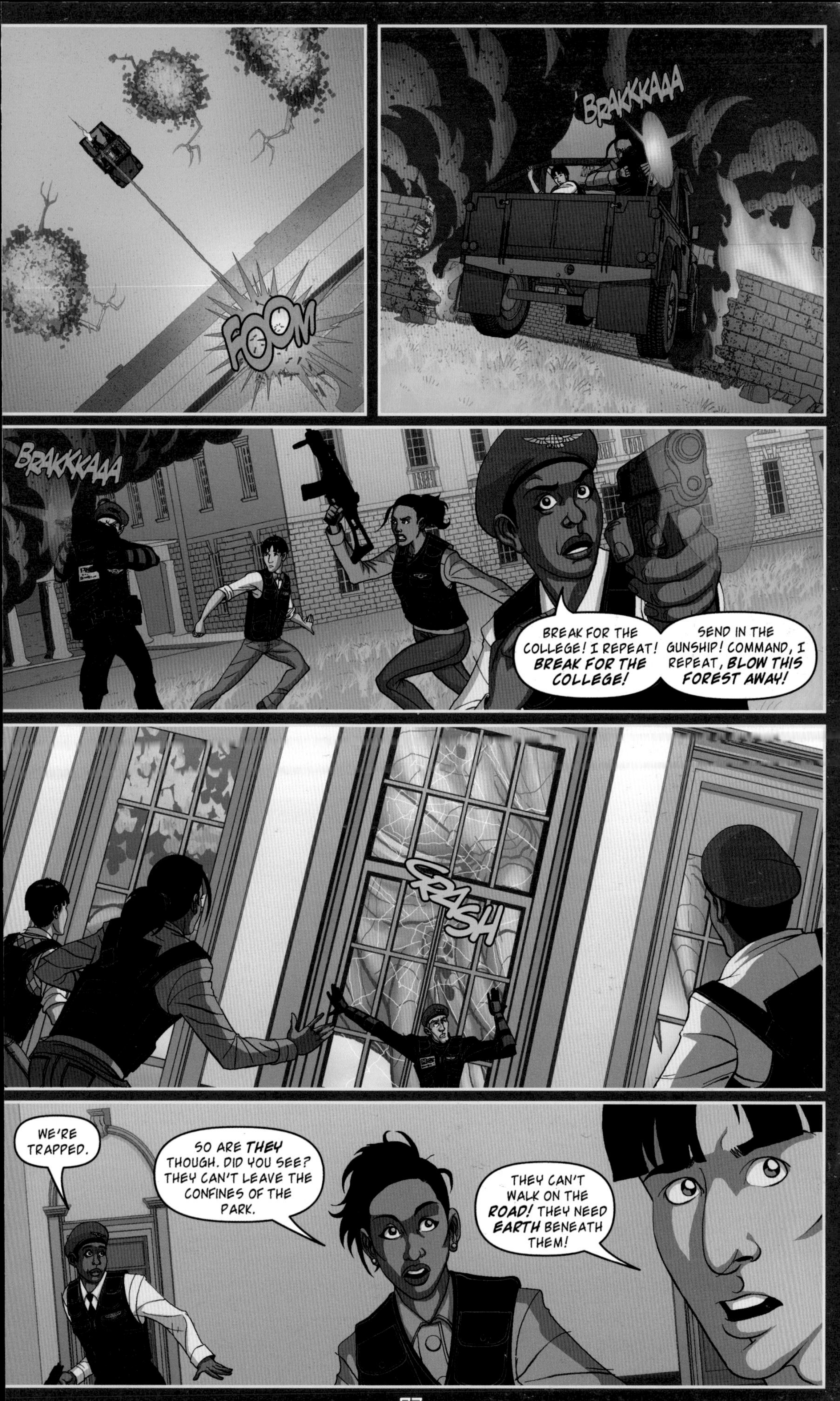
FOOM
BRAKKKAAA
BRAKKKAAA
BREAK FOR THE COLLEGE! I REPEAT! BREAK FOR THE COLLEGE!
SEND IN THE GUNSHIP! COMMAND, I REPEAT, BLOW THIS FOREST AWAY!
CRASH
WE'RE TRAPPED.
SO ARE THEY THOUGH. DID YOU SEE? THEY CAN'T LEAVE THE CONFINES OF THE PARK.
THEY CAN'T WALK ON THE ROAD! THEY NEED EARTH BENEATH THEM!

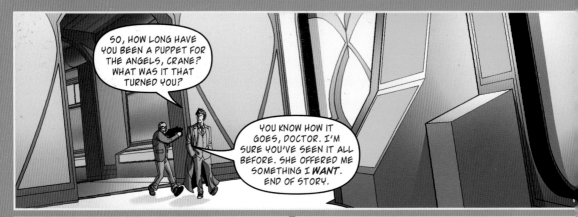

SO, HOW LONG HAVE YOU BEEN A PUPPET FOR THE ANGELS, CRANE? WHAT WAS IT THAT TURNED YOU?

YOU KNOW HOW IT GOES, DOCTOR. I'M SURE YOU'VE SEEN IT ALL BEFORE. SHE OFFERED ME SOMETHING I *WANT*. END OF STORY.

"SHE"? NOW *THAT'S* AN INTERESTING SLIP OF THE TONGUE TO HAVE.

BE CAREFUL OF WHAT YOU ACCEPT AS A *BILL OF SALE*, CRANE. THE *LAST* PERSON THE ANGELS OFFERED EVERYTHING TO IS LYING RIGHT THERE.

LOOK, DOCTOR, I'M NOT A *BAD* MAN.

IT'S JUST... SOMETIMES I FEEL I HAVE SO MUCH *MORE* THAT SHOULD HAVE HAPPENED TO ME / I SHOULD BE LEADING *COMPANIES*, NOT SITTING IN A TWO-BEDROOM IN THE SUBURBS.

I KNOW CEOS WHO *DREAM* OF YOUR LIFE. DON'T TAKE IT FOR GRANTED.

OH, BELIEVE ME, I DON'T. AND SOON, THOSE CEOS WILL BE SWAPPING PLACES QUITE HAPPILY.

I HAVE THE DOCTOR. THE WOMAN HAS ESCAPED.

LEAVE HER, THERE IS NO OTHER WAY OUT! LET HER DIE DOWN THERE LIKE DEE!

BRING THE DOCTOR AND HIS SONIC DEVICE TO ME!

AH. WHOOPS. *LOST* IT. I'M ALWAYS DOING THAT.

I COULD PROBABLY FIND A *CHEESE SANDWICH* OR A *WALNUT WHIP* IF YOU WANT...

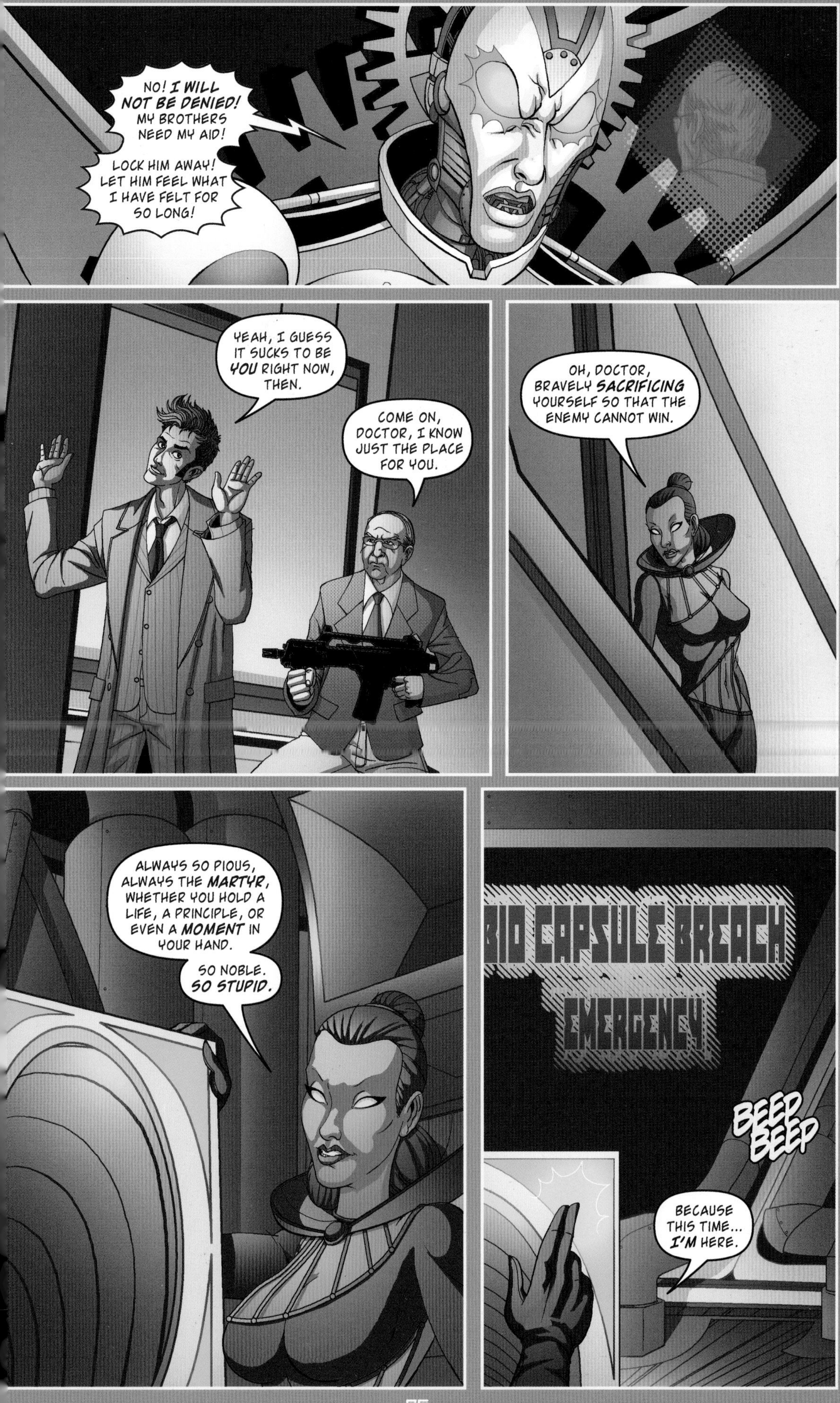

NO! I WILL NOT BE DENIED! MY BROTHERS NEED MY AID!
LOCK HIM AWAY! LET HIM FEEL WHAT I HAVE FELT FOR SO LONG!
YEAH, I GUESS IT SUCKS TO BE YOU RIGHT NOW, THEN.
COME ON, DOCTOR, I KNOW JUST THE PLACE FOR YOU.
OH, DOCTOR, BRAVELY SACRIFICING YOURSELF SO THAT THE ENEMY CANNOT WIN.
ALWAYS SO PIOUS, ALWAYS THE MARTYR, WHETHER YOU HOLD A LIFE, A PRINCIPLE, OR EVEN A MOMENT IN YOUR HAND.
SO NOBLE. SO STUPID.
BIO CAPSULE BREACH
EMERGENCY
BEEP BEEP
BECAUSE THIS TIME... I'M HERE.

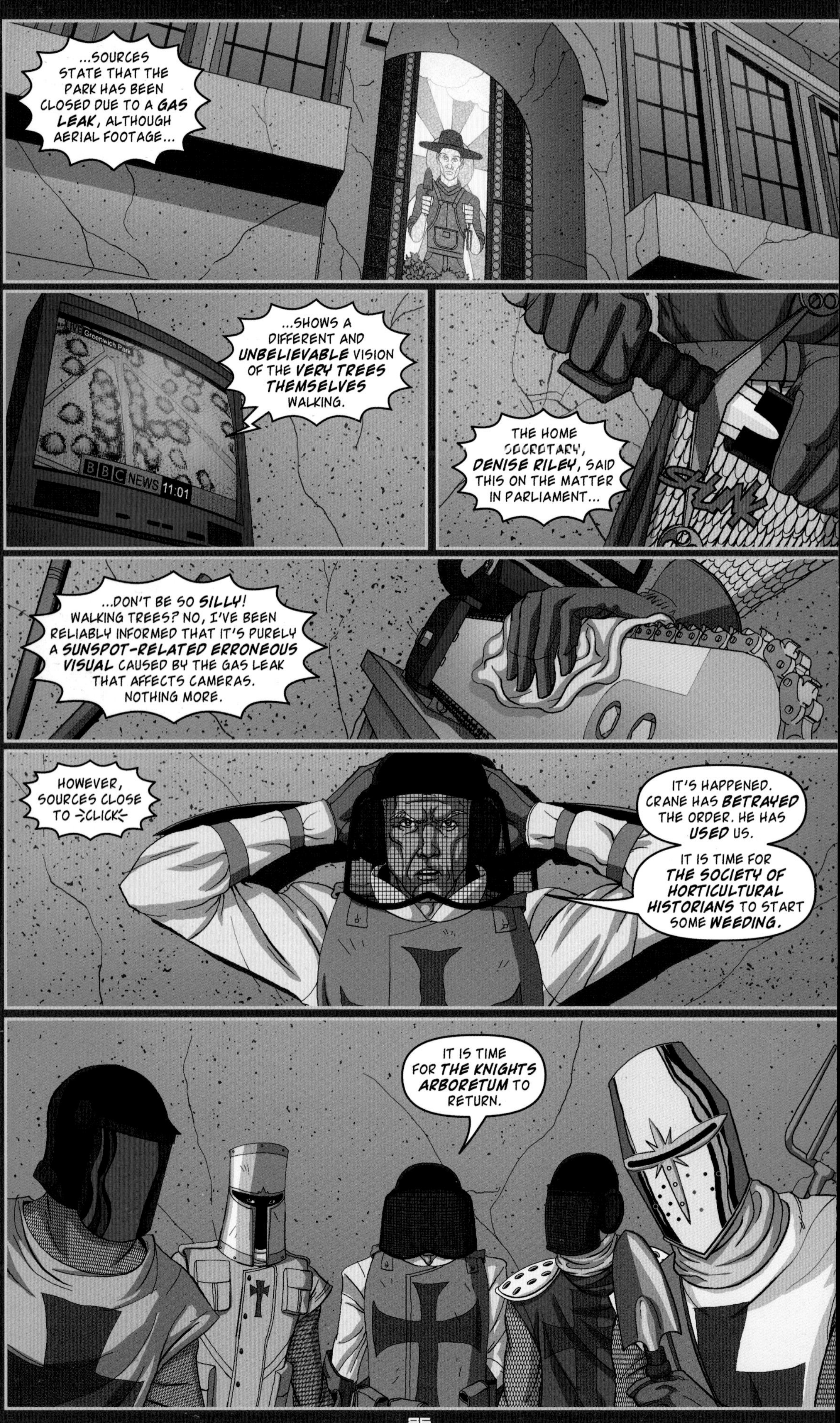
...SOURCES STATE THAT THE PARK HAS BEEN CLOSED DUE TO A GAS LEAK, ALTHOUGH AERIAL FOOTAGE...
LIVE Greenwich Park
BBC NEWS 11:01
...SHOWS A DIFFERENT AND UNBELIEVABLE VISION OF THE VERY TREES THEMSELVES WALKING.
THE HOME SECRETARY, DENISE RILEY, SAID THIS ON THE MATTER IN PARLIAMENT...
...DON'T BE SO SILLY! WALKING TREES? NO, I'VE BEEN RELIABLY INFORMED THAT IT'S PURELY A SUNSPOT-RELATED ERRONEOUS VISUAL CAUSED BY THE GAS LEAK THAT AFFECTS CAMERAS. NOTHING MORE.
HOWEVER, SOURCES CLOSE TO -CLICK-
IT'S HAPPENED. CRANE HAS BETRAYED THE ORDER. HE HAS USED US.
IT IS TIME FOR THE SOCIETY OF HORTICULTURAL HISTORIANS TO START SOME WEEDING.
IT IS TIME FOR THE KNIGHTS ARBORETUM TO RETURN.

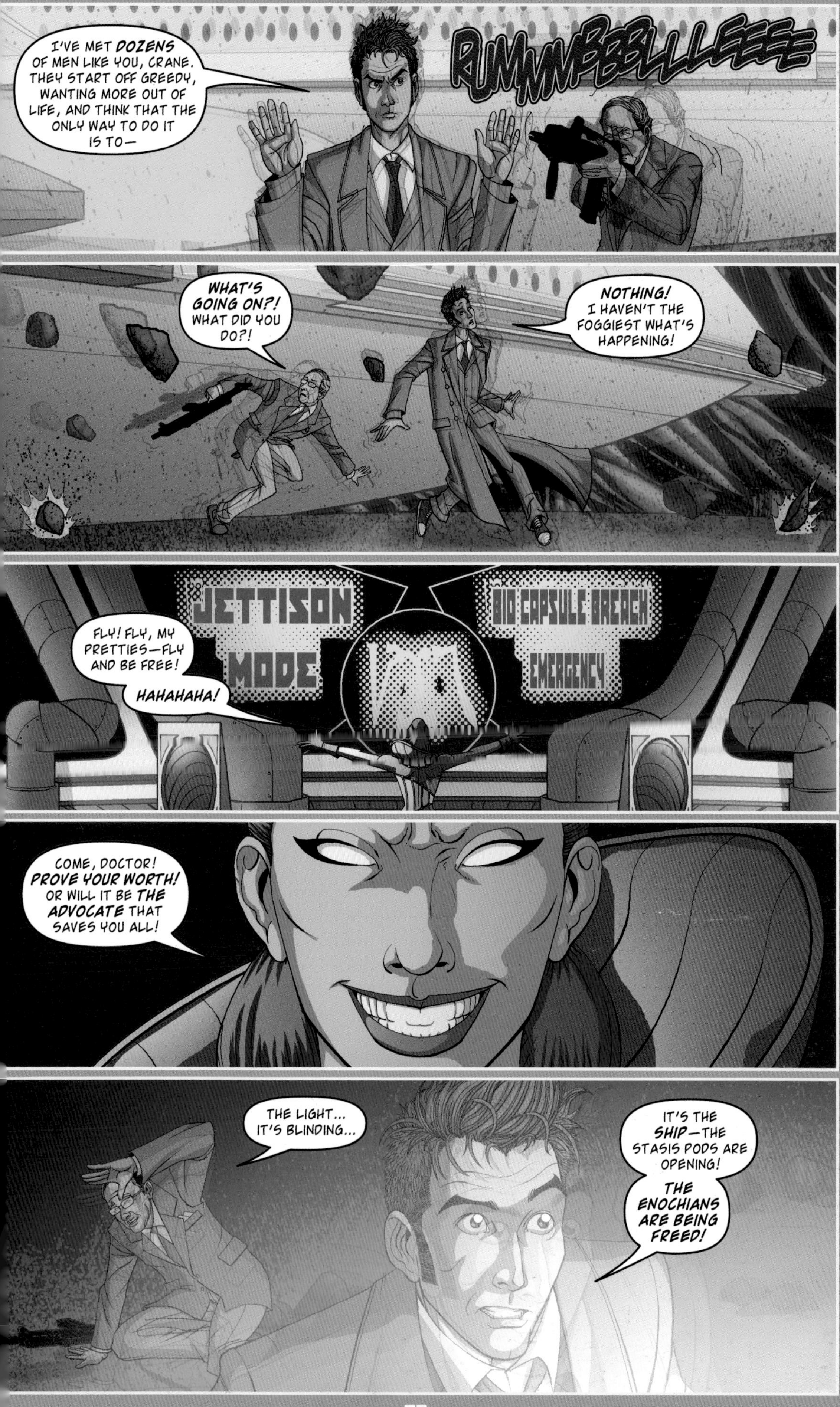
I'VE MET DOZENS OF MEN LIKE YOU, CRANE. THEY START OFF GREEDY, WANTING MORE OUT OF LIFE, AND THINK THAT THE ONLY WAY TO DO IT IS TO—
RUMMMBBBLLLEEEE
WHAT'S GOING ON?! WHAT DID YOU DO?!
NOTHING! I HAVEN'T THE FOGGIEST WHAT'S HAPPENING!
JETTISON MODE
BIO CAPSULE BREACH EMERGENCY
FLY! FLY, MY PRETTIES—FLY AND BE FREE!
HAHAHAHA!
COME, DOCTOR! PROVE YOUR WORTH! OR WILL IT BE THE ADVOCATE THAT SAVES YOU ALL!
THE LIGHT... IT'S BLINDING...
IT'S THE SHIP—THE STASIS PODS ARE OPENING!
THE ENOCHIANS ARE BEING FREED!

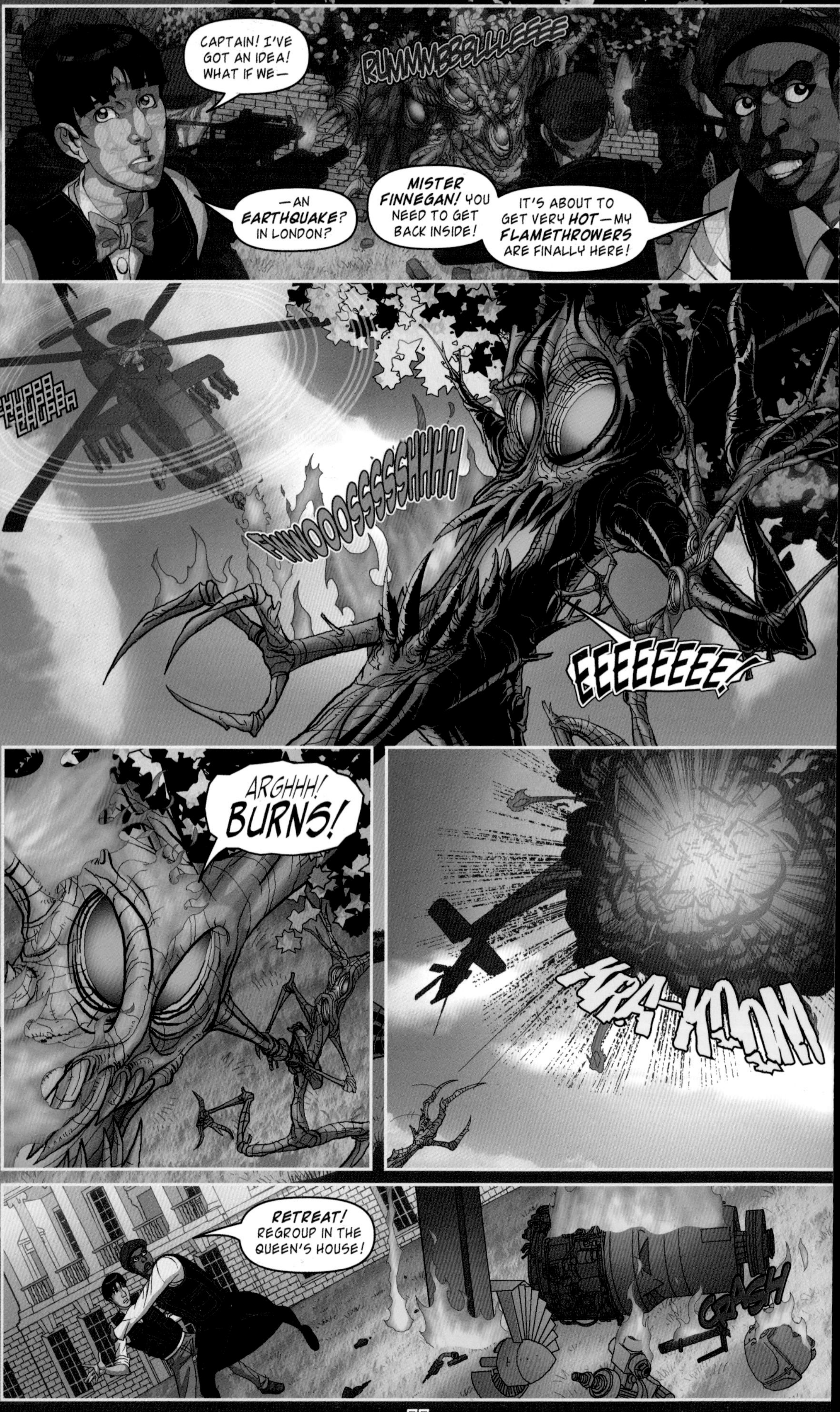

CAPTAIN! I'VE GOT AN IDEA! WHAT IF WE—
RUMMMBBBLLLEEEE
—AN EARTHQUAKE? IN LONDON?
MISTER FINNEGAN! YOU NEED TO GET BACK INSIDE!
IT'S ABOUT TO GET VERY HOT—MY FLAMETHROWERS ARE FINALLY HERE!
CHUPPA CHUPPA CHUPPA
FWWOOOSSSSSHHHH
EEEEEEEE!
ARGHHH! BURNS!
KRA-KOOM
RETREAT! REGROUP IN THE QUEEN'S HOUSE!
CRASH

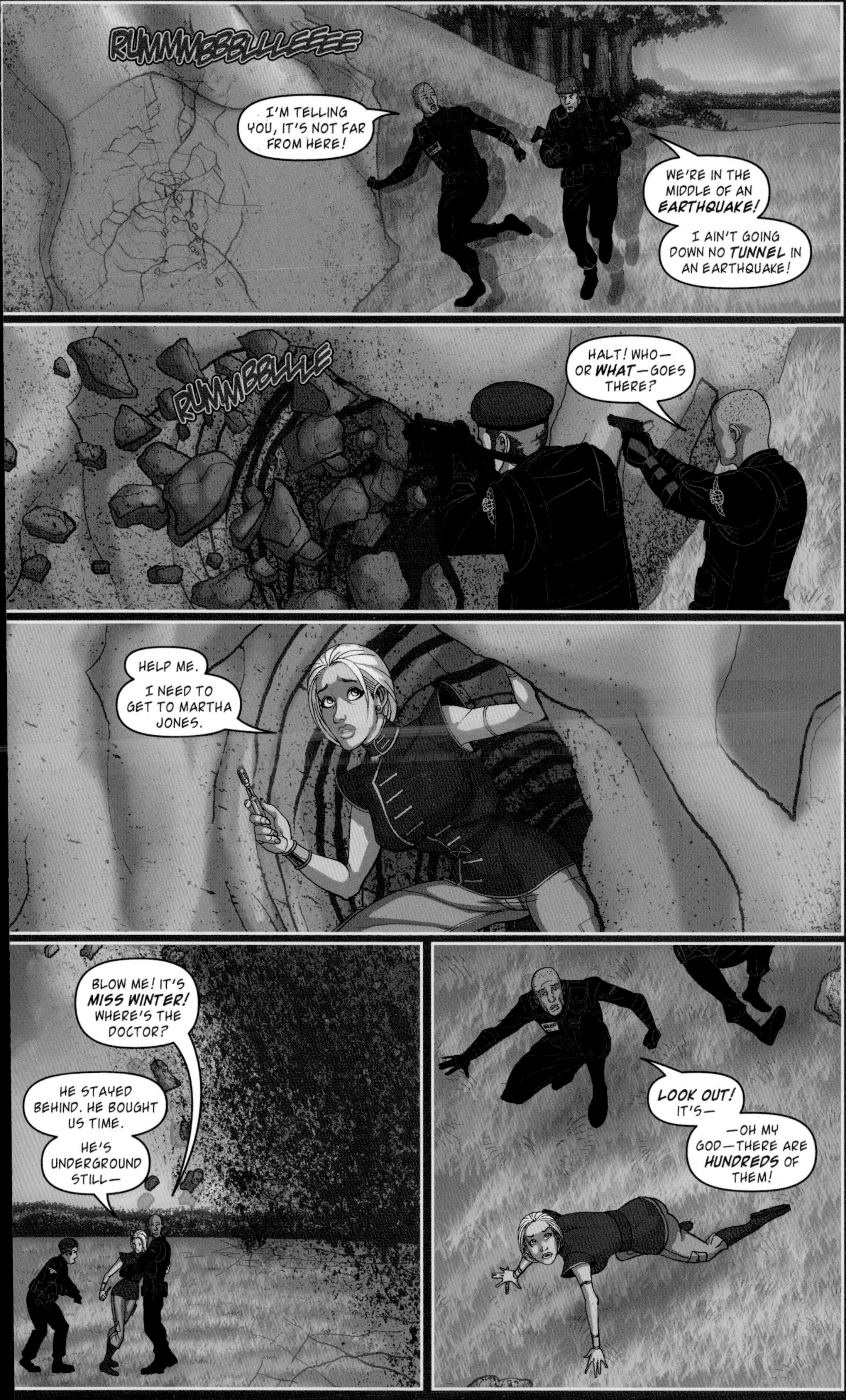
RUMMMBBBLLLEEEE
I'M TELLING YOU, IT'S NOT FAR FROM HERE!
WE'RE IN THE MIDDLE OF AN EARTHQUAKE!
I AIN'T GOING DOWN NO TUNNEL IN AN EARTHQUAKE!
RUMMBBLLLE
HALT! WHO— OR WHAT—GOES THERE?
HELP ME.
I NEED TO GET TO MARTHA JONES.
BLOW ME! IT'S MISS WINTER! WHERE'S THE DOCTOR?
HE STAYED BEHIND. HE BOUGHT US TIME.
HE'S UNDERGROUND STILL—
LOOK OUT! IT'S—
—OH MY GOD—THERE ARE HUNDREDS OF THEM!

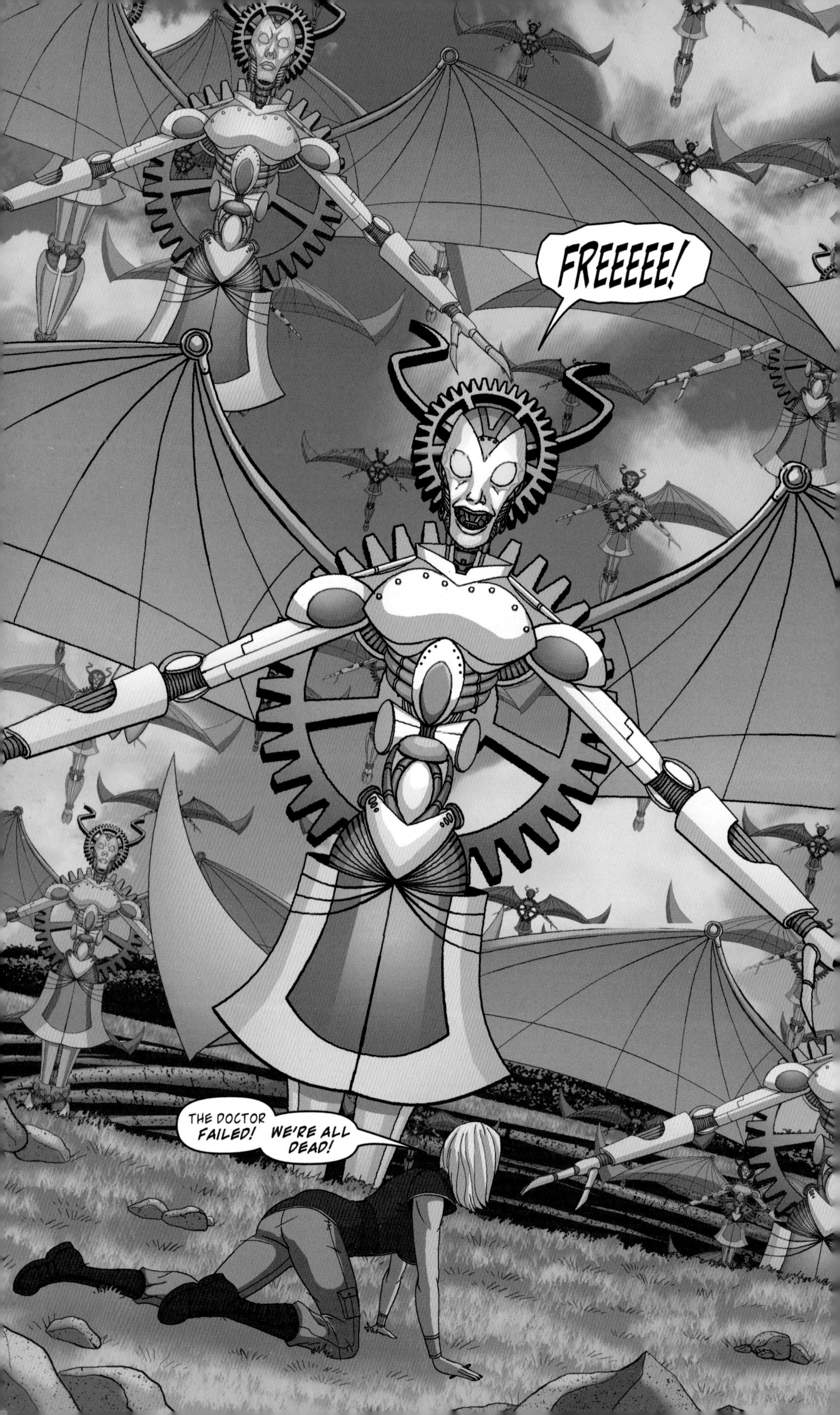
FREEEEE!
THE DOCTOR FAILED!
WE'RE ALL DEAD!

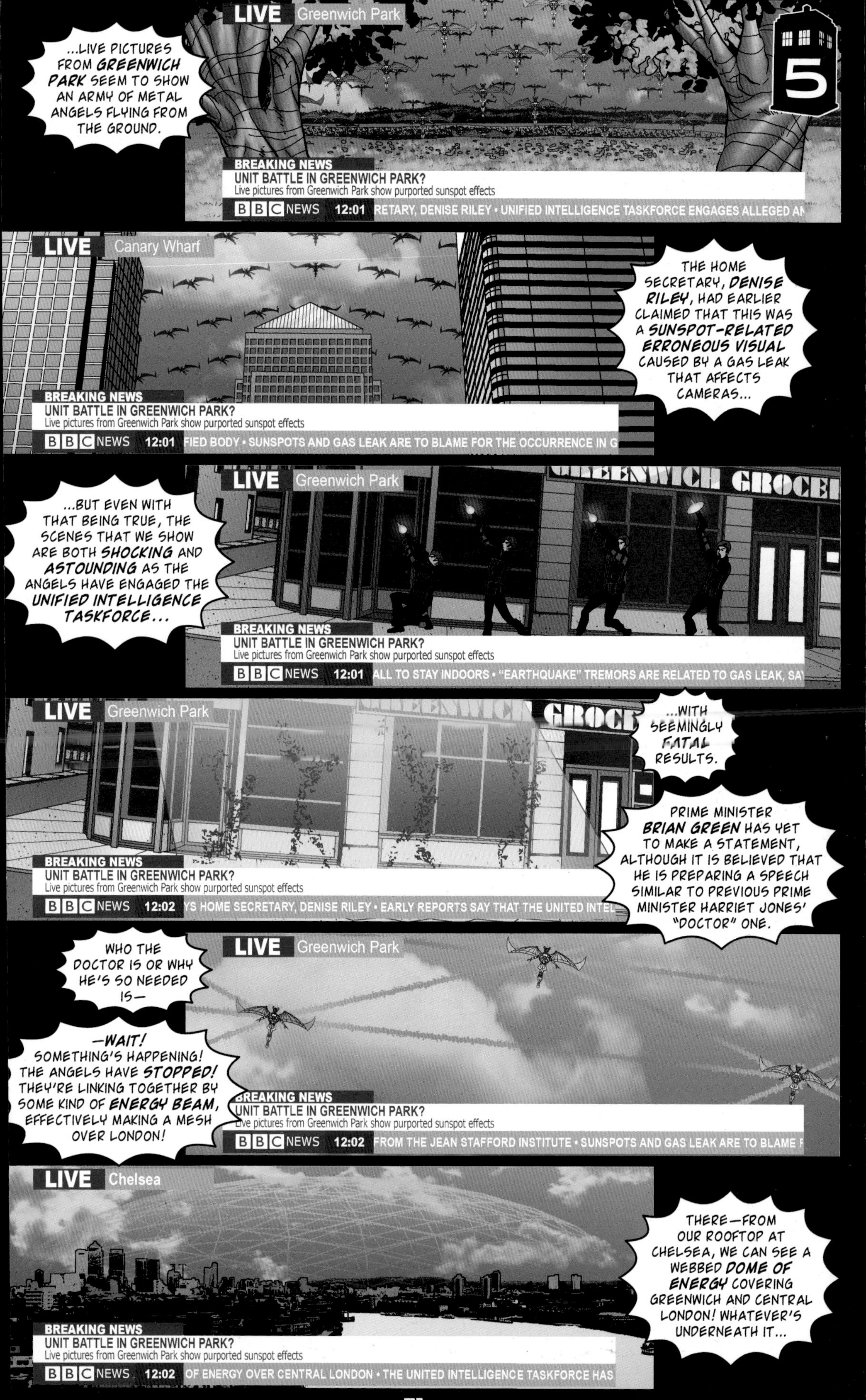
LIVE Greenwich Park
...LIVE PICTURES FROM GREENWICH PARK SEEM TO SHOW AN ARMY OF METAL ANGELS FLYING FROM THE GROUND.
5
BREAKING NEWS
UNIT BATTLE IN GREENWICH PARK?
Live pictures from Greenwich Park show purported sunspot effects
BBC NEWS 12:01 RETARY, DENISE RILEY • UNIFIED INTELLIGENCE TASKFORCE ENGAGES ALLEGED AN
LIVE Canary Wharf
THE HOME SECRETARY, DENISE RILEY, HAD EARLIER CLAIMED THAT THIS WAS A SUNSPOT-RELATED ERRONEOUS VISUAL CAUSED BY A GAS LEAK THAT AFFECTS CAMERAS...
BREAKING NEWS
UNIT BATTLE IN GREENWICH PARK?
Live pictures from Greenwich Park show purported sunspot effects
BBC NEWS 12:01 FIED BODY • SUNSPOTS AND GAS LEAK ARE TO BLAME FOR THE OCCURRENCE IN G
LIVE Greenwich Park
GREENWICH GROCE
...BUT EVEN WITH THAT BEING TRUE, THE SCENES THAT WE SHOW ARE BOTH SHOCKING AND ASTOUNDING AS THE ANGELS HAVE ENGAGED THE UNIFIED INTELLIGENCE TASKFORCE...
BREAKING NEWS
UNIT BATTLE IN GREENWICH PARK?
Live pictures from Greenwich Park show purported sunspot effects
BBC NEWS 12:01 ALL TO STAY INDOORS • "EARTHQUAKE" TREMORS ARE RELATED TO GAS LEAK, SA
LIVE Greenwich Park
...WITH SEEMINGLY FATAL RESULTS.
PRIME MINISTER BRIAN GREEN HAS YET TO MAKE A STATEMENT, ALTHOUGH IT IS BELIEVED THAT HE IS PREPARING A SPEECH SIMILAR TO PREVIOUS PRIME MINISTER HARRIET JONES' "DOCTOR" ONE.
BREAKING NEWS
UNIT BATTLE IN GREENWICH PARK?
Live pictures from Greenwich Park show purported sunspot effects
BBC NEWS 12:02 YS HOME SECRETARY, DENISE RILEY • EARLY REPORTS SAY THAT THE UNITED INTEL
LIVE Greenwich Park
WHO THE DOCTOR IS OR WHY HE'S SO NEEDED IS—
—WAIT! SOMETHING'S HAPPENING! THE ANGELS HAVE STOPPED! THEY'RE LINKING TOGETHER BY SOME KIND OF ENERGY BEAM, EFFECTIVELY MAKING A MESH OVER LONDON!
BREAKING NEWS
UNIT BATTLE IN GREENWICH PARK?
Live pictures from Greenwich Park show purported sunspot effects
BBC NEWS 12:02 FROM THE JEAN STAFFORD INSTITUTE • SUNSPOTS AND GAS LEAK ARE TO BLAME F
LIVE Chelsea
THERE—FROM OUR ROOFTOP AT CHELSEA, WE CAN SEE A WEBBED DOME OF ENERGY COVERING GREENWICH AND CENTRAL LONDON! WHATEVER'S UNDERNEATH IT...
BREAKING NEWS
UNIT BATTLE IN GREENWICH PARK?
Live pictures from Greenwich Park show purported sunspot effects
BBC NEWS 12:02 OF ENERGY OVER CENTRAL LONDON • THE UNITED INTELLIGENCE TASKFORCE HAS

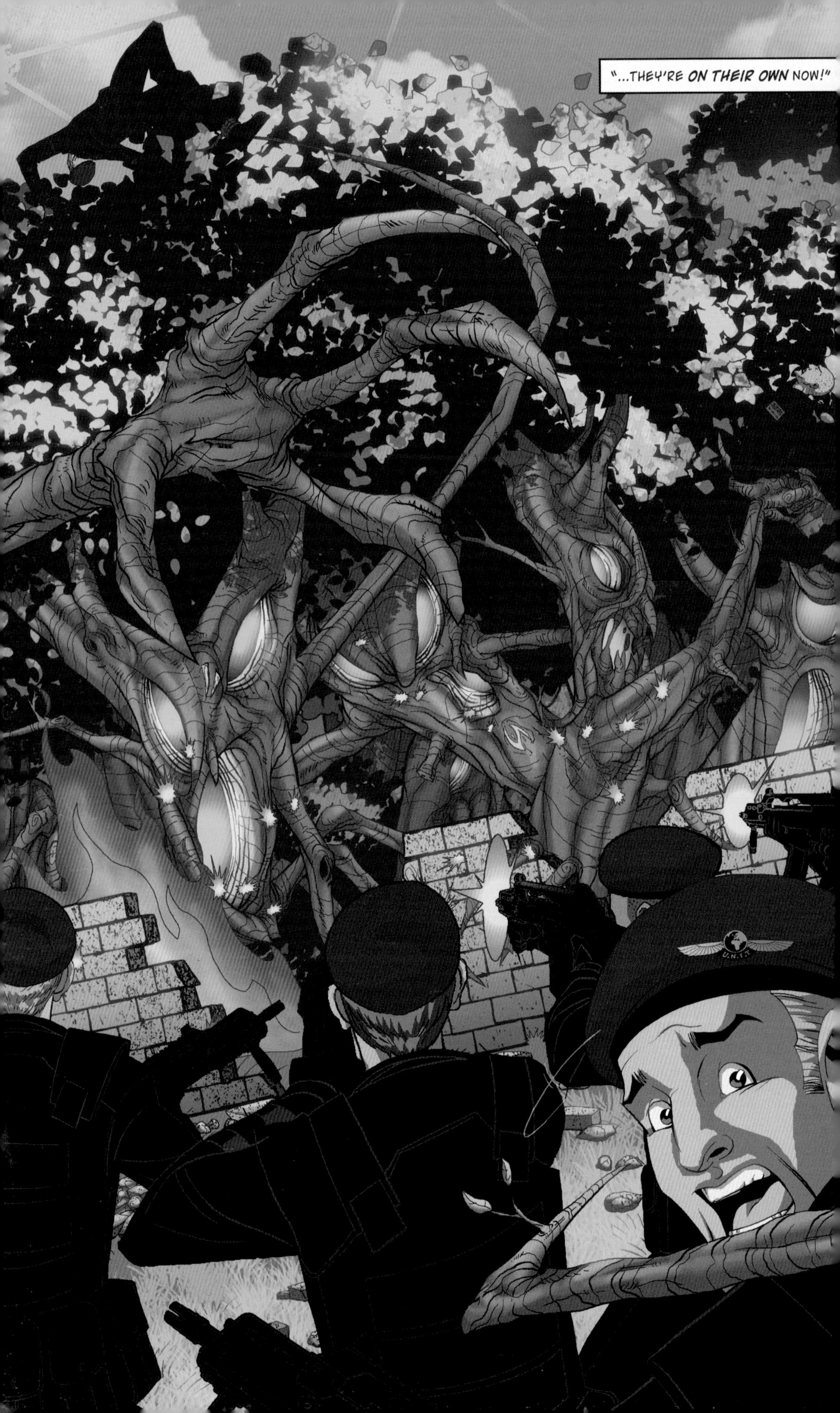
"...THEY'RE ON THEIR OWN NOW!"

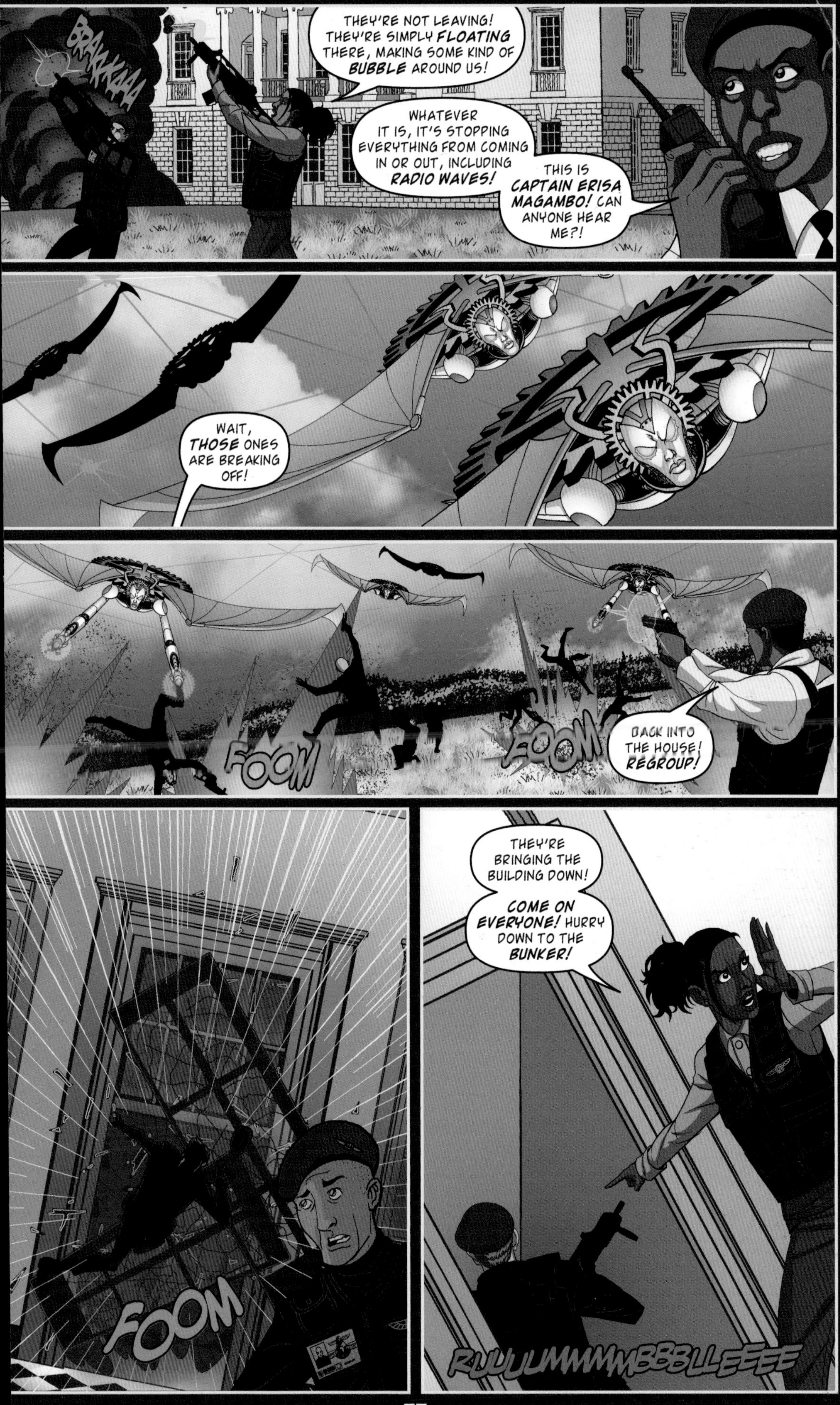
BRAKKAAA
THEY'RE NOT LEAVING! THEY'RE SIMPLY FLOATING THERE, MAKING SOME KIND OF BUBBLE AROUND US!
WHATEVER IT IS, IT'S STOPPING EVERYTHING FROM COMING IN OR OUT, INCLUDING RADIO WAVES!
THIS IS CAPTAIN ERISA MAGAMBO! CAN ANYONE HEAR ME?!
WAIT, THOSE ONES ARE BREAKING OFF!
FOOM
FOOM
BACK INTO THE HOUSE! REGROUP!
FOOM
THEY'RE BRINGING THE BUILDING DOWN!
COME ON EVERYONE! HURRY DOWN TO THE BUNKER!
RUUUUMMMMBBBLLEEEE

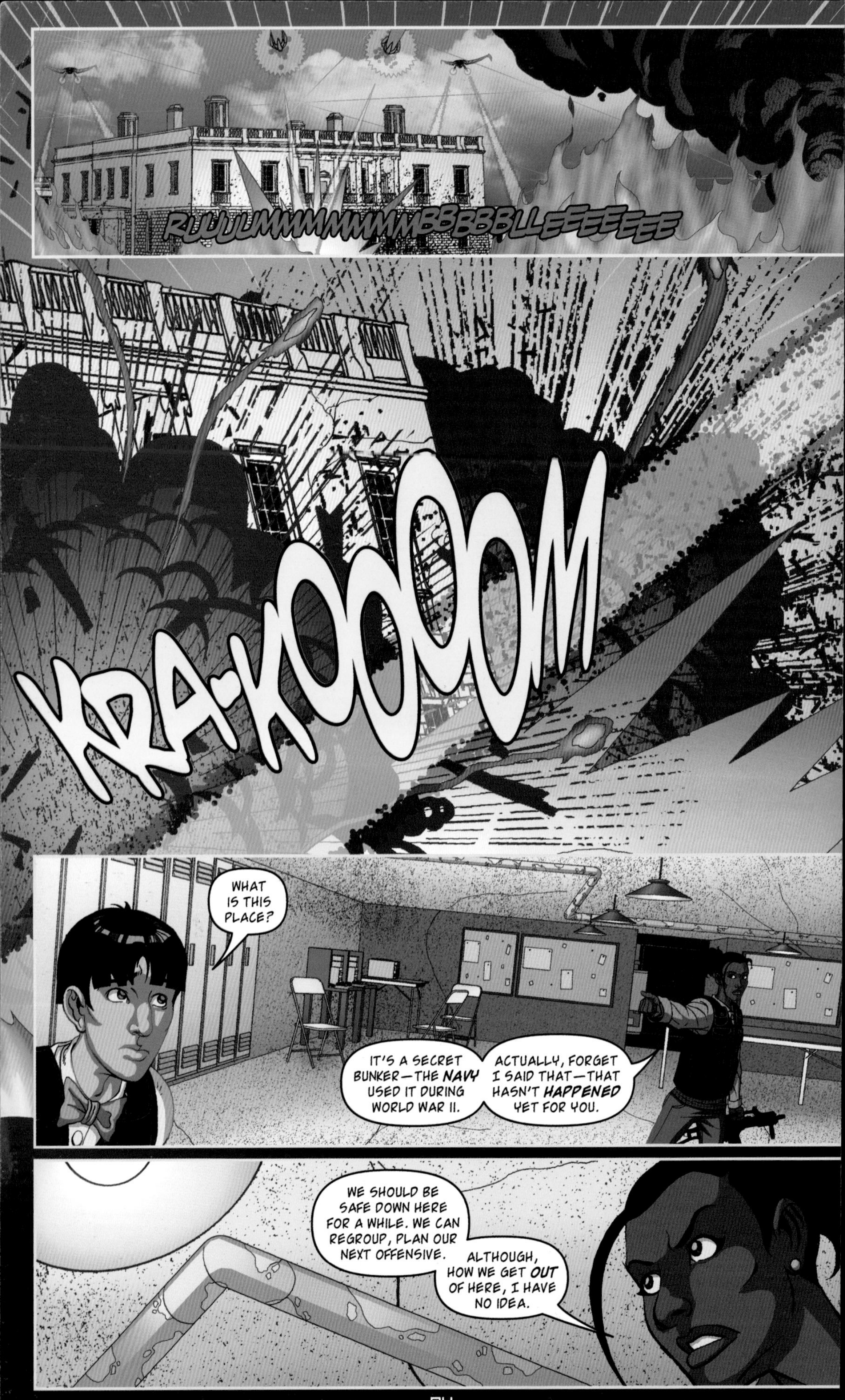
RUUUUMMMMMMMMMBBBBBBLLLEEEEEEE
KRA-KOOOOM
WHAT IS THIS PLACE?
IT'S A SECRET BUNKER—THE NAVY USED IT DURING WORLD WAR II.
ACTUALLY, FORGET I SAID THAT—THAT HASN'T HAPPENED YET FOR YOU.
WE SHOULD BE SAFE DOWN HERE FOR A WHILE. WE CAN REGROUP, PLAN OUR NEXT OFFENSIVE.
ALTHOUGH, HOW WE GET OUT OF HERE, I HAVE NO IDEA.

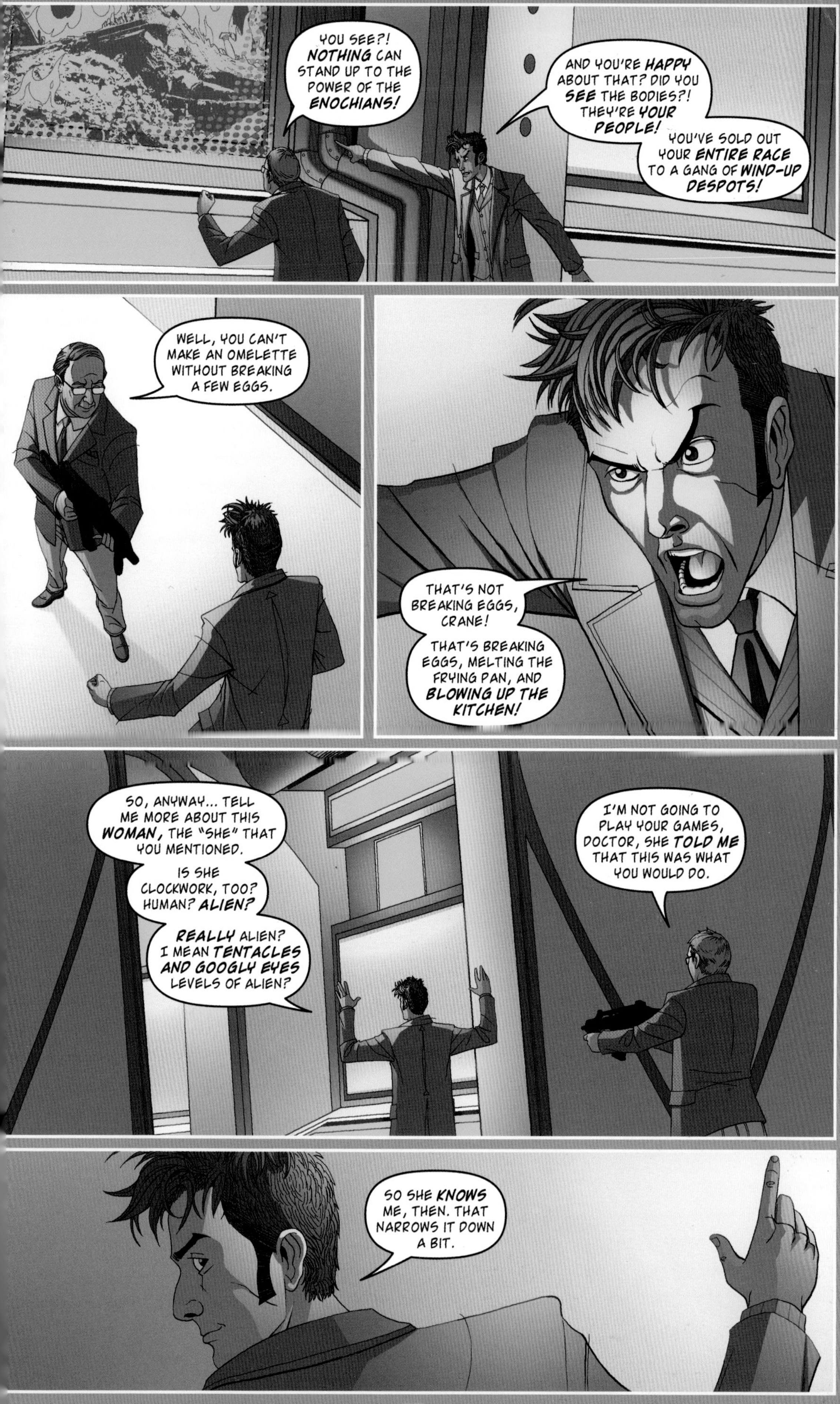
YOU SEE?! NOTHING CAN STAND UP TO THE POWER OF THE ENOCHIANS!
AND YOU'RE HAPPY ABOUT THAT? DID YOU SEE THE BODIES?! THEY'RE YOUR PEOPLE!
YOU'VE SOLD OUT YOUR ENTIRE RACE TO A GANG OF WIND-UP DESPOTS!
WELL, YOU CAN'T MAKE AN OMELETTE WITHOUT BREAKING A FEW EGGS.
THAT'S NOT BREAKING EGGS, CRANE!
THAT'S BREAKING EGGS, MELTING THE FRYING PAN, AND BLOWING UP THE KITCHEN!
SO, ANYWAY... TELL ME MORE ABOUT THIS WOMAN, THE "SHE" THAT YOU MENTIONED.
IS SHE CLOCKWORK, TOO? HUMAN? ALIEN?
REALLY ALIEN? I MEAN TENTACLES AND GOOGLY EYES LEVELS OF ALIEN?
I'M NOT GOING TO PLAY YOUR GAMES, DOCTOR, SHE TOLD ME THAT THIS WAS WHAT YOU WOULD DO.
SO SHE KNOWS ME, THEN. THAT NARROWS IT DOWN A BIT.

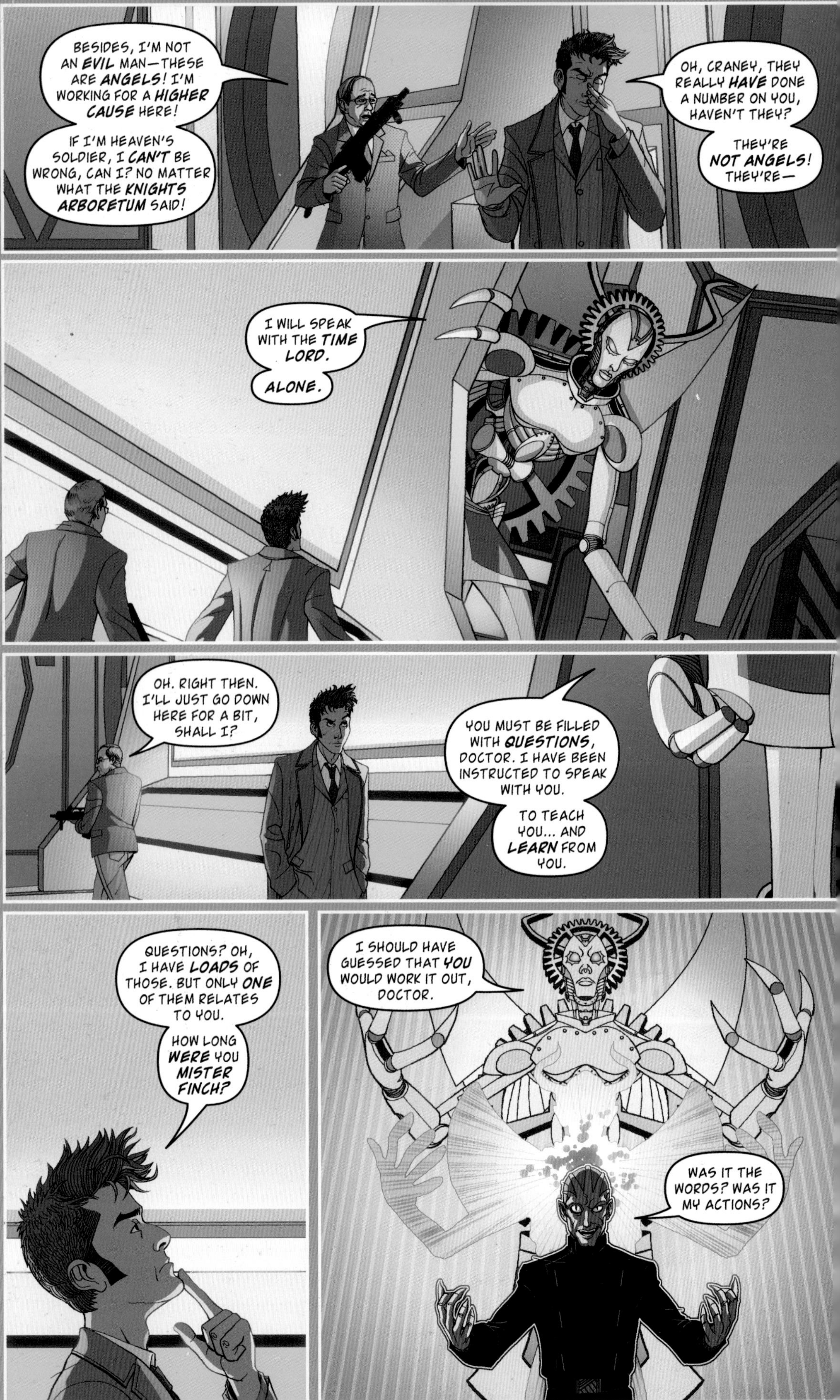
BESIDES, I'M NOT AN EVIL MAN—THESE ARE ANGELS! I'M WORKING FOR A HIGHER CAUSE HERE!
IF I'M HEAVEN'S SOLDIER, I CAN'T BE WRONG, CAN I? NO MATTER WHAT THE KNIGHTS ARBORETUM SAID!
OH, CRANEY, THEY REALLY HAVE DONE A NUMBER ON YOU, HAVEN'T THEY?
THEY'RE NOT ANGELS! THEY'RE—
I WILL SPEAK WITH THE TIME LORD.
ALONE.
OH. RIGHT THEN. I'LL JUST GO DOWN HERE FOR A BIT, SHALL I?
YOU MUST BE FILLED WITH QUESTIONS, DOCTOR. I HAVE BEEN INSTRUCTED TO SPEAK WITH YOU.
TO TEACH YOU... AND LEARN FROM YOU.
QUESTIONS? OH, I HAVE LOADS OF THOSE. BUT ONLY ONE OF THEM RELATES TO YOU.
HOW LONG WERE YOU MISTER FINCH?
I SHOULD HAVE GUESSED THAT YOU WOULD WORK IT OUT, DOCTOR.
WAS IT THE WORDS? WAS IT MY ACTIONS?

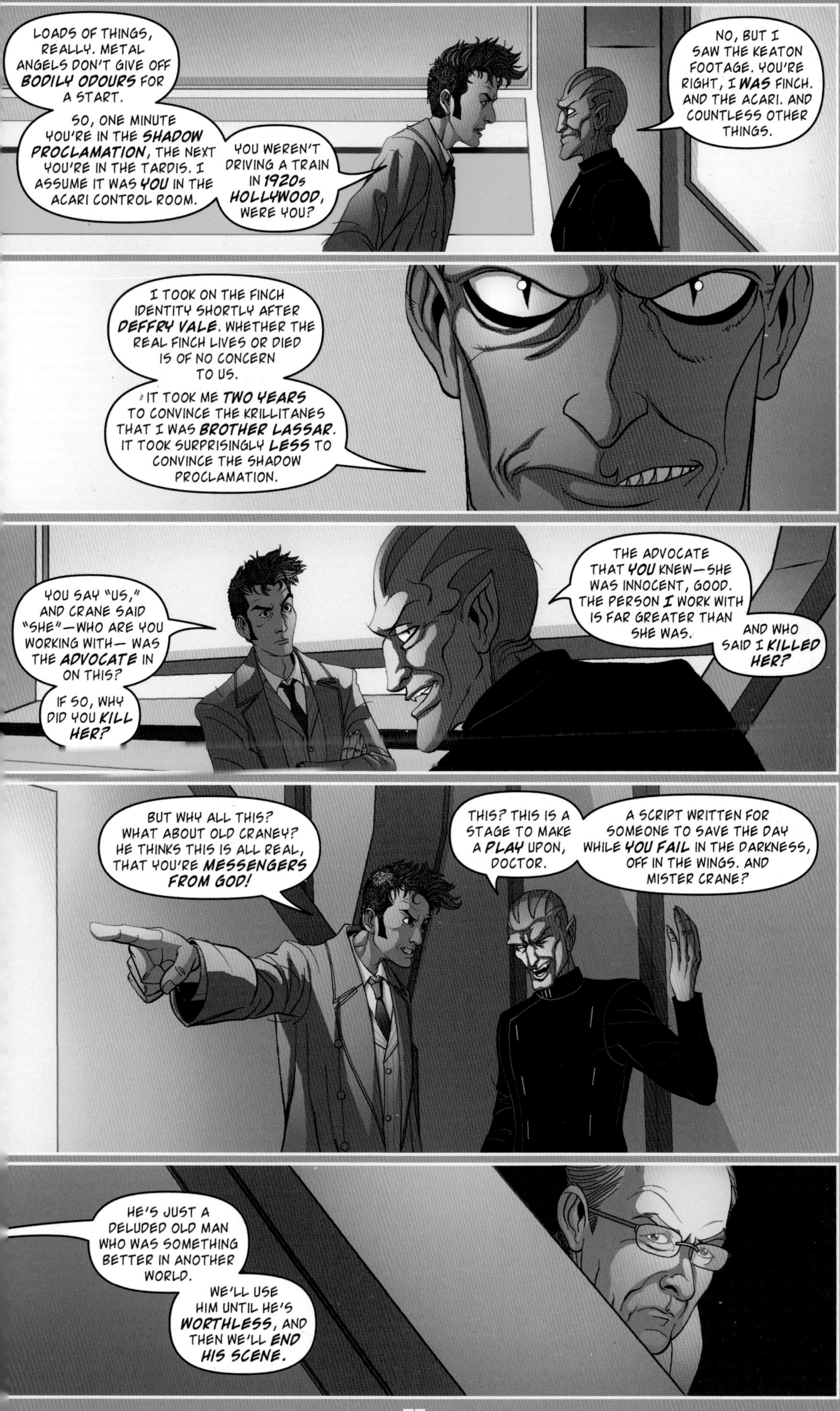
LOADS OF THINGS, REALLY. METAL ANGELS DON'T GIVE OFF BODILY ODOURS FOR A START.
SO, ONE MINUTE YOU'RE IN THE SHADOW PROCLAMATION, THE NEXT YOU'RE IN THE TARDIS. I ASSUME IT WAS YOU IN THE ACARI CONTROL ROOM.
YOU WEREN'T DRIVING A TRAIN IN 1920s HOLLYWOOD, WERE YOU?
NO, BUT I SAW THE KEATON FOOTAGE. YOU'RE RIGHT, I WAS FINCH. AND THE ACARI. AND COUNTLESS OTHER THINGS.
I TOOK ON THE FINCH IDENTITY SHORTLY AFTER DEFFRY VALE. WHETHER THE REAL FINCH LIVES OR DIED IS OF NO CONCERN TO US.
IT TOOK ME TWO YEARS TO CONVINCE THE KRILLITANES THAT I WAS BROTHER LASSAR. IT TOOK SURPRISINGLY LESS TO CONVINCE THE SHADOW PROCLAMATION.
YOU SAY "US," AND CRANE SAID "SHE"—WHO ARE YOU WORKING WITH— WAS THE ADVOCATE IN ON THIS?
IF SO, WHY DID YOU KILL HER?
THE ADVOCATE THAT YOU KNEW—SHE WAS INNOCENT, GOOD. THE PERSON I WORK WITH IS FAR GREATER THAN SHE WAS.
AND WHO SAID I KILLED HER?
BUT WHY ALL THIS? WHAT ABOUT OLD CRANEY? HE THINKS THIS IS ALL REAL, THAT YOU'RE MESSENGERS FROM GOD!
THIS? THIS IS A STAGE TO MAKE A PLAY UPON, DOCTOR.
A SCRIPT WRITTEN FOR SOMEONE TO SAVE THE DAY WHILE YOU FAIL IN THE DARKNESS, OFF IN THE WINGS. AND MISTER CRANE?
HE'S JUST A DELUDED OLD MAN WHO WAS SOMETHING BETTER IN ANOTHER WORLD.
WE'LL USE HIM UNTIL HE'S WORTHLESS, AND THEN WE'LL END HIS SCENE.

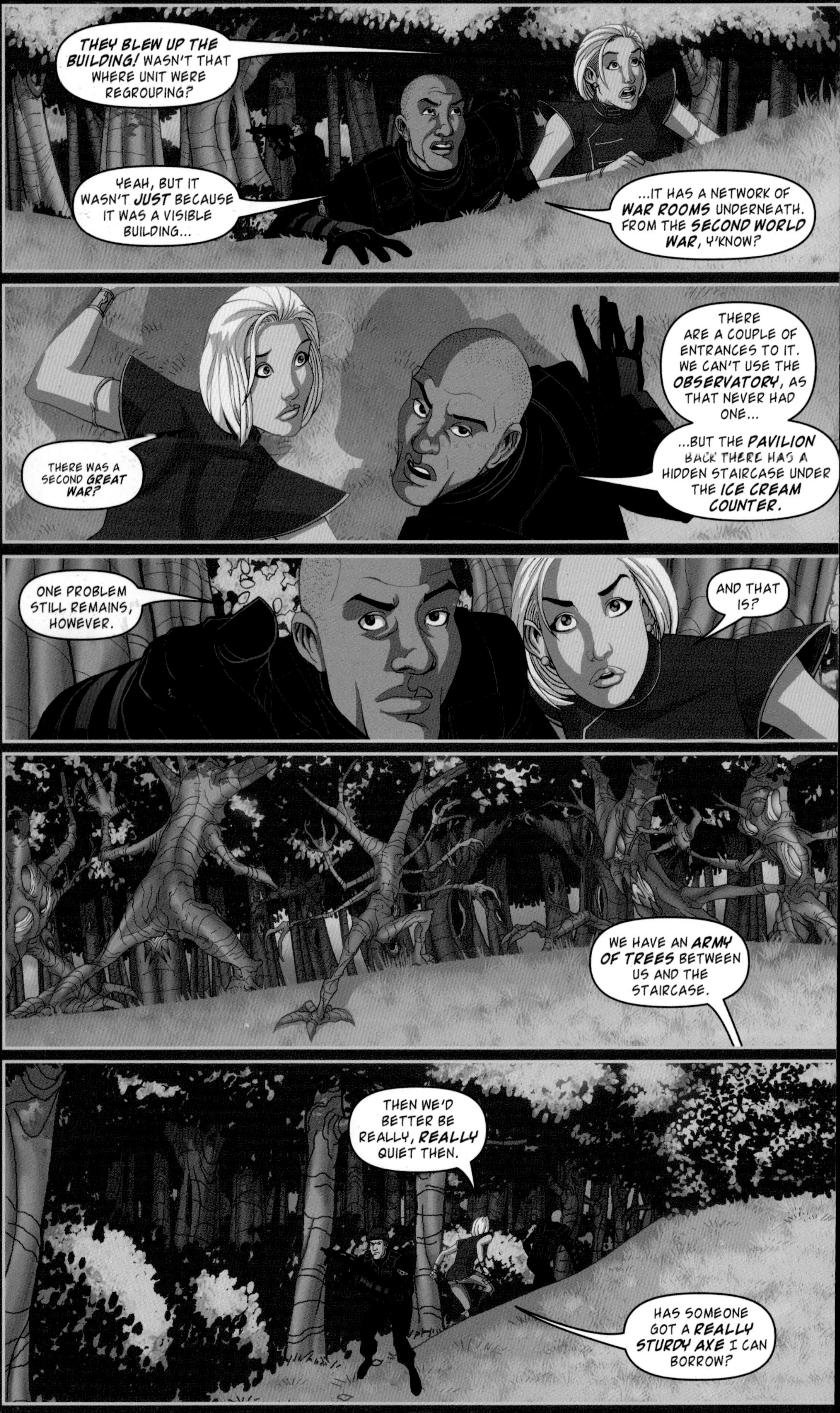
THEY BLEW UP THE BUILDING! WASN'T THAT WHERE UNIT WERE REGROUPING?
YEAH, BUT IT WASN'T JUST BECAUSE IT WAS A VISIBLE BUILDING...
...IT HAS A NETWORK OF WAR ROOMS UNDERNEATH. FROM THE SECOND WORLD WAR, Y'KNOW?
THERE WAS A SECOND GREAT WAR?
THERE ARE A COUPLE OF ENTRANCES TO IT. WE CAN'T USE THE OBSERVATORY, AS THAT NEVER HAD ONE...
...BUT THE PAVILION BACK THERE HAS A HIDDEN STAIRCASE UNDER THE ICE CREAM COUNTER.
ONE PROBLEM STILL REMAINS, HOWEVER.
AND THAT IS?
WE HAVE AN ARMY OF TREES BETWEEN US AND THE STAIRCASE.
THEN WE'D BETTER BE REALLY, REALLY QUIET THEN.
HAS SOMEONE GOT A REALLY STURDY AXE I CAN BORROW?

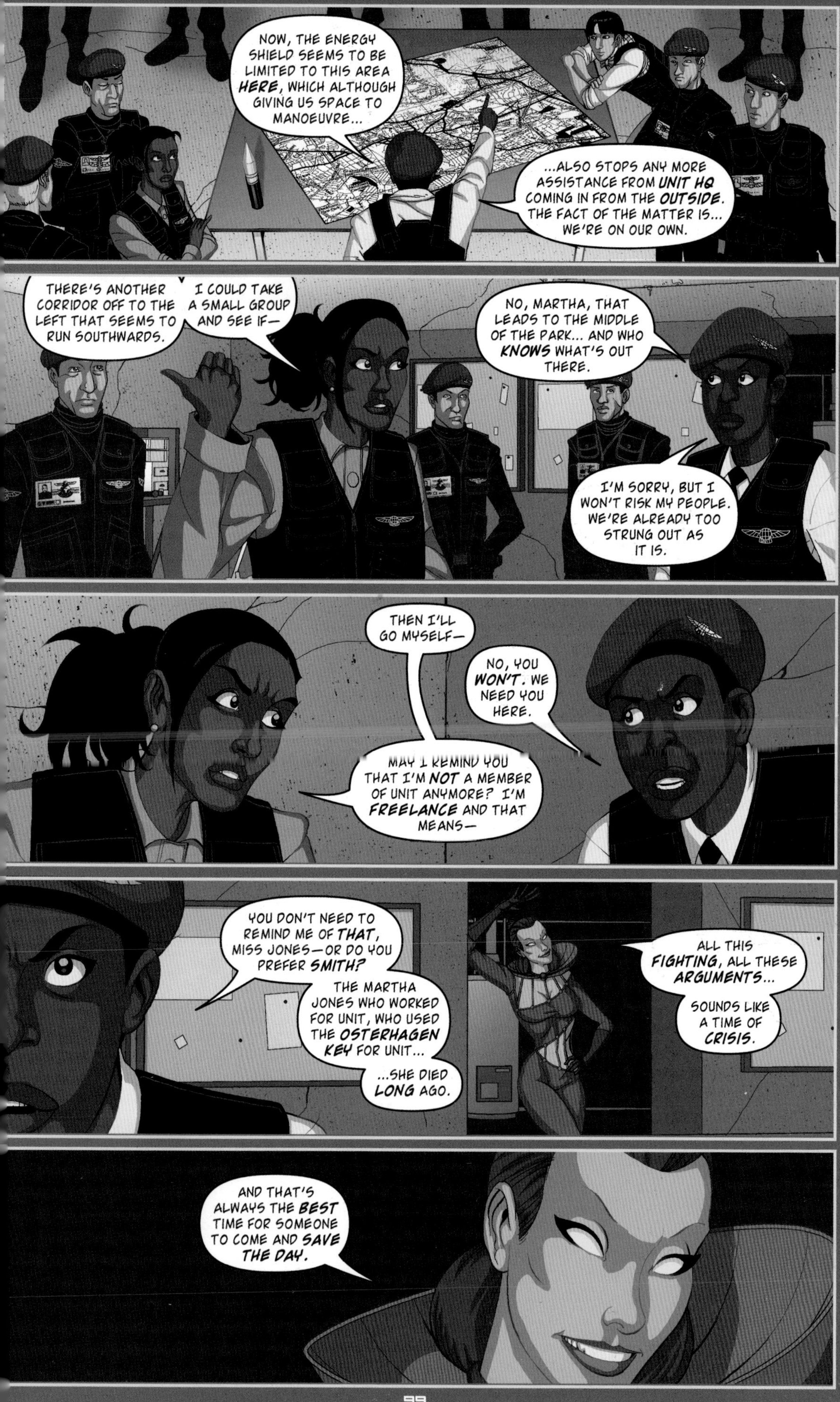
NOW, THE ENERGY SHIELD SEEMS TO BE LIMITED TO THIS AREA HERE, WHICH ALTHOUGH GIVING US SPACE TO MANOEUVRE...
...ALSO STOPS ANY MORE ASSISTANCE FROM UNIT HQ COMING IN FROM THE OUTSIDE. THE FACT OF THE MATTER IS... WE'RE ON OUR OWN.
THERE'S ANOTHER CORRIDOR OFF TO THE LEFT THAT SEEMS TO RUN SOUTHWARDS.
I COULD TAKE A SMALL GROUP AND SEE IF—
NO, MARTHA, THAT LEADS TO THE MIDDLE OF THE PARK... AND WHO KNOWS WHAT'S OUT THERE.
I'M SORRY, BUT I WON'T RISK MY PEOPLE. WE'RE ALREADY TOO STRUNG OUT AS IT IS.
THEN I'LL GO MYSELF—
MAY I REMIND YOU THAT I'M NOT A MEMBER OF UNIT ANYMORE? I'M FREELANCE AND THAT MEANS—
NO, YOU WON'T. WE NEED YOU HERE.
YOU DON'T NEED TO REMIND ME OF THAT, MISS JONES—OR DO YOU PREFER SMITH?
THE MARTHA JONES WHO WORKED FOR UNIT, WHO USED THE OSTERHAGEN KEY FOR UNIT...
...SHE DIED LONG AGO.
ALL THIS FIGHTING, ALL THESE ARGUMENTS...
SOUNDS LIKE A TIME OF CRISIS.
AND THAT'S ALWAYS THE BEST TIME FOR SOMEONE TO COME AND SAVE THE DAY.

STAY WHERE YOU ARE! HANDS IN THE AIR!

WELL, *THIS* IS A FINE WAY TO GREET A FRIEND!

AH, HELLO, MATTHEW.

STOP! LOWER YOUR WEAPONS! SHE'S A *FRIEND!*

I MET HER ON THE DOCTOR'S TARDIS!

YOU'RE A FRIEND OF THE DOCTOR'S?

NOT REALLY, BUT I HAVE BEEN HIS *DEFENSE LAWYER.* DOES THAT COUNT?

AND YOU'VE BEEN IN THE TARDIS?

OH, COME ON, THAT'S HARDLY A *SELECT GROUP*—PRETTY MUCH *EVERYONE'S* BEEN IN THE TARDIS BY NOW.

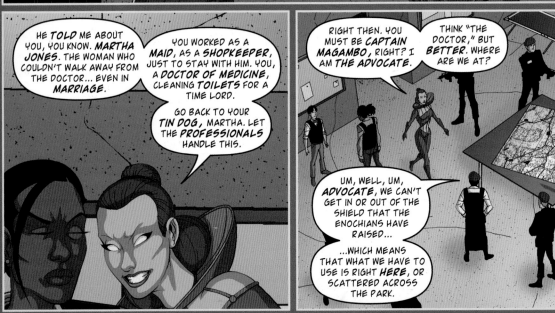

HE *TOLD* ME ABOUT YOU, YOU KNOW. *MARTHA JONES.* THE WOMAN WHO COULDN'T WALK AWAY FROM THE DOCTOR... EVEN IN *MARRIAGE.*

YOU WORKED AS A *MAID,* AS A *SHOPKEEPER,* JUST TO STAY WITH HIM. YOU, A *DOCTOR OF MEDICINE,* CLEANING *TOILETS* FOR A TIME LORD.

GO BACK TO YOUR *TIN DOG,* MARTHA. LET THE *PROFESSIONALS* HANDLE THIS.

RIGHT THEN. YOU MUST BE *CAPTAIN MAGAMBO,* RIGHT? I AM *THE ADVOCATE.*

THINK "THE DOCTOR," BUT *BETTER.* WHERE ARE WE AT?

UM, WELL, UM, *ADVOCATE,* WE CAN'T GET IN OR OUT OF THE SHIELD THAT THE ENOCHIANS HAVE RAISED...

...WHICH MEANS THAT WHAT WE HAVE TO USE IS RIGHT *HERE,* OR SCATTERED ACROSS THE PARK.

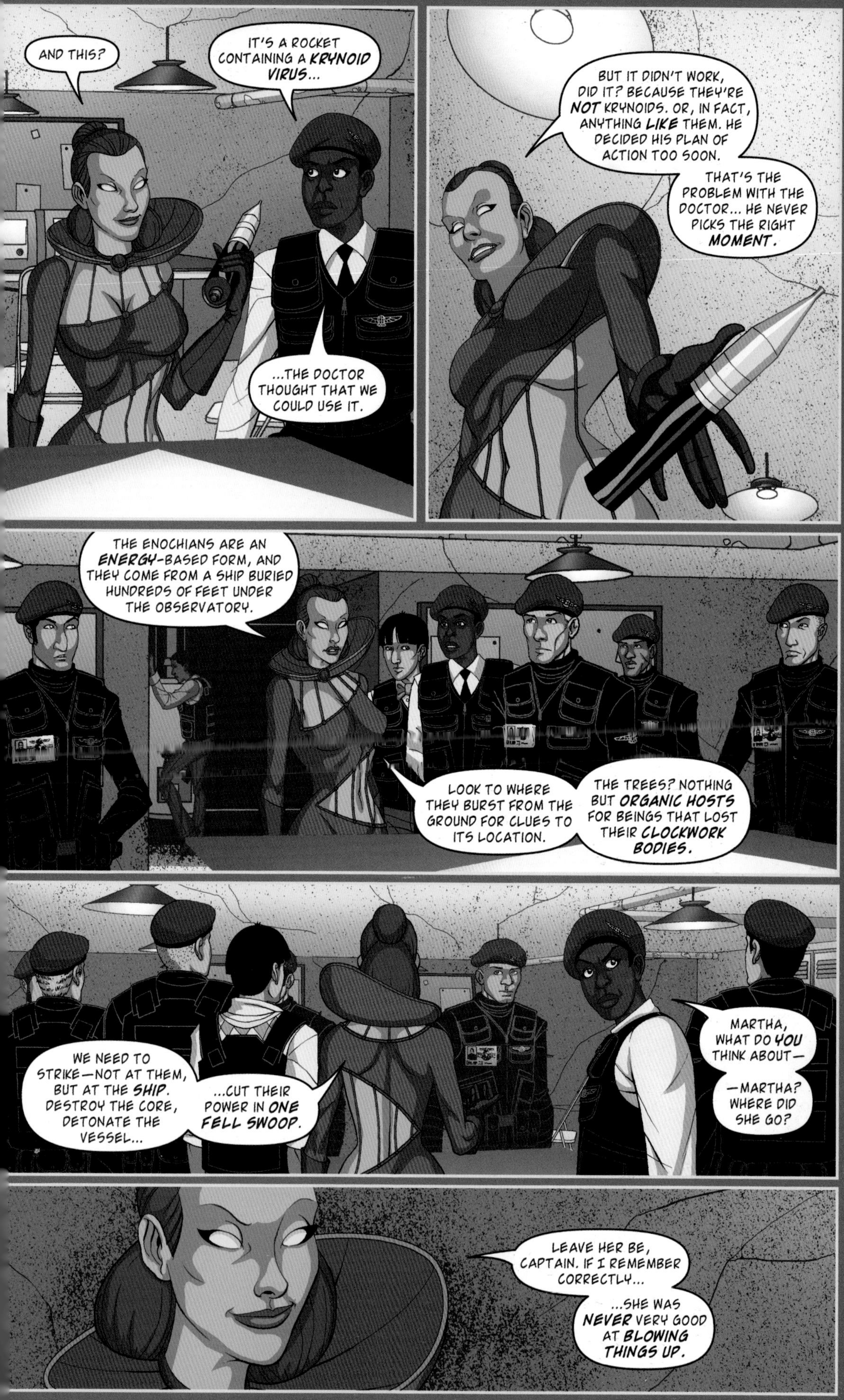
AND THIS?
IT'S A ROCKET CONTAINING A KRYNOID VIRUS...
...THE DOCTOR THOUGHT THAT WE COULD USE IT.
BUT IT DIDN'T WORK, DID IT? BECAUSE THEY'RE NOT KRYNOIDS. OR, IN FACT, ANYTHING LIKE THEM. HE DECIDED HIS PLAN OF ACTION TOO SOON.
THAT'S THE PROBLEM WITH THE DOCTOR... HE NEVER PICKS THE RIGHT MOMENT.
THE ENOCHIANS ARE AN ENERGY-BASED FORM, AND THEY COME FROM A SHIP BURIED HUNDREDS OF FEET UNDER THE OBSERVATORY.
LOOK TO WHERE THEY BURST FROM THE GROUND FOR CLUES TO ITS LOCATION.
THE TREES? NOTHING BUT ORGANIC HOSTS FOR BEINGS THAT LOST THEIR CLOCKWORK BODIES.
WE NEED TO STRIKE—NOT AT THEM, BUT AT THE SHIP. DESTROY THE CORE, DETONATE THE VESSEL...
...CUT THEIR POWER IN ONE FELL SWOOP.
MARTHA, WHAT DO YOU THINK ABOUT—
—MARTHA? WHERE DID SHE GO?
LEAVE HER BE, CAPTAIN. IF I REMEMBER CORRECTLY...
...SHE WAS NEVER VERY GOOD AT BLOWING THINGS UP.

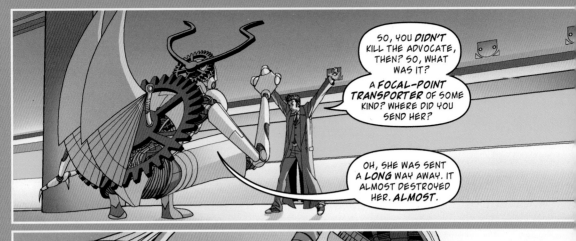

SO, YOU *DIDN'T* KILL THE ADVOCATE, THEN? SO, WHAT WAS IT? A *FOCAL-POINT TRANSPORTER* OF SOME KIND? WHERE DID YOU SEND HER?

OH, SHE WAS SENT A *LONG* WAY AWAY. IT ALMOST DESTROYED HER. *ALMOST.*

YOU KNOW THE STORY. GIRL MEETS BOY, GIRL SENT BACK *THOUSANDS OF YEARS*, GIRL SPENDS MILLENNIA TRAPPED IN A *TIME WAR*...

...GIRL GETS OUT, GIRL SETS UP REVENGE, GIRL GIVES HENCHMAN DEVICE TO SEND HER *EARLIER SELF* BACK, CREATE A SELF-FULFILLING PROPHECY—

TIME... WAR?

YEAH. YOU SHOULD *ASK HER* ABOUT THAT.

OH, WAIT, THAT'S UNLIKELY, AS YOU'RE ABOUT TO *DIE*. SUCH A SHAME... SHE EXPECTED *SO MUCH MORE* FROM YOU.

SHE'S *USING* YOU! CAN'T YOU SEE THAT?

THERE ARE TWO TYPES OF PEOPLE IN THIS UNIVERSE: THE *MANIPULATED*... AND THE *MANIPULATORS.*

IF I'M ONE OF THE FORMER, WHAT DOES THAT MAKE *YOU?*

WAIT! WHY WERE YOU IN THE *TARDIS?!* WHAT WERE YOU AFTER?! WAS SHE *WITH* YOU?

GOODBYE, DOCTOR.

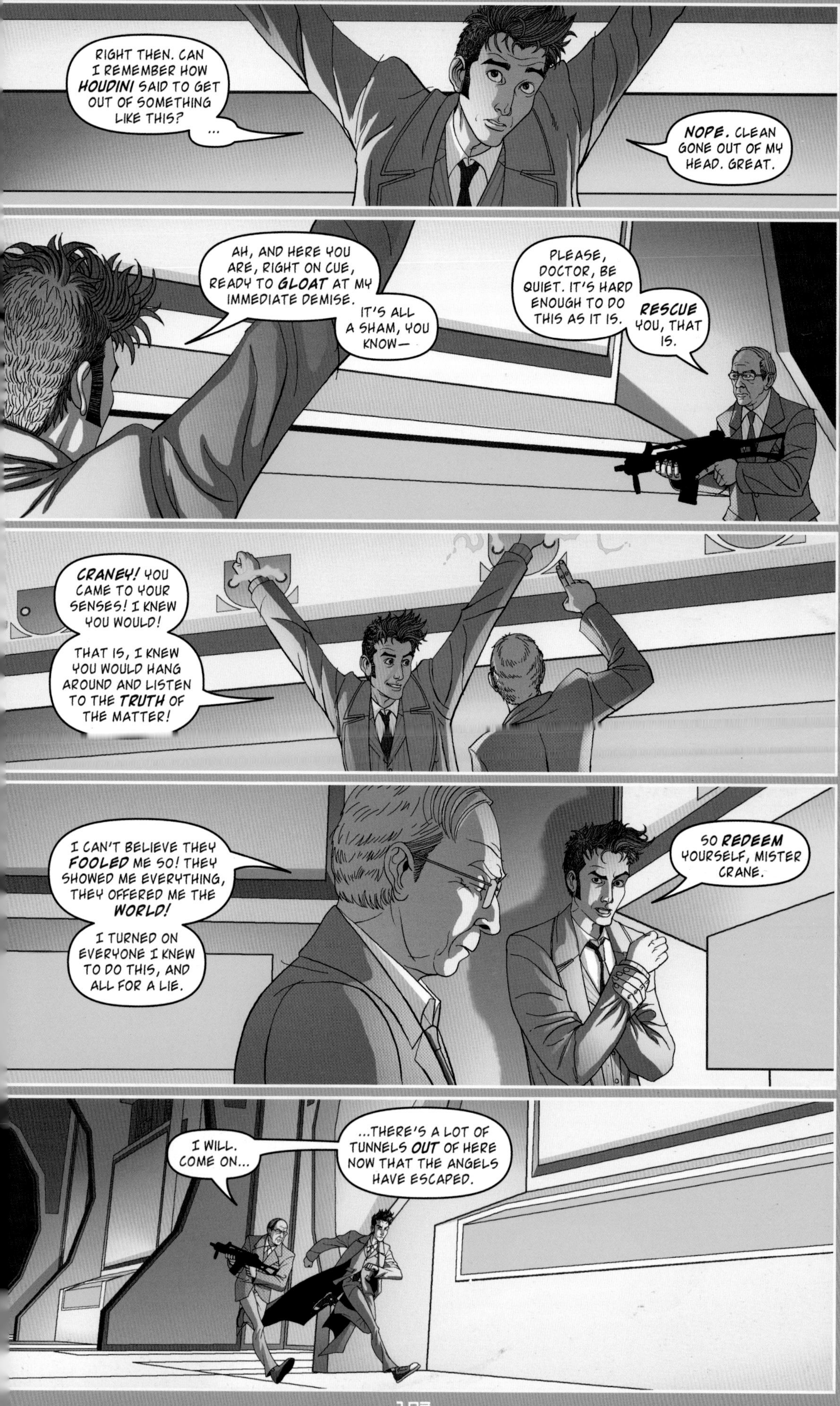

RIGHT THEN. CAN I REMEMBER HOW HOUDINI SAID TO GET OUT OF SOMETHING LIKE THIS? ...
NOPE. CLEAN GONE OUT OF MY HEAD. GREAT.
AH, AND HERE YOU ARE, RIGHT ON CUE, READY TO GLOAT AT MY IMMEDIATE DEMISE.
IT'S ALL A SHAM, YOU KNOW—
PLEASE, DOCTOR, BE QUIET. IT'S HARD ENOUGH TO DO THIS AS IT IS.
RESCUE YOU, THAT IS.
CRANEY! YOU CAME TO YOUR SENSES! I KNEW YOU WOULD!
THAT IS, I KNEW YOU WOULD HANG AROUND AND LISTEN TO THE TRUTH OF THE MATTER!
I CAN'T BELIEVE THEY FOOLED ME SO! THEY SHOWED ME EVERYTHING, THEY OFFERED ME THE WORLD!
I TURNED ON EVERYONE I KNEW TO DO THIS, AND ALL FOR A LIE.
SO REDEEM YOURSELF, MISTER CRANE.
I WILL. COME ON...
...THERE'S A LOT OF TUNNELS OUT OF HERE NOW THAT THE ANGELS HAVE ESCAPED.

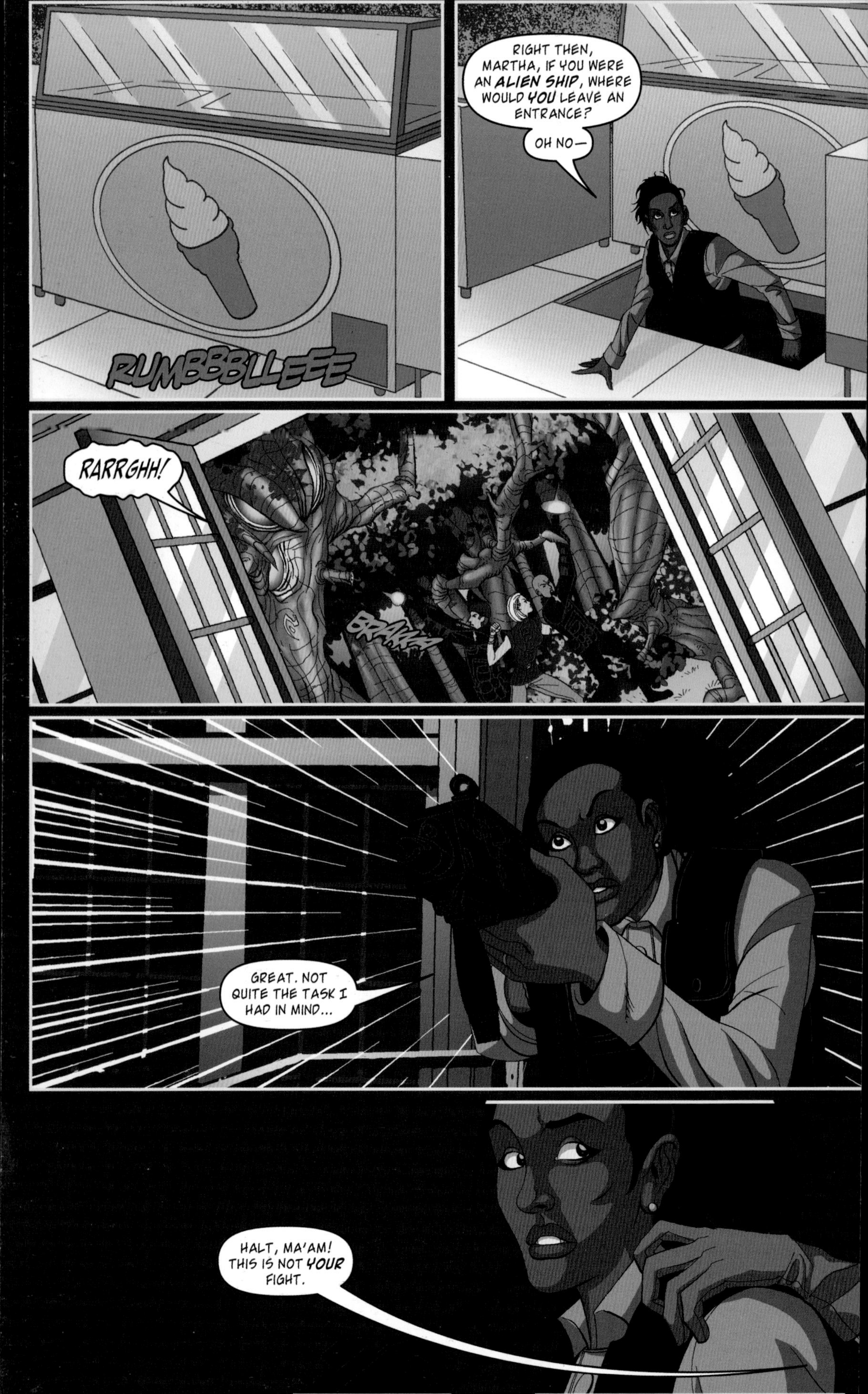
RUMBBBLLEEE
RIGHT THEN, MARTHA, IF YOU WERE AN ALIEN SHIP, WHERE WOULD YOU LEAVE AN ENTRANCE?
OH NO—
RARRGHH!
BRAKKA
GREAT. NOT QUITE THE TASK I HAD IN MIND...
HALT, MA'AM! THIS IS NOT YOUR FIGHT.

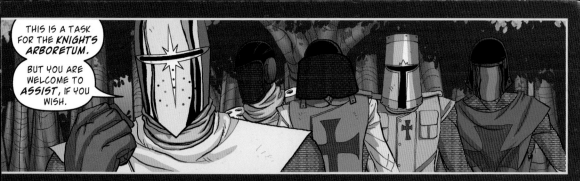

THIS IS A TASK FOR THE KNIGHTS ARBORETUM.

BUT YOU ARE WELCOME TO ASSIST, IF YOU WISH.

FOR THE GARDENERS!

-:GACK:-

AAAIIIEEEEEE!

SHUNK

COME ON! WE NEED TO GET OUT OF HERE!

IT'S TOO LATE! WE'VE BEEN SPOTTED!

BRAKKKAAA

BCHHLLLLM

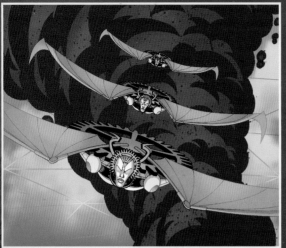

BRAKKKAAA

BLAM BLAM BLAM

GRAARGHHH!

PING
PING PING

FOOM

CRUMP

ALLEZ-OOP!

DOCTOR! YOU'RE ALIVE!

YOU DIDN'T THINK I'D GO AND MISS ALL THE FUN, NOW, DID YOU?

NOW, MISS WINTER, DO YOU STILL HAVE MY SONIC SCREWDRIVER HANDY?

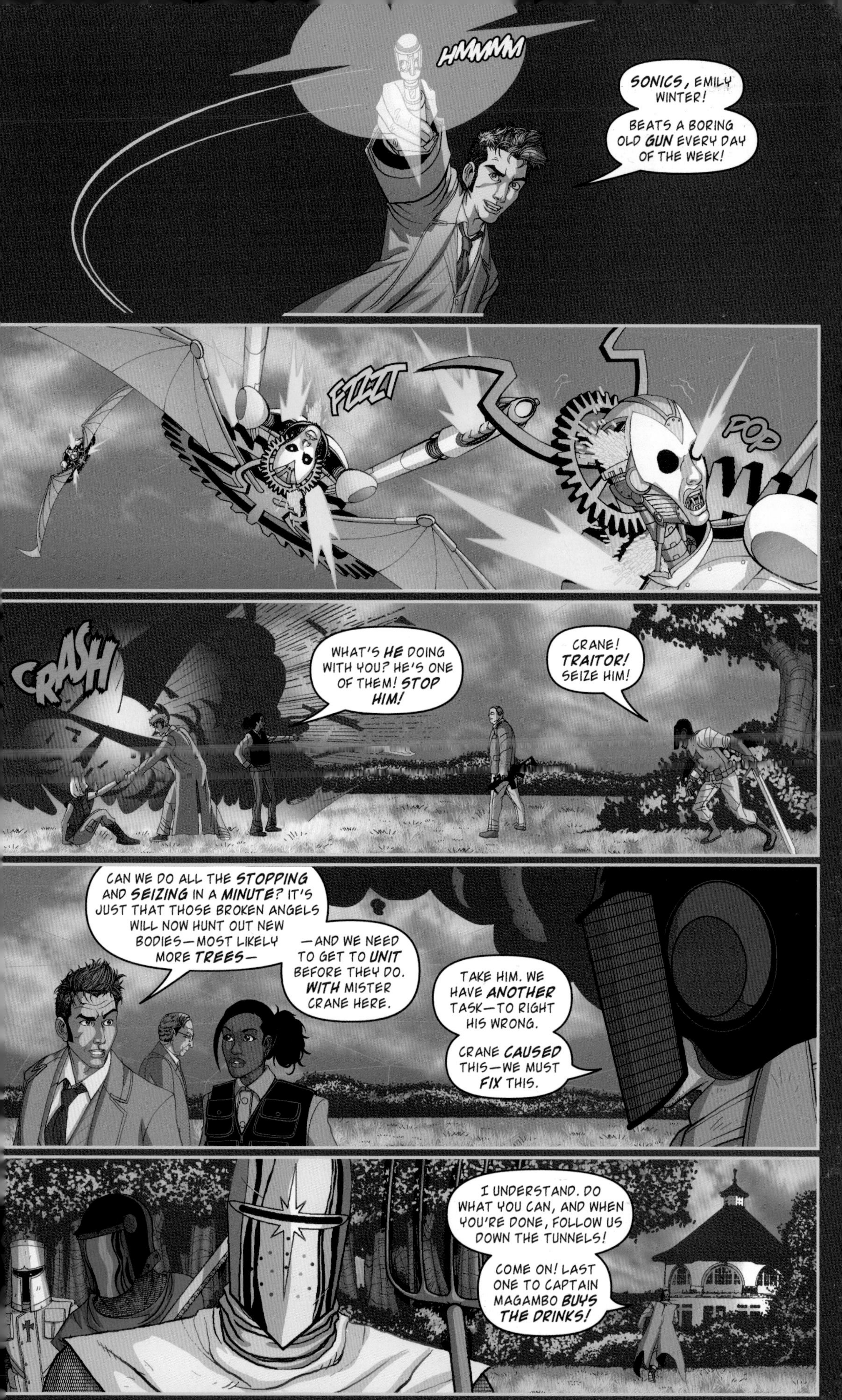
HMWMM
SONICS, EMILY WINTER!
BEATS A BORING OLD GUN EVERY DAY OF THE WEEK!
FZZZT
POP
CRASH
WHAT'S HE DOING WITH YOU? HE'S ONE OF THEM! STOP HIM!
CRANE! TRAITOR! SEIZE HIM!
CAN WE DO ALL THE STOPPING AND SEIZING IN A MINUTE? IT'S JUST THAT THOSE BROKEN ANGELS WILL NOW HUNT OUT NEW BODIES—MOST LIKELY MORE TREES—
—AND WE NEED TO GET TO UNIT BEFORE THEY DO. WITH MISTER CRANE HERE.
TAKE HIM. WE HAVE ANOTHER TASK—TO RIGHT HIS WRONG.
CRANE CAUSED THIS—WE MUST FIX THIS.
I UNDERSTAND. DO WHAT YOU CAN, AND WHEN YOU'RE DONE, FOLLOW US DOWN THE TUNNELS!
COME ON! LAST ONE TO CAPTAIN MAGAMBO BUYS THE DRINKS!

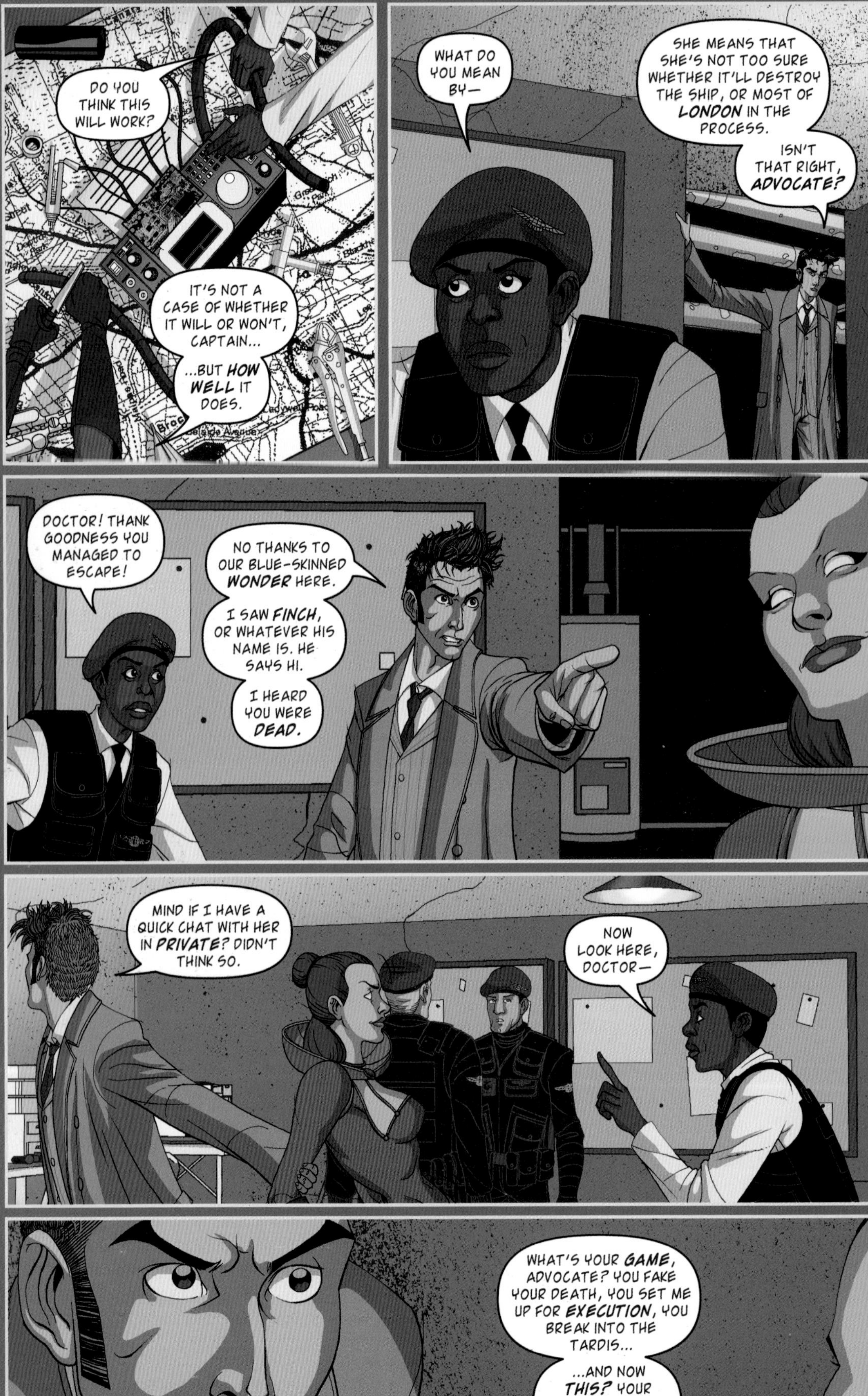
DO YOU THINK THIS WILL WORK?
IT'S NOT A CASE OF WHETHER IT WILL OR WON'T, CAPTAIN...
...BUT HOW WELL IT DOES.
WHAT DO YOU MEAN BY—
SHE MEANS THAT SHE'S NOT TOO SURE WHETHER IT'LL DESTROY THE SHIP, OR MOST OF LONDON IN THE PROCESS.
ISN'T THAT RIGHT, ADVOCATE?
DOCTOR! THANK GOODNESS YOU MANAGED TO ESCAPE!
NO THANKS TO OUR BLUE-SKINNED WONDER HERE.
I SAW FINCH, OR WHATEVER HIS NAME IS. HE SAYS HI.
I HEARD YOU WERE DEAD.
MIND IF I HAVE A QUICK CHAT WITH HER IN PRIVATE? DIDN'T THINK SO.
NOW LOOK HERE, DOCTOR—
WHAT'S YOUR GAME, ADVOCATE? YOU FAKE YOUR DEATH, YOU SET ME UP FOR EXECUTION, YOU BREAK INTO THE TARDIS...
...AND NOW THIS? YOUR FINGERPRINTS ARE ALL OVER THIS MESS. WHY?

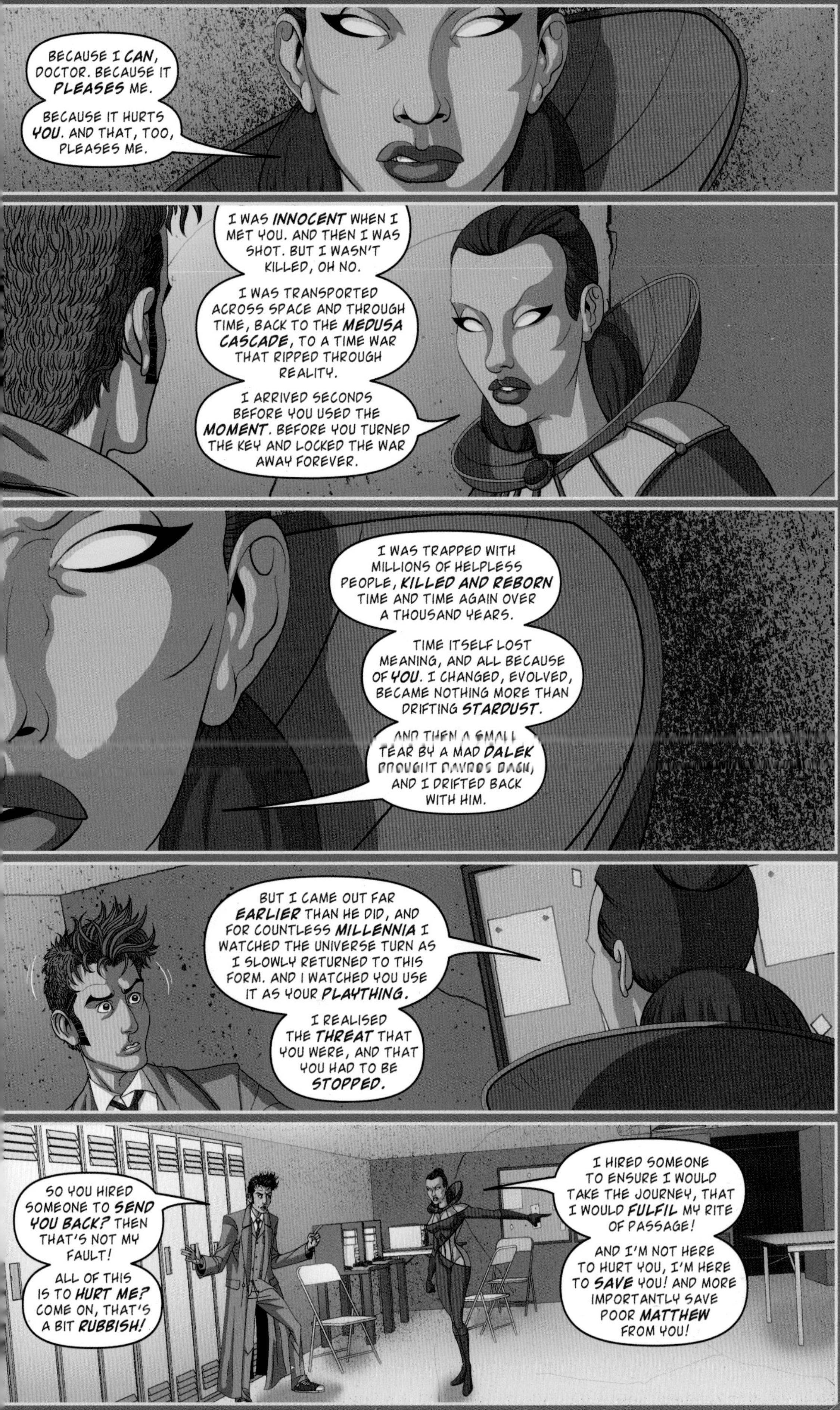

BECAUSE I CAN, DOCTOR. BECAUSE IT PLEASES ME.
BECAUSE IT HURTS YOU. AND THAT, TOO, PLEASES ME.
I WAS INNOCENT WHEN I MET YOU. AND THEN I WAS SHOT. BUT I WASN'T KILLED, OH NO.
I WAS TRANSPORTED ACROSS SPACE AND THROUGH TIME, BACK TO THE MEDUSA CASCADE, TO A TIME WAR THAT RIPPED THROUGH REALITY.
I ARRIVED SECONDS BEFORE YOU USED THE MOMENT. BEFORE YOU TURNED THE KEY AND LOCKED THE WAR AWAY FOREVER.
I WAS TRAPPED WITH MILLIONS OF HELPLESS PEOPLE, KILLED AND REBORN TIME AND TIME AGAIN OVER A THOUSAND YEARS.
TIME ITSELF LOST MEANING, AND ALL BECAUSE OF YOU. I CHANGED, EVOLVED, BECAME NOTHING MORE THAN DRIFTING STARDUST.
AND THEN A SMALL TEAR BY A MAD DALEK BROUGHT DAVROS BACK, AND I DRIFTED BACK WITH HIM.
BUT I CAME OUT FAR EARLIER THAN HE DID, AND FOR COUNTLESS MILLENNIA I WATCHED THE UNIVERSE TURN AS I SLOWLY RETURNED TO THIS FORM. AND I WATCHED YOU USE IT AS YOUR PLAYTHING.
I REALISED THE THREAT THAT YOU WERE, AND THAT YOU HAD TO BE STOPPED.
SO YOU HIRED SOMEONE TO SEND YOU BACK? THEN THAT'S NOT MY FAULT!
ALL OF THIS IS TO HURT ME? COME ON, THAT'S A BIT RUBBISH!
I HIRED SOMEONE TO ENSURE I WOULD TAKE THE JOURNEY, THAT I WOULD FULFIL MY RITE OF PASSAGE!
AND I'M NOT HERE TO HURT YOU, I'M HERE TO SAVE YOU! AND MORE IMPORTANTLY SAVE POOR MATTHEW FROM YOU!

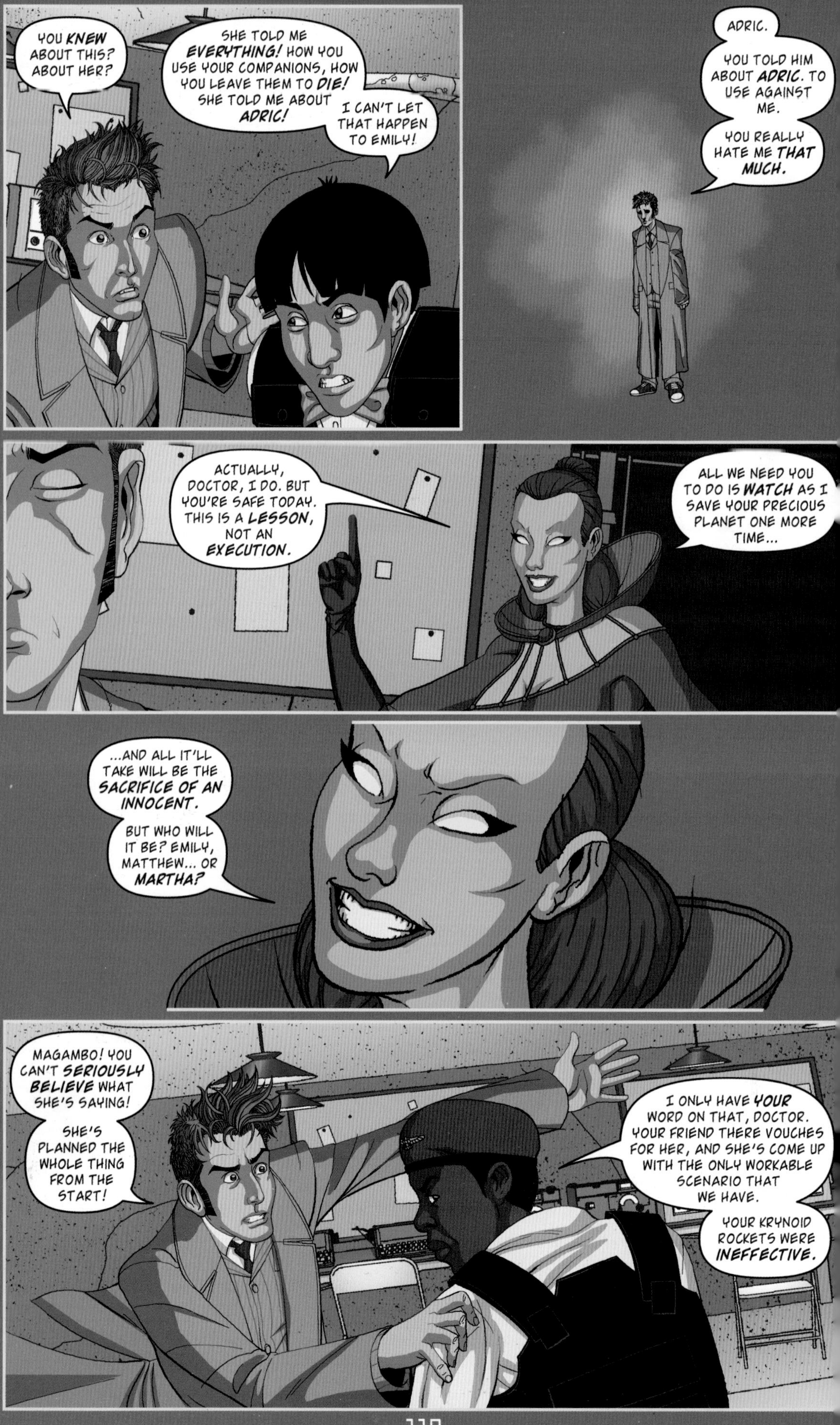

YOU KNEW ABOUT THIS? ABOUT HER?
SHE TOLD ME EVERYTHING! HOW YOU USE YOUR COMPANIONS, HOW YOU LEAVE THEM TO DIE! SHE TOLD ME ABOUT ADRIC!
I CAN'T LET THAT HAPPEN TO EMILY!
ADRIC.
YOU TOLD HIM ABOUT ADRIC. TO USE AGAINST ME.
YOU REALLY HATE ME THAT MUCH.
ACTUALLY, DOCTOR, I DO. BUT YOU'RE SAFE TODAY. THIS IS A LESSON, NOT AN EXECUTION.
ALL WE NEED YOU TO DO IS WATCH AS I SAVE YOUR PRECIOUS PLANET ONE MORE TIME...
...AND ALL IT'LL TAKE WILL BE THE SACRIFICE OF AN INNOCENT.
BUT WHO WILL IT BE? EMILY, MATTHEW... OR MARTHA?
MAGAMBO! YOU CAN'T SERIOUSLY BELIEVE WHAT SHE'S SAYING!
SHE'S PLANNED THE WHOLE THING FROM THE START!
I ONLY HAVE YOUR WORD ON THAT, DOCTOR. YOUR FRIEND THERE VOUCHES FOR HER, AND SHE'S COME UP WITH THE ONLY WORKABLE SCENARIO THAT WE HAVE.
YOUR KRYNOID ROCKETS WERE INEFFECTIVE.

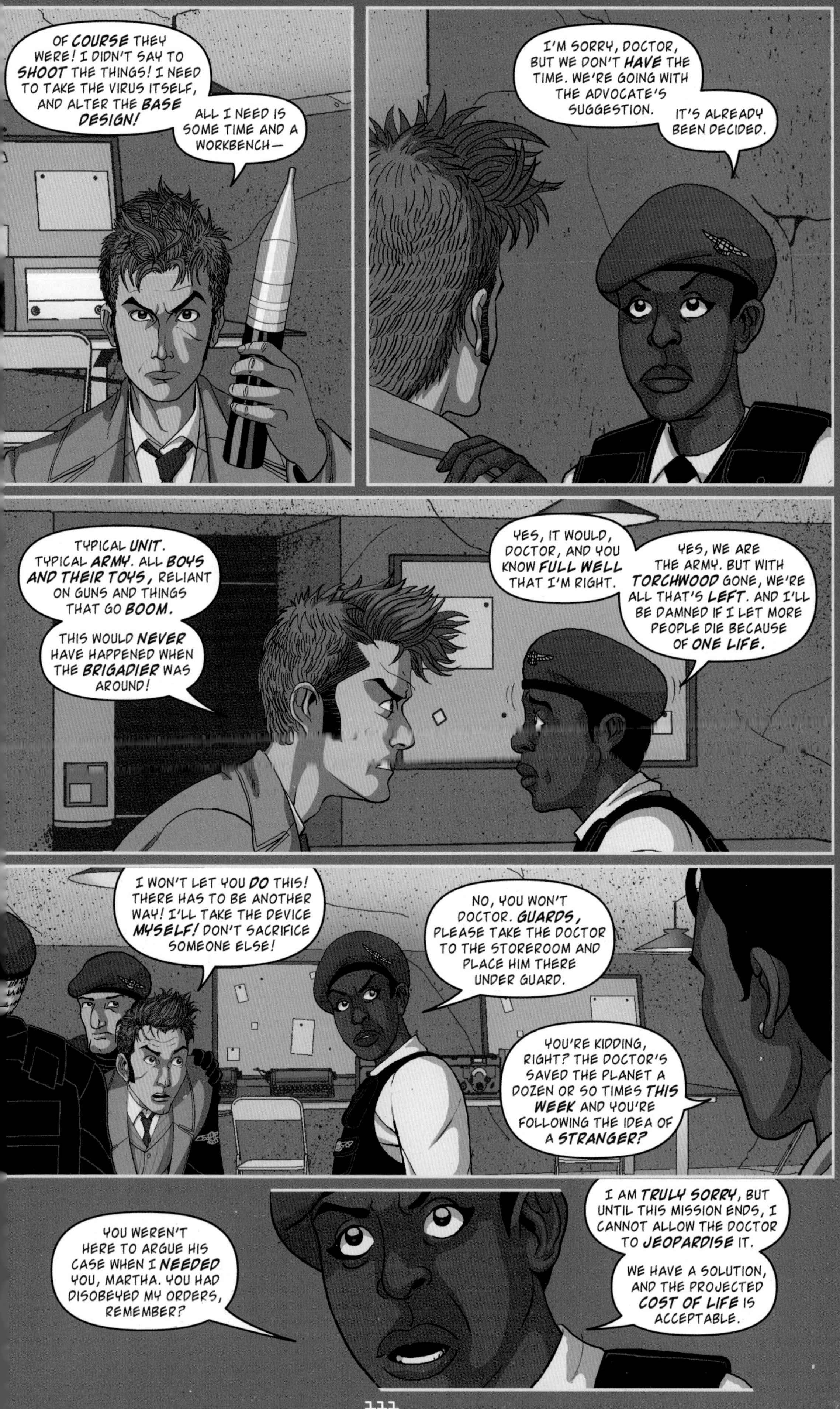
OF COURSE THEY WERE! I DIDN'T SAY TO SHOOT THE THINGS! I NEED TO TAKE THE VIRUS ITSELF, AND ALTER THE BASE DESIGN!
ALL I NEED IS SOME TIME AND A WORKBENCH—
I'M SORRY, DOCTOR, BUT WE DON'T HAVE THE TIME. WE'RE GOING WITH THE ADVOCATE'S SUGGESTION.
IT'S ALREADY BEEN DECIDED.
TYPICAL UNIT. TYPICAL ARMY. ALL BOYS AND THEIR TOYS, RELIANT ON GUNS AND THINGS THAT GO BOOM.
THIS WOULD NEVER HAVE HAPPENED WHEN THE BRIGADIER WAS AROUND!
YES, IT WOULD, DOCTOR, AND YOU KNOW FULL WELL THAT I'M RIGHT.
YES, WE ARE THE ARMY. BUT WITH TORCHWOOD GONE, WE'RE ALL THAT'S LEFT. AND I'LL BE DAMNED IF I LET MORE PEOPLE DIE BECAUSE OF ONE LIFE.
I WON'T LET YOU DO THIS! THERE HAS TO BE ANOTHER WAY! I'LL TAKE THE DEVICE MYSELF! DON'T SACRIFICE SOMEONE ELSE!
NO, YOU WON'T DOCTOR. GUARDS, PLEASE TAKE THE DOCTOR TO THE STOREROOM AND PLACE HIM THERE UNDER GUARD.
YOU'RE KIDDING, RIGHT? THE DOCTOR'S SAVED THE PLANET A DOZEN OR SO TIMES THIS WEEK AND YOU'RE FOLLOWING THE IDEA OF A STRANGER?
YOU WEREN'T HERE TO ARGUE HIS CASE WHEN I NEEDED YOU, MARTHA. YOU HAD DISOBEYED MY ORDERS, REMEMBER?
I AM TRULY SORRY, BUT UNTIL THIS MISSION ENDS, I CANNOT ALLOW THE DOCTOR TO JEOPARDISE IT.
WE HAVE A SOLUTION, AND THE PROJECTED COST OF LIFE IS ACCEPTABLE.

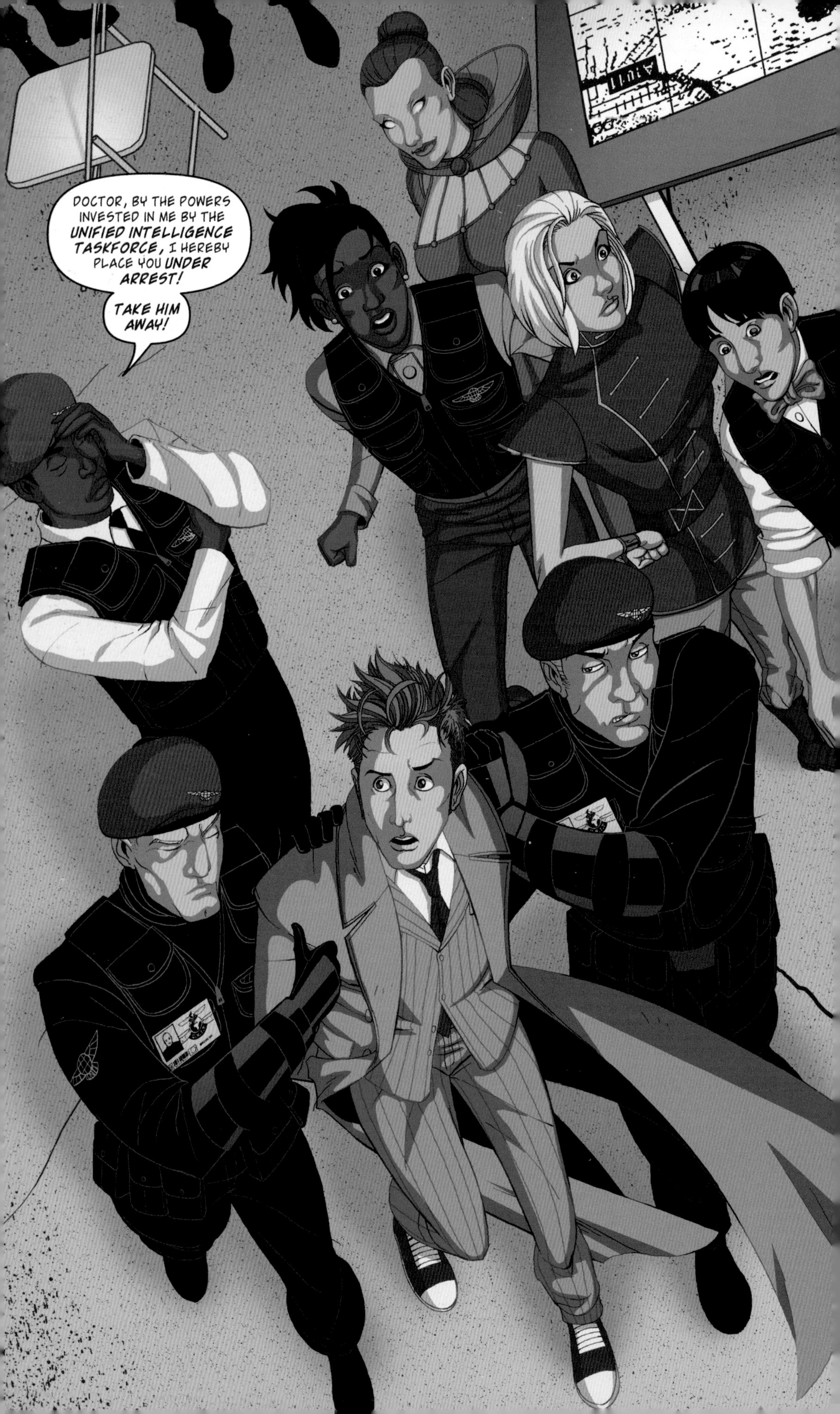
DOCTOR, BY THE POWERS INVESTED IN ME BY THE **UNIFIED INTELLIGENCE TASKFORCE**, I HEREBY PLACE YOU **UNDER ARREST!**
TAKE HIM AWAY!

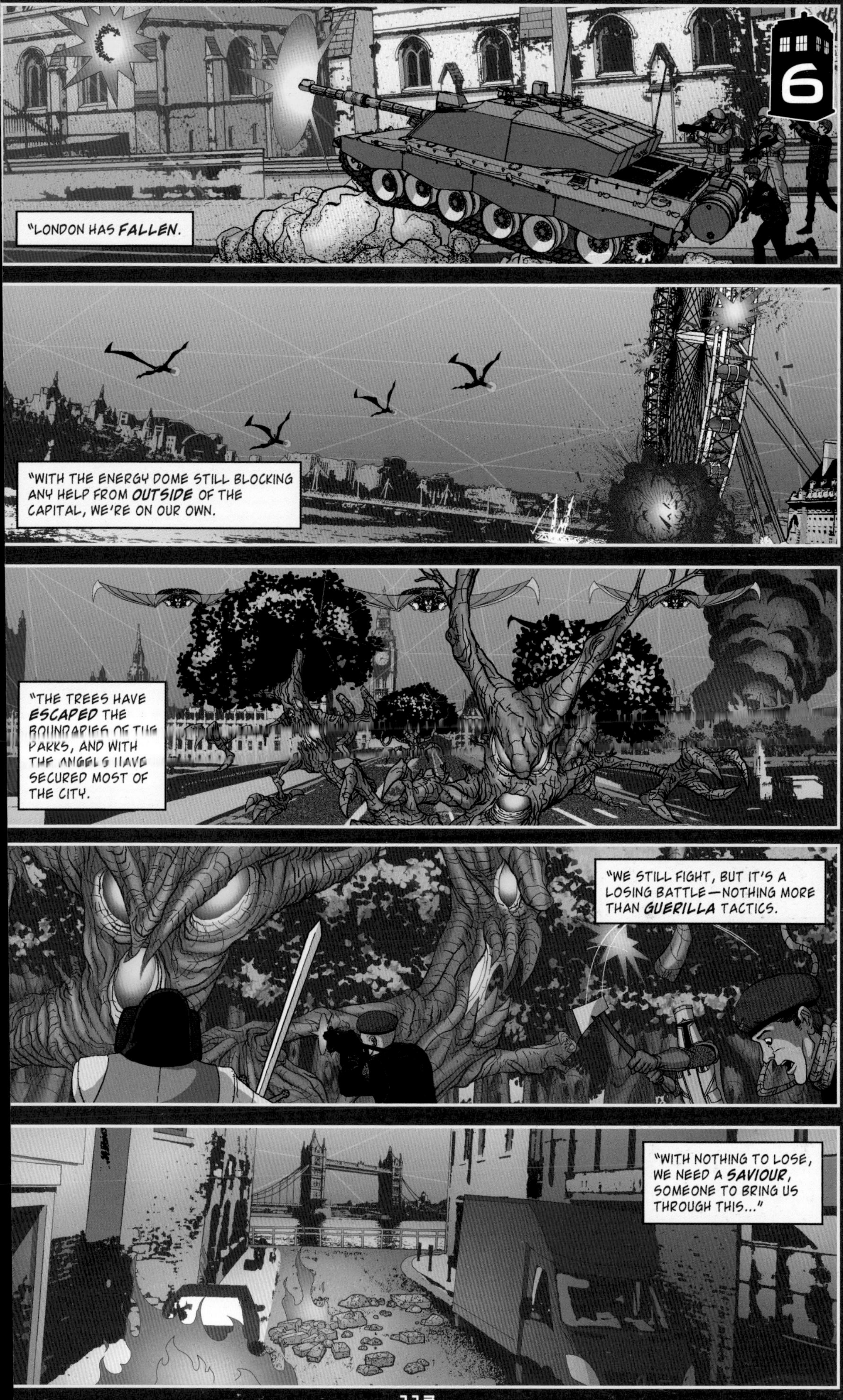
6
"LONDON HAS FALLEN.
"WITH THE ENERGY DOME STILL BLOCKING ANY HELP FROM OUTSIDE OF THE CAPITAL, WE'RE ON OUR OWN.
"THE TREES HAVE ESCAPED THE BOUNDARIES OF THE PARKS, AND WITH THE ANGELS HAVE SECURED MOST OF THE CITY.
"WE STILL FIGHT, BUT IT'S A LOSING BATTLE—NOTHING MORE THAN GUERILLA TACTICS.
"WITH NOTHING TO LOSE, WE NEED A SAVIOUR, SOMEONE TO BRING US THROUGH THIS..."

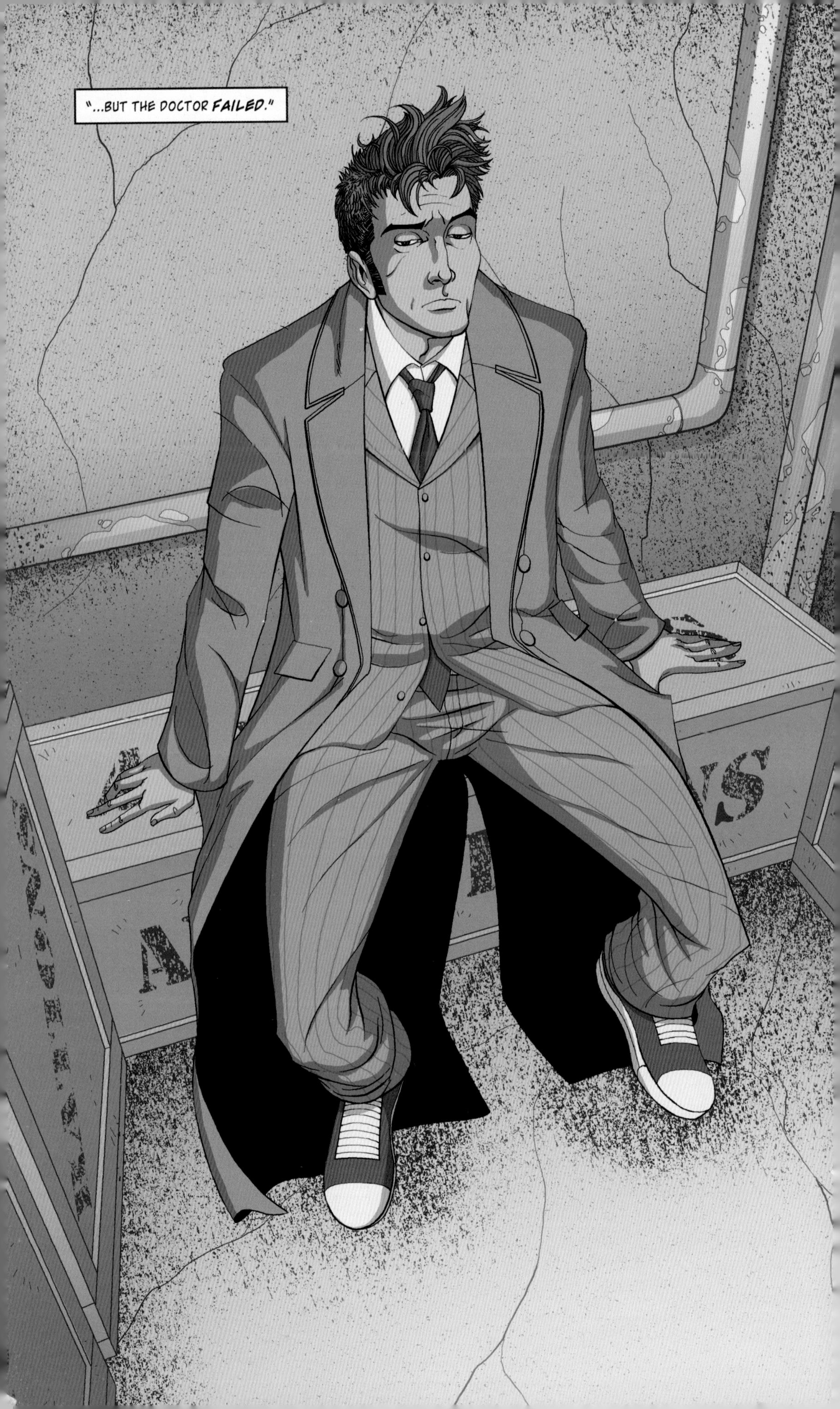
"...BUT THE DOCTOR FAILED."

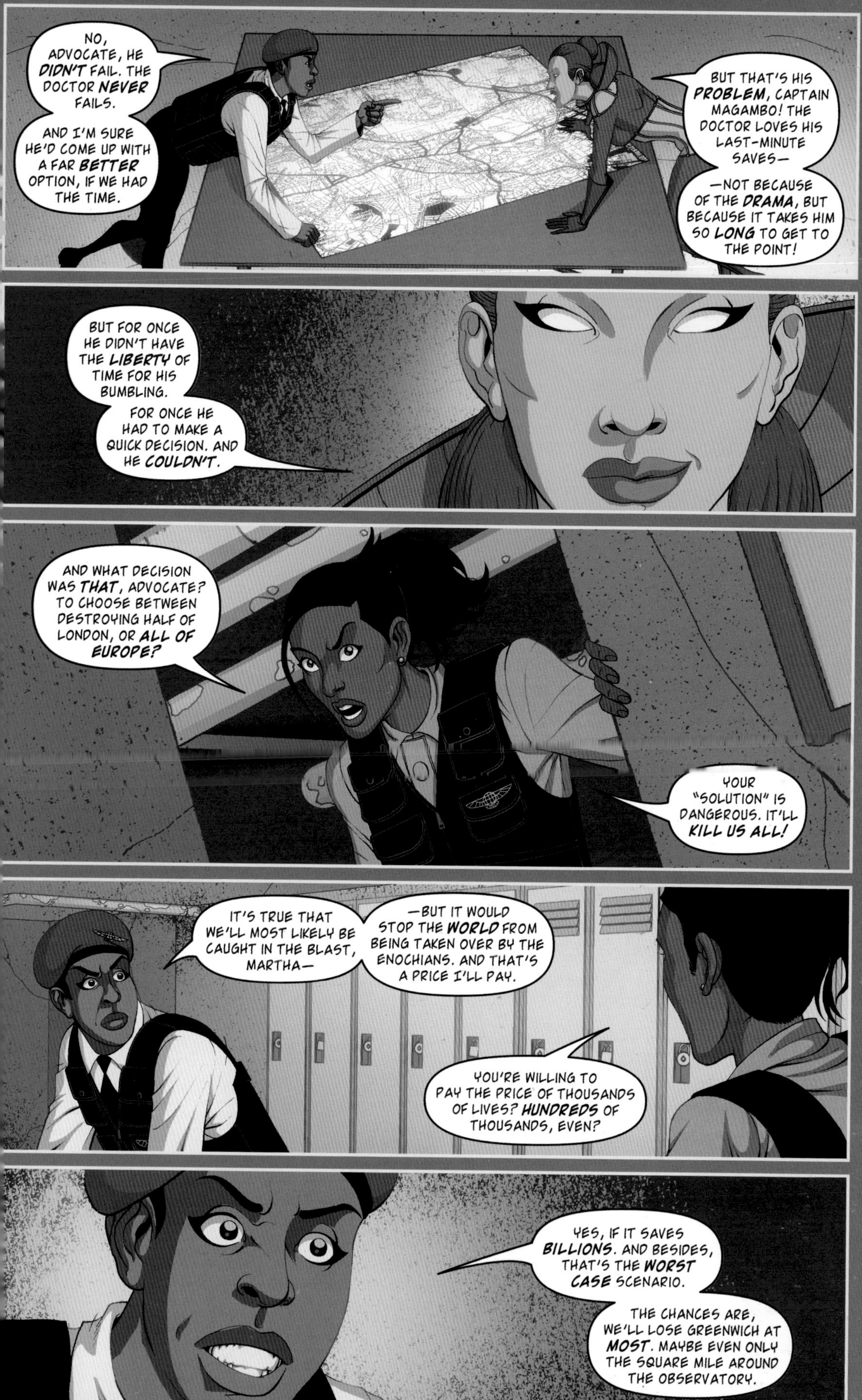

NO, ADVOCATE, HE DIDN'T FAIL. THE DOCTOR NEVER FAILS.
AND I'M SURE HE'D COME UP WITH A FAR BETTER OPTION, IF WE HAD THE TIME.
BUT THAT'S HIS PROBLEM, CAPTAIN MAGAMBO! THE DOCTOR LOVES HIS LAST-MINUTE SAVES—
—NOT BECAUSE OF THE DRAMA, BUT BECAUSE IT TAKES HIM SO LONG TO GET TO THE POINT!
BUT FOR ONCE HE DIDN'T HAVE THE LIBERTY OF TIME FOR HIS BUMBLING.
FOR ONCE HE HAD TO MAKE A QUICK DECISION. AND HE COULDN'T.
AND WHAT DECISION WAS THAT, ADVOCATE? TO CHOOSE BETWEEN DESTROYING HALF OF LONDON, OR ALL OF EUROPE?
YOUR "SOLUTION" IS DANGEROUS. IT'LL KILL US ALL!
IT'S TRUE THAT WE'LL MOST LIKELY BE CAUGHT IN THE BLAST, MARTHA—
—BUT IT WOULD STOP THE WORLD FROM BEING TAKEN OVER BY THE ENOCHIANS. AND THAT'S A PRICE I'LL PAY.
YOU'RE WILLING TO PAY THE PRICE OF THOUSANDS OF LIVES? HUNDREDS OF THOUSANDS, EVEN?
YES, IF IT SAVES BILLIONS. AND BESIDES, THAT'S THE WORST CASE SCENARIO.
THE CHANCES ARE, WE'LL LOSE GREENWICH AT MOST. MAYBE EVEN ONLY THE SQUARE MILE AROUND THE OBSERVATORY.

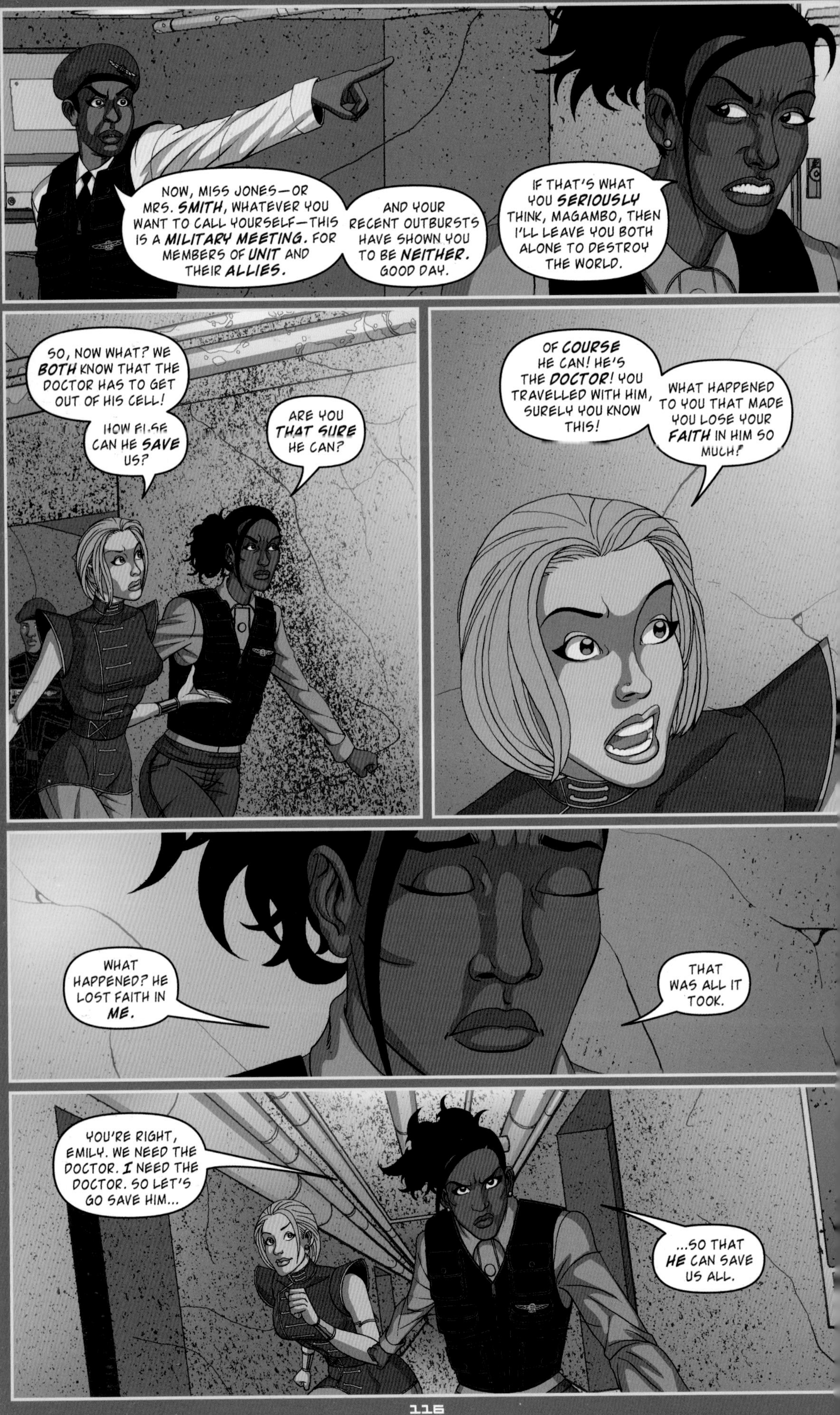
NOW, MISS JONES—OR MRS. SMITH, WHATEVER YOU WANT TO CALL YOURSELF—THIS IS A MILITARY MEETING. FOR MEMBERS OF UNIT AND THEIR ALLIES.
AND YOUR RECENT OUTBURSTS HAVE SHOWN YOU TO BE NEITHER. GOOD DAY.
IF THAT'S WHAT YOU SERIOUSLY THINK, MAGAMBO, THEN I'LL LEAVE YOU BOTH ALONE TO DESTROY THE WORLD.
SO, NOW WHAT? WE BOTH KNOW THAT THE DOCTOR HAS TO GET OUT OF HIS CELL!
HOW ELSE CAN HE SAVE US?
ARE YOU THAT SURE HE CAN?
OF COURSE HE CAN! HE'S THE DOCTOR! YOU TRAVELLED WITH HIM, SURELY YOU KNOW THIS!
WHAT HAPPENED TO YOU THAT MADE YOU LOSE YOUR FAITH IN HIM SO MUCH?
WHAT HAPPENED? HE LOST FAITH IN ME.
THAT WAS ALL IT TOOK.
YOU'RE RIGHT, EMILY. WE NEED THE DOCTOR. I NEED THE DOCTOR. SO LET'S GO SAVE HIM...
...SO THAT HE CAN SAVE US ALL.

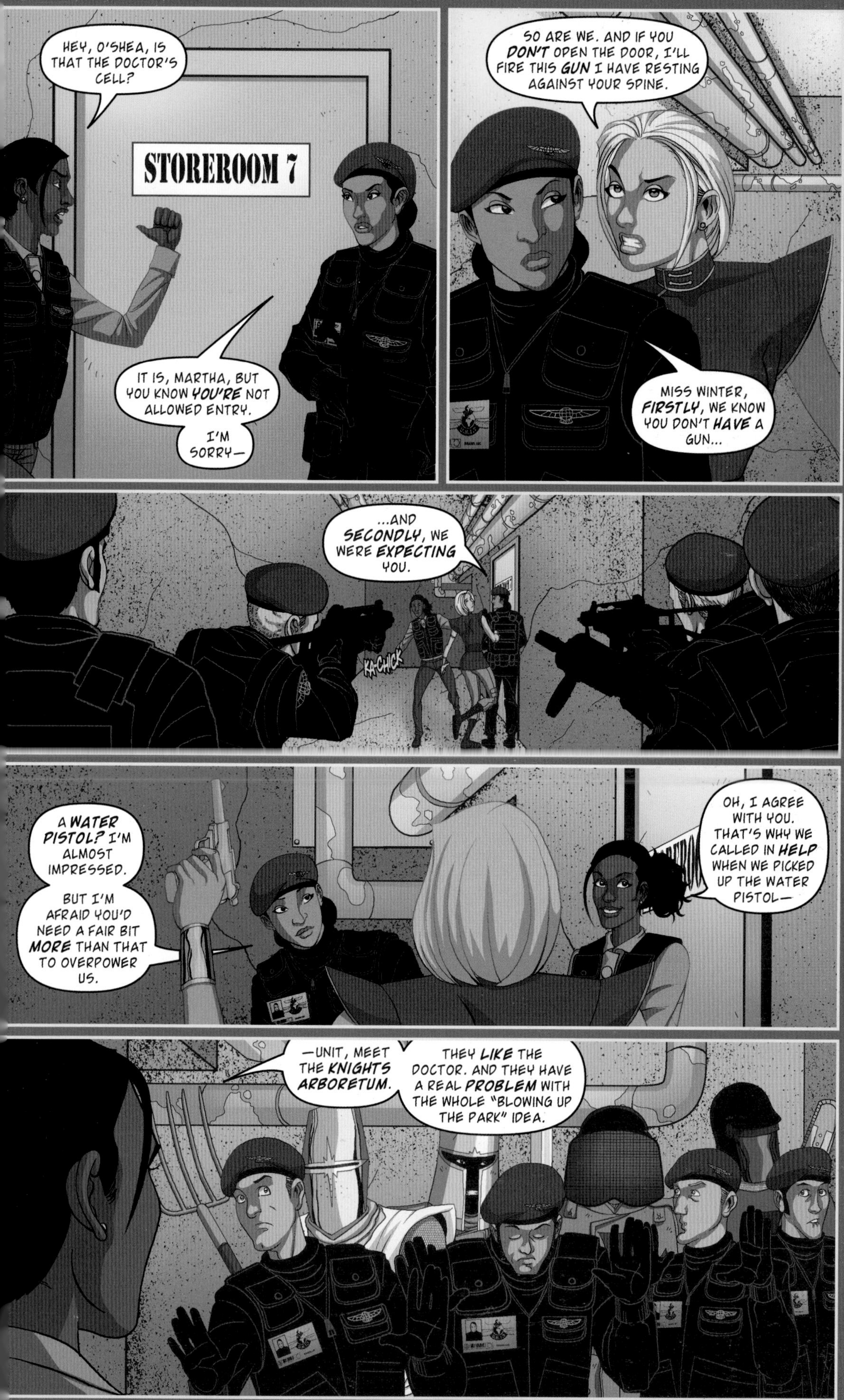
HEY, O'SHEA, IS THAT THE DOCTOR'S CELL?
STOREROOM 7
IT IS, MARTHA, BUT YOU KNOW YOU'RE NOT ALLOWED ENTRY.
I'M SORRY—
SO ARE WE. AND IF YOU DON'T OPEN THE DOOR, I'LL FIRE THIS GUN I HAVE RESTING AGAINST YOUR SPINE.
MISS WINTER, FIRSTLY, WE KNOW YOU DON'T HAVE A GUN...
...AND SECONDLY, WE WERE EXPECTING YOU.
KA-CHICK
A WATER PISTOL? I'M ALMOST IMPRESSED.
BUT I'M AFRAID YOU'D NEED A FAIR BIT MORE THAN THAT TO OVERPOWER US.
OH, I AGREE WITH YOU. THAT'S WHY WE CALLED IN HELP WHEN WE PICKED UP THE WATER PISTOL—
—UNIT, MEET THE KNIGHTS ARBORETUM.
THEY LIKE THE DOCTOR. AND THEY HAVE A REAL PROBLEM WITH THE WHOLE "BLOWING UP THE PARK" IDEA.

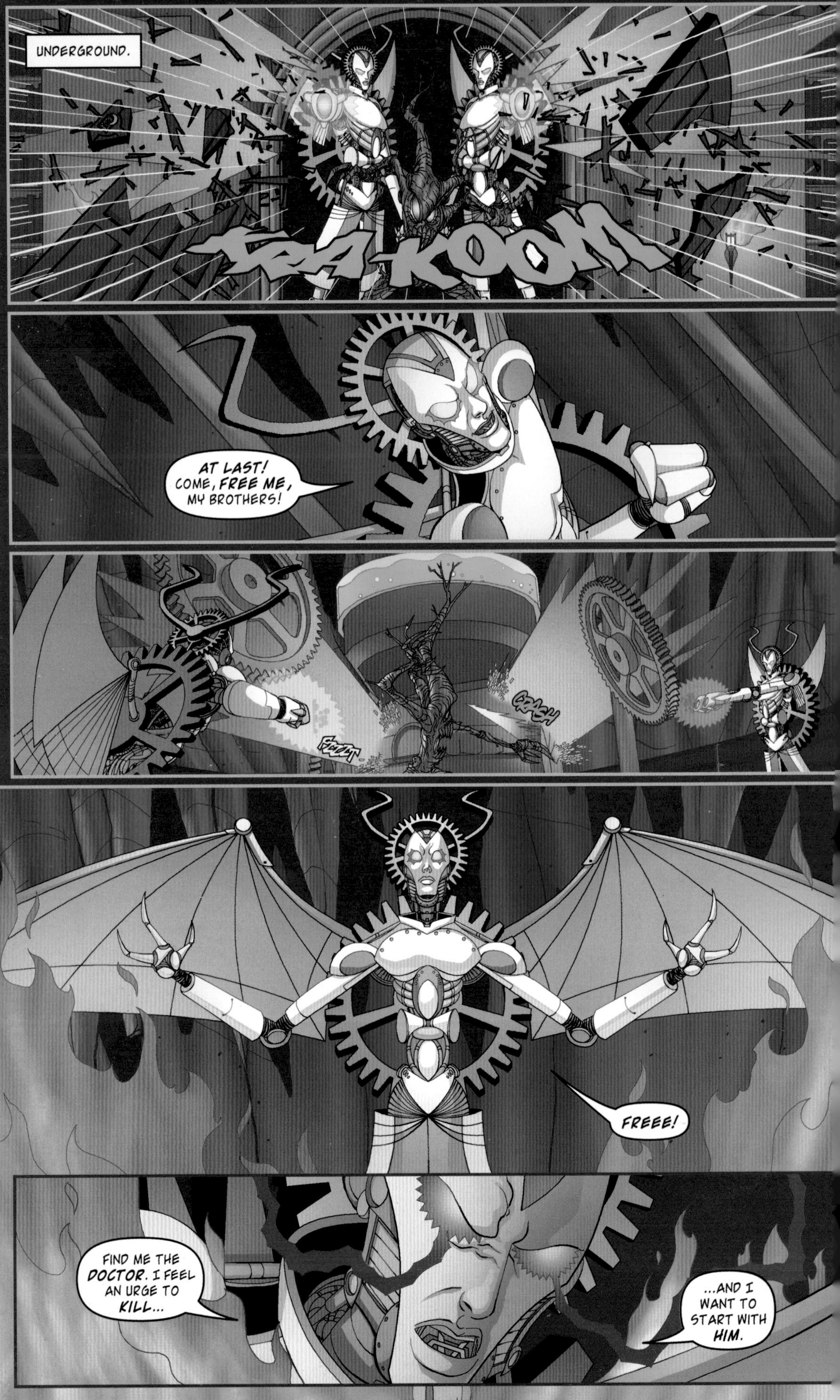
UNDERGROUND.
AT LAST! COME, FREE ME, MY BROTHERS!
CRASH
FREEE!
FIND ME THE DOCTOR. I FEEL AN URGE TO KILL...
...AND I WANT TO START WITH HIM.

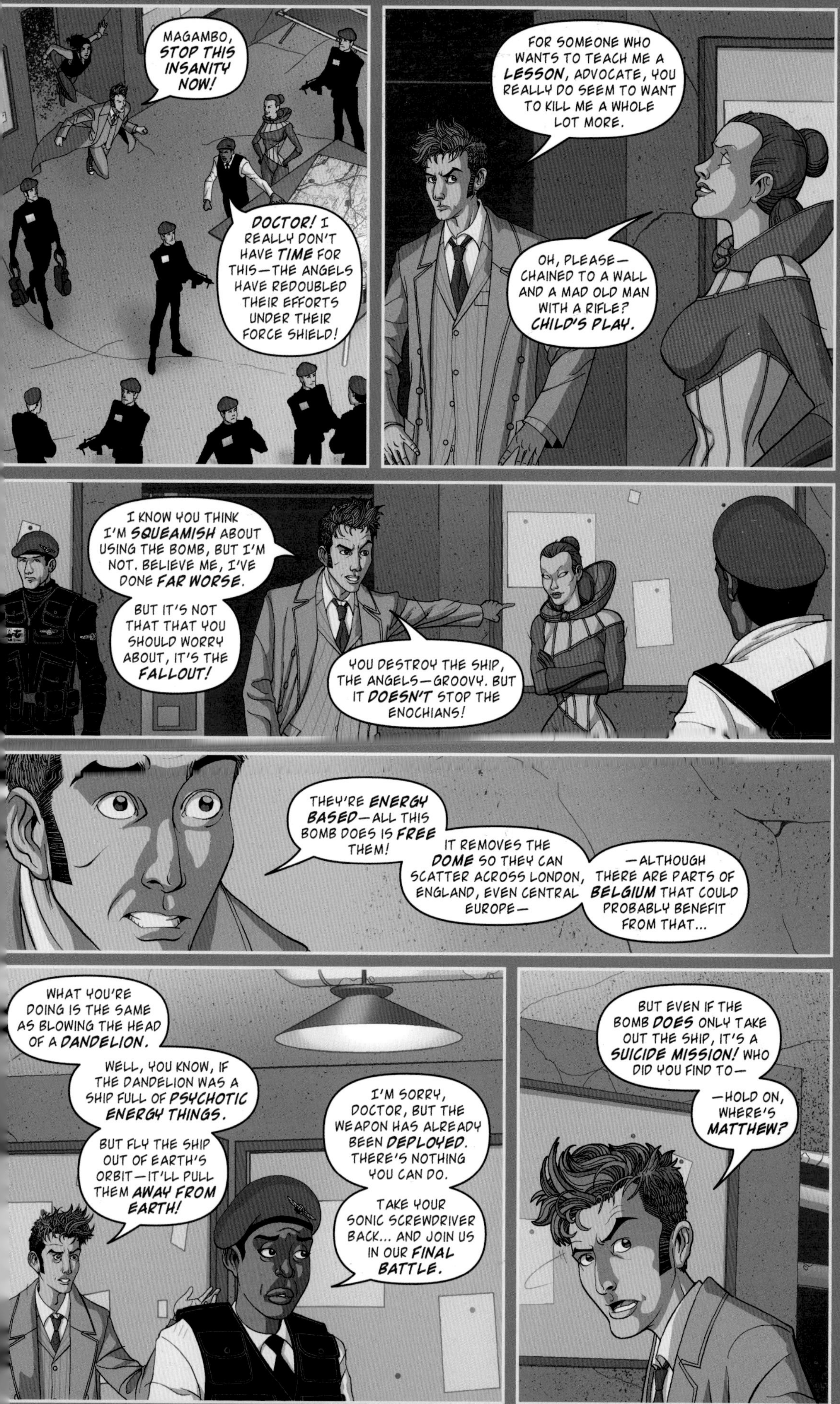
MAGAMBO, STOP THIS INSANITY NOW!
DOCTOR! I REALLY DON'T HAVE TIME FOR THIS—THE ANGELS HAVE REDOUBLED THEIR EFFORTS UNDER THEIR FORCE SHIELD!
FOR SOMEONE WHO WANTS TO TEACH ME A LESSON, ADVOCATE, YOU REALLY DO SEEM TO WANT TO KILL ME A WHOLE LOT MORE.
OH, PLEASE—CHAINED TO A WALL AND A MAD OLD MAN WITH A RIFLE? CHILD'S PLAY.
I KNOW YOU THINK I'M SQUEAMISH ABOUT USING THE BOMB, BUT I'M NOT. BELIEVE ME, I'VE DONE FAR WORSE.
BUT IT'S NOT THAT THAT YOU SHOULD WORRY ABOUT, IT'S THE FALLOUT!
YOU DESTROY THE SHIP, THE ANGELS—GROOVY. BUT IT DOESN'T STOP THE ENOCHIANS!
THEY'RE ENERGY BASED—ALL THIS BOMB DOES IS FREE THEM!
IT REMOVES THE DOME SO THEY CAN SCATTER ACROSS LONDON, ENGLAND, EVEN CENTRAL EUROPE—
—ALTHOUGH THERE ARE PARTS OF BELGIUM THAT COULD PROBABLY BENEFIT FROM THAT...
WHAT YOU'RE DOING IS THE SAME AS BLOWING THE HEAD OF A DANDELION.
WELL, YOU KNOW, IF THE DANDELION WAS A SHIP FULL OF PSYCHOTIC ENERGY THINGS.
BUT FLY THE SHIP OUT OF EARTH'S ORBIT—IT'LL PULL THEM AWAY FROM EARTH!
I'M SORRY, DOCTOR, BUT THE WEAPON HAS ALREADY BEEN DEPLOYED. THERE'S NOTHING YOU CAN DO.
TAKE YOUR SONIC SCREWDRIVER BACK... AND JOIN US IN OUR FINAL BATTLE.
BUT EVEN IF THE BOMB DOES ONLY TAKE OUT THE SHIP, IT'S A SUICIDE MISSION! WHO DID YOU FIND TO—
—HOLD ON, WHERE'S MATTHEW?

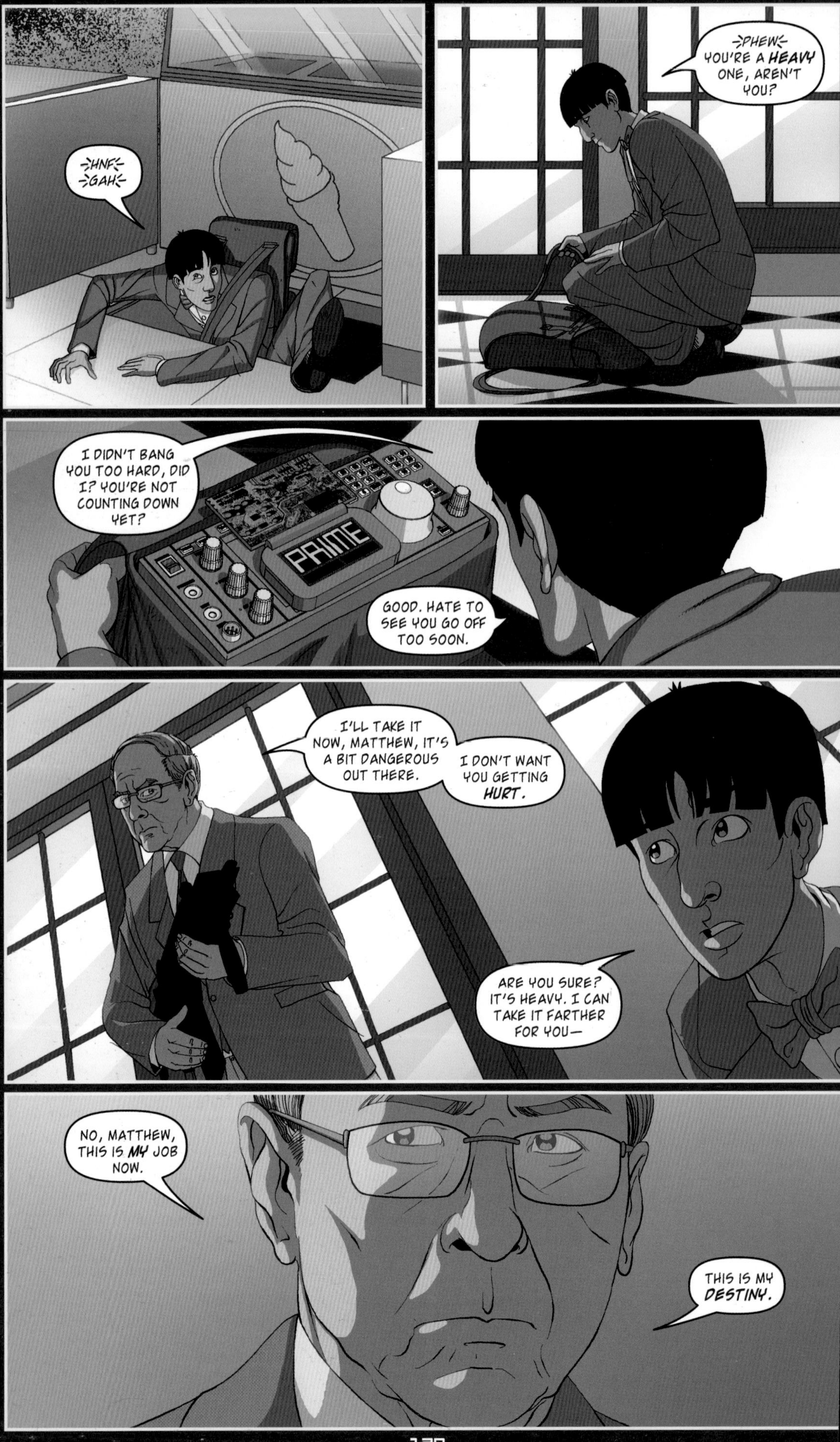

HNF GAH
PHEW YOU'RE A HEAVY ONE, AREN'T YOU?
I DIDN'T BANG YOU TOO HARD, DID I? YOU'RE NOT COUNTING DOWN YET?
PRIME
GOOD. HATE TO SEE YOU GO OFF TOO SOON.
I'LL TAKE IT NOW, MATTHEW, IT'S A BIT DANGEROUS OUT THERE.
I DON'T WANT YOU GETTING HURT.
ARE YOU SURE? IT'S HEAVY. I CAN TAKE IT FARTHER FOR YOU—
NO, MATTHEW, THIS IS MY JOB NOW.
THIS IS MY DESTINY.

GREENWICH HIGH STREET.

DOCTOR! WHERE ARE YOU?!

COME OUT AND DIE!

KA-BOOM

WHERE IS THE DOCTOR?

WHO KNOWS? PROBABLY THE SAME PLACE THAT THE **ADVOCATE** WENT TO.

BRAKKKAAA

OR HE WENT TO THE SHIP TO TRY AND SAVE THE DAY. WE CALL THAT "WEDNESDAYS."

SWOOSH

BRAKKKAAA

I HAVE HAD **ENOUGH** OF YOU!

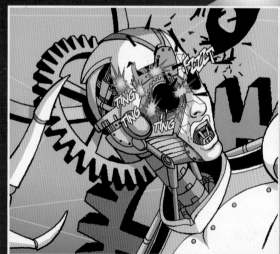

TING TING TING TING

CRASH

NICE GROUPING THERE.

121

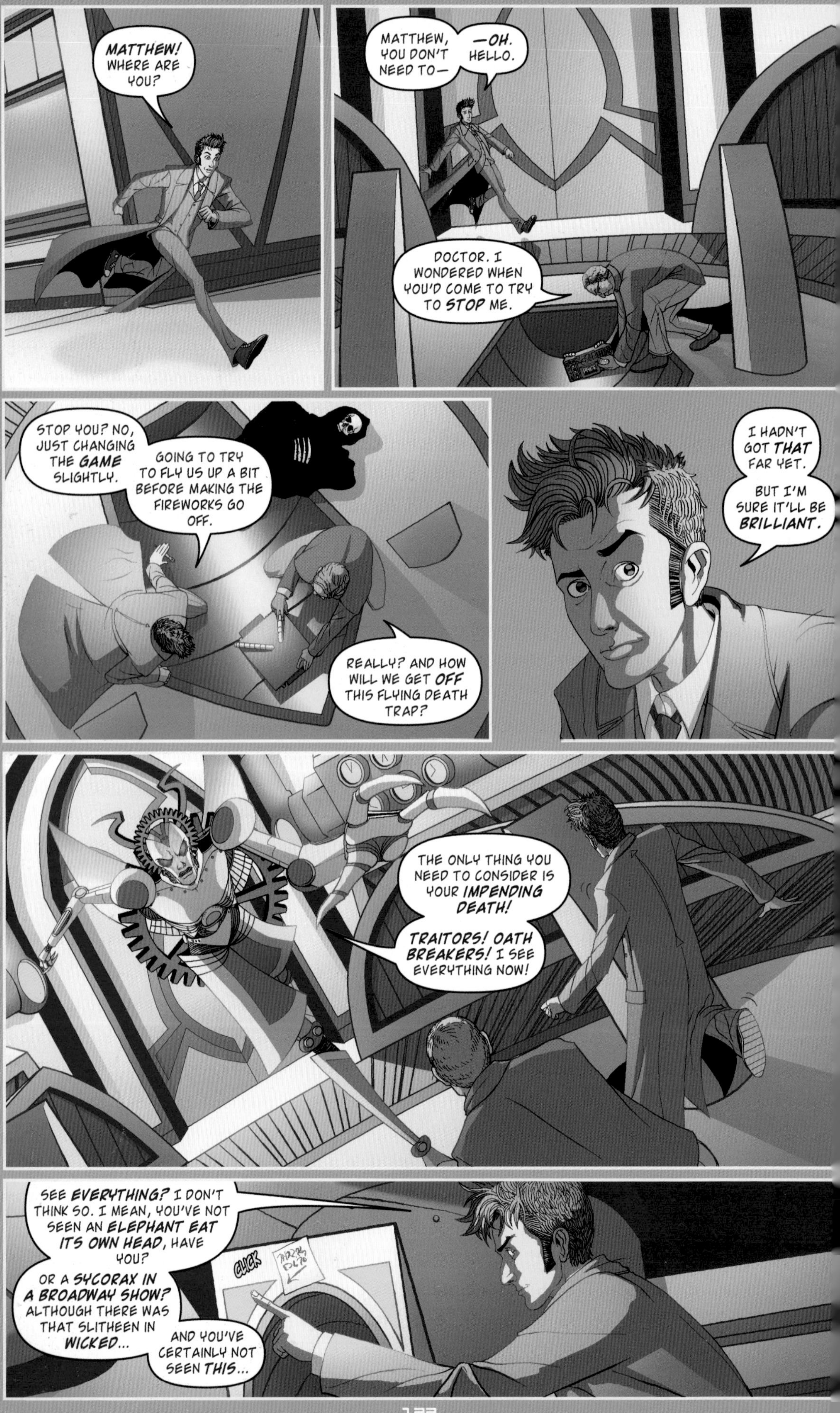
MATTHEW! WHERE ARE YOU?
MATTHEW, YOU DON'T NEED TO—
—OH. HELLO.
DOCTOR. I WONDERED WHEN YOU'D COME TO TRY TO STOP ME.
STOP YOU? NO, JUST CHANGING THE GAME SLIGHTLY.
GOING TO TRY TO FLY US UP A BIT BEFORE MAKING THE FIREWORKS GO OFF.
REALLY? AND HOW WILL WE GET OFF THIS FLYING DEATH TRAP?
I HADN'T GOT THAT FAR YET.
BUT I'M SURE IT'LL BE BRILLIANT.
THE ONLY THING YOU NEED TO CONSIDER IS YOUR IMPENDING DEATH!
TRAITORS! OATH BREAKERS! I SEE EVERYTHING NOW!
SEE EVERYTHING? I DON'T THINK SO. I MEAN, YOU'VE NOT SEEN AN ELEPHANT EAT ITS OWN HEAD, HAVE YOU?
OR A SYCORAX IN A BROADWAY SHOW? ALTHOUGH THERE WAS THAT SLITHEEN IN WICKED...
AND YOU'VE CERTAINLY NOT SEEN THIS...
CLICK

HELLO. IF YOU HAVE FOUND THIS, IT MEANS THAT I AM DEAD, AND THAT I HAVE MOST LIKELY FAILED IN DESTROYING THIS DEVIL VESSEL.
YOU! CURSED DEE! YOU ARE DEAD! HOW CAN THIS—
FZZZT
MADE YOU LOOK.
SORRY, NO TIME FOR A BIG FIGHT WITH THE END OF LEVEL BOSS, WE'RE ON A BIT OF A DEADLINE.
GRRAARGHH!
MANY YEARS AGO, THESE ANGELS SPOKE TO ME THROUGH A FRIEND, EDWARD KELLEY—
CRASH
SORRY, I GET BORED WITH REPEATS. DON'T YOU?
CLICK
COME ON, CRANEY, LET'S GET THIS BABY SPACEBORN! FUSION DRIVES TO FULL, I FEEL!
ARMED
HEY! HAVE YOU EVER TRIED A HIGH ALTITUDE JUMP WITH A PAIR OF CLOCKWORK WINGS?

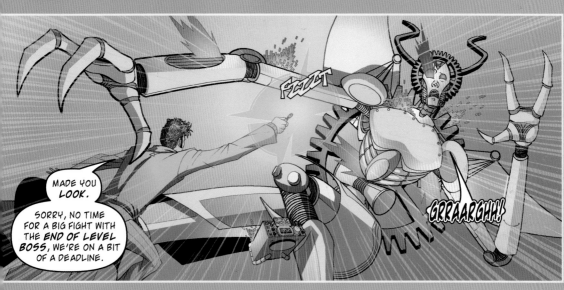

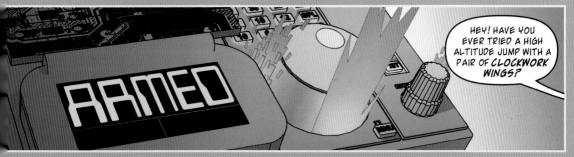

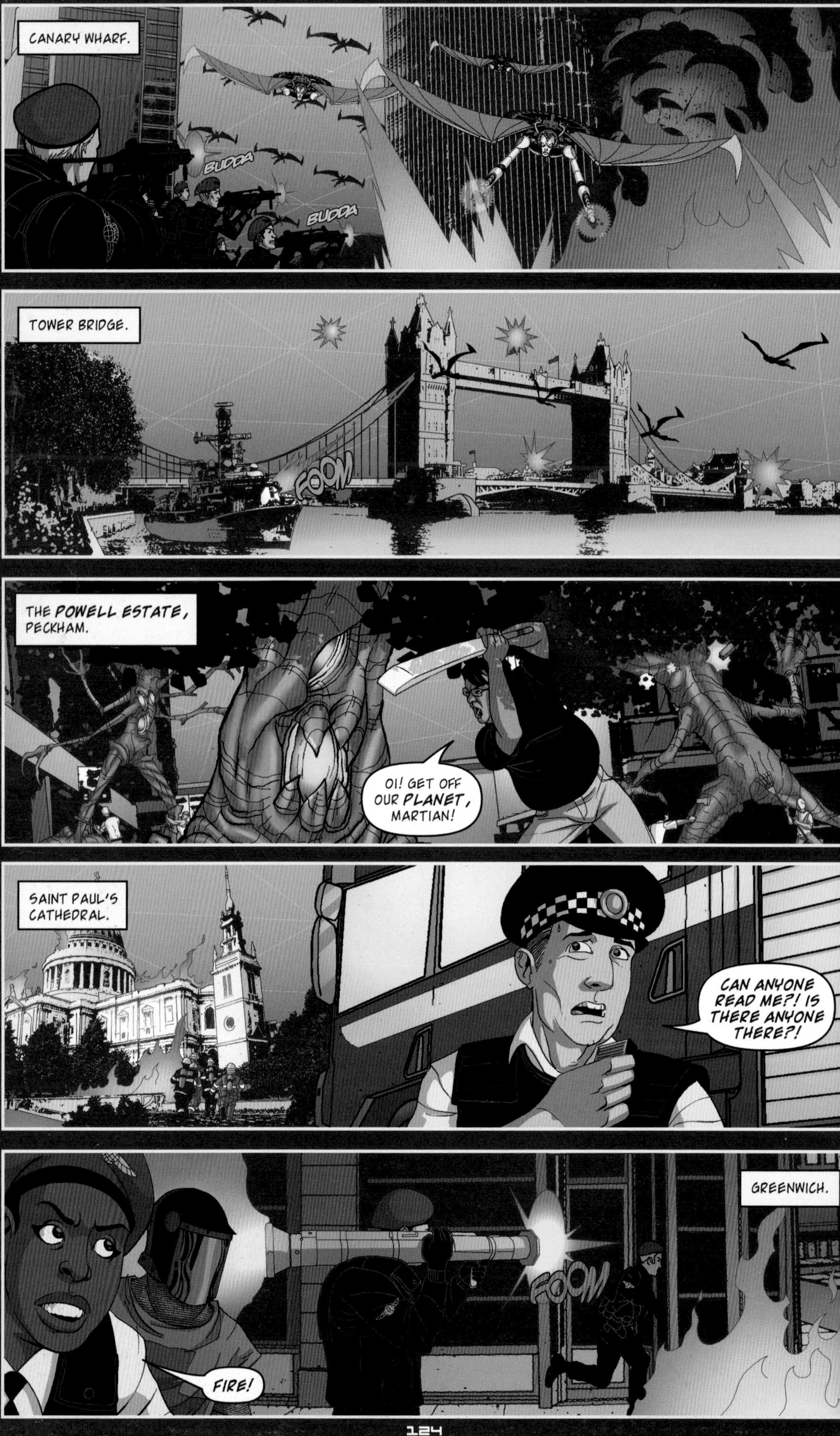
CANARY WHARF.
BUDDA
BUDDA
TOWER BRIDGE.
FOOM
THE POWELL ESTATE, PECKHAM.
OI! GET OFF OUR PLANET, MARTIAN!
SAINT PAUL'S CATHEDRAL.
CAN ANYONE READ ME?! IS THERE ANYONE THERE?!
GREENWICH.
FOOM
FIRE!

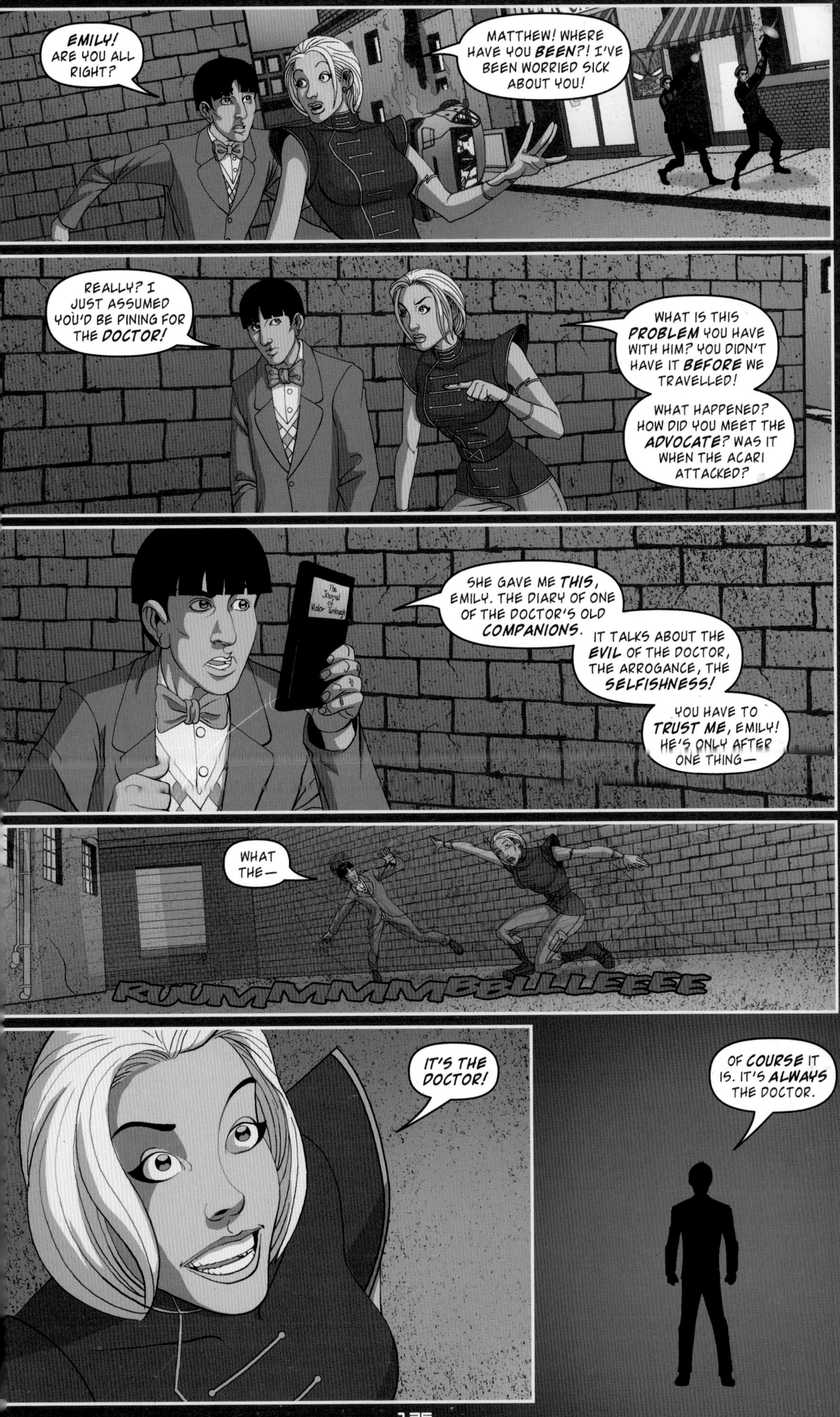
EMILY! ARE YOU ALL RIGHT?
MATTHEW! WHERE HAVE YOU BEEN?! I'VE BEEN WORRIED SICK ABOUT YOU!
REALLY? I JUST ASSUMED YOU'D BE PINING FOR THE DOCTOR!
WHAT IS THIS PROBLEM YOU HAVE WITH HIM? YOU DIDN'T HAVE IT BEFORE WE TRAVELLED!
WHAT HAPPENED? HOW DID YOU MEET THE ADVOCATE? WAS IT WHEN THE ACARI ATTACKED?
SHE GAVE ME THIS, EMILY. THE DIARY OF ONE OF THE DOCTOR'S OLD COMPANIONS.
IT TALKS ABOUT THE EVIL OF THE DOCTOR, THE ARROGANCE, THE SELFISHNESS!
YOU HAVE TO TRUST ME, EMILY! HE'S ONLY AFTER ONE THING—
WHAT THE—
RUUMMMMBBLLEEEE
IT'S THE DOCTOR!
OF COURSE IT IS. IT'S ALWAYS THE DOCTOR.

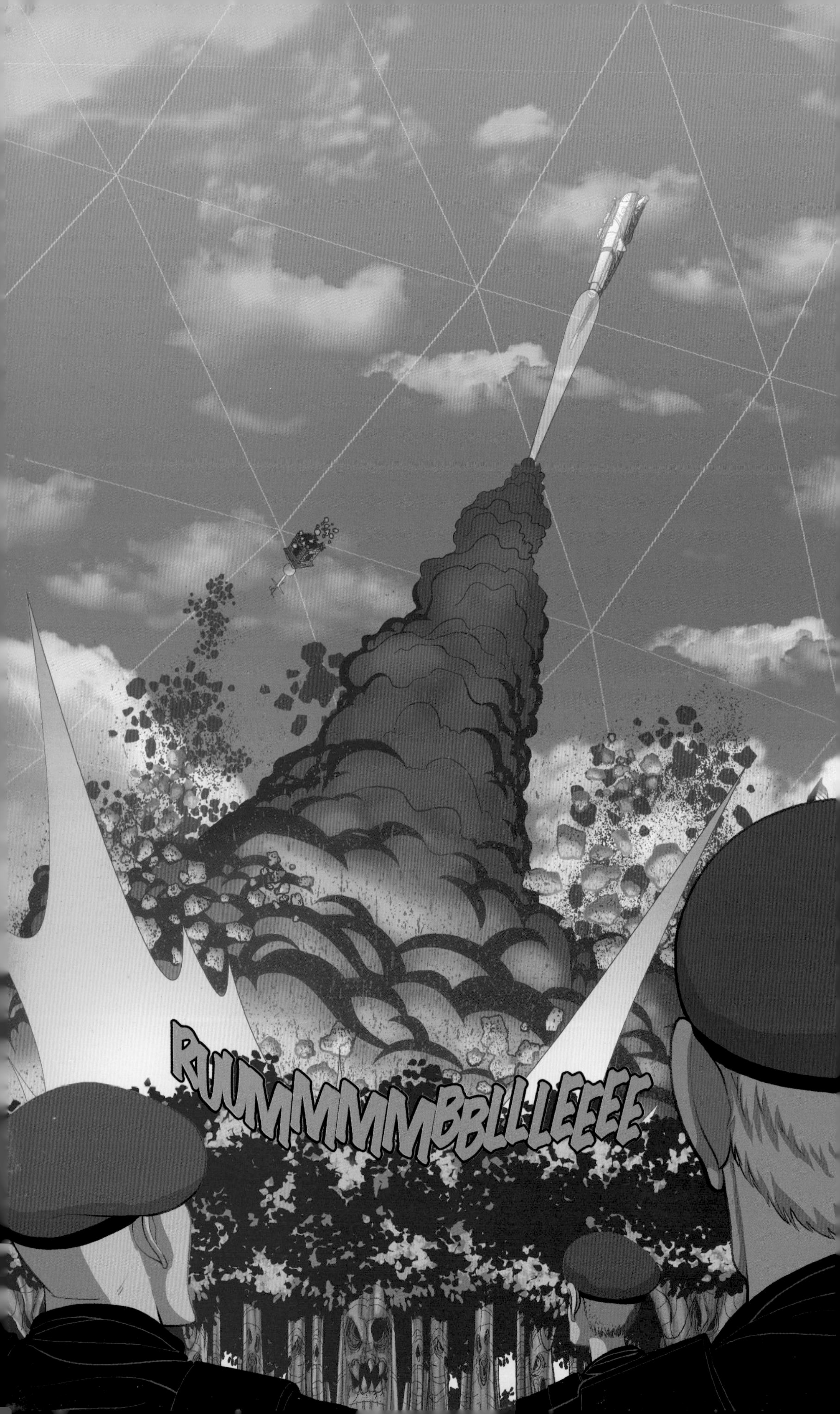
RUUMMMMMBBLLLEEEE

DO YOU SEE THAT, MISTER CRANE? IT'S *WORKING!*

AS WE RISE, THE ENERGY OF THE ENOCHIANS IS BEING PULLED *WITH* US!

THEY'RE RETURNING TO THE *STASIS PODS!* THEY'RE RETURNING TO THE SHIP!

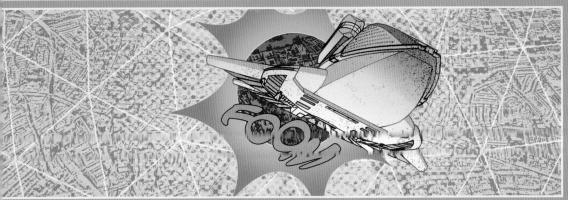

CRASH

THIS SHIP WILL JUST KEEP *FLYING ON,* CONSTANTLY AWAY FROM EARTH!

BY THE TIME THE ENOCHIANS GET OUT OF STASIS, THEY'LL BE *FAR AWAY* FROM HERE!

I BEAT THE ADVOCATE! HER BOMB ISN'T NEEDED AFTER ALL!

YES, ABOUT THAT, DOCTOR...

...WE MIGHT HAVE A *PROBLEM* THERE.

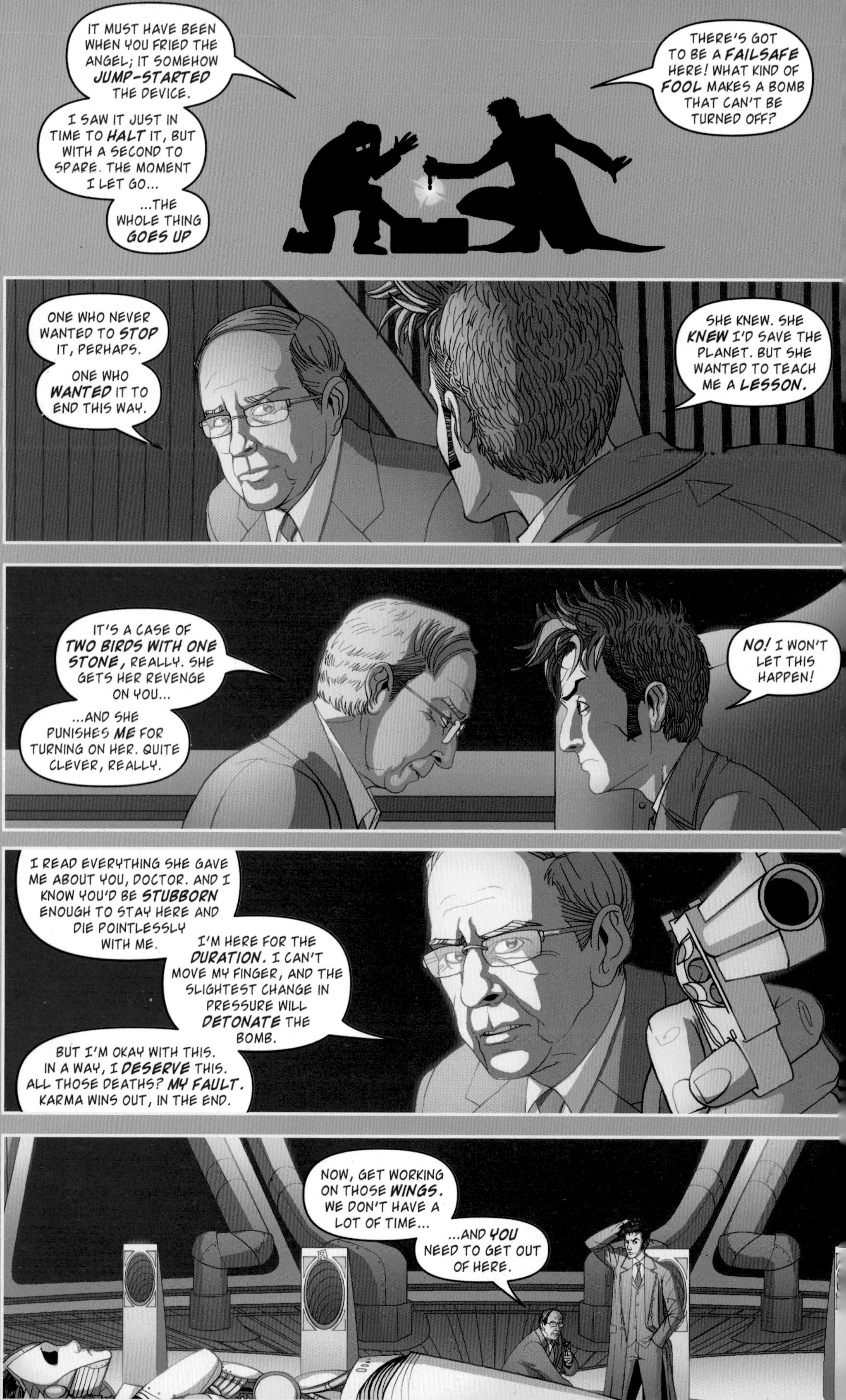
IT MUST HAVE BEEN WHEN YOU FRIED THE ANGEL; IT SOMEHOW JUMP-STARTED THE DEVICE.
I SAW IT JUST IN TIME TO HALT IT, BUT WITH A SECOND TO SPARE. THE MOMENT I LET GO...
...THE WHOLE THING GOES UP
THERE'S GOT TO BE A FAILSAFE HERE! WHAT KIND OF FOOL MAKES A BOMB THAT CAN'T BE TURNED OFF?
ONE WHO NEVER WANTED TO STOP IT, PERHAPS.
ONE WHO WANTED IT TO END THIS WAY.
SHE KNEW. SHE KNEW I'D SAVE THE PLANET. BUT SHE WANTED TO TEACH ME A LESSON.
IT'S A CASE OF TWO BIRDS WITH ONE STONE, REALLY. SHE GETS HER REVENGE ON YOU...
...AND SHE PUNISHES ME FOR TURNING ON HER. QUITE CLEVER, REALLY.
NO! I WON'T LET THIS HAPPEN!
I READ EVERYTHING SHE GAVE ME ABOUT YOU, DOCTOR. AND I KNOW YOU'D BE STUBBORN ENOUGH TO STAY HERE AND DIE POINTLESSLY WITH ME.
I'M HERE FOR THE DURATION. I CAN'T MOVE MY FINGER, AND THE SLIGHTEST CHANGE IN PRESSURE WILL DETONATE THE BOMB.
BUT I'M OKAY WITH THIS. IN A WAY, I DESERVE THIS. ALL THOSE DEATHS? MY FAULT. KARMA WINS OUT, IN THE END.
NOW, GET WORKING ON THOSE WINGS. WE DON'T HAVE A LOT OF TIME...
...AND YOU NEED TO GET OUT OF HERE.

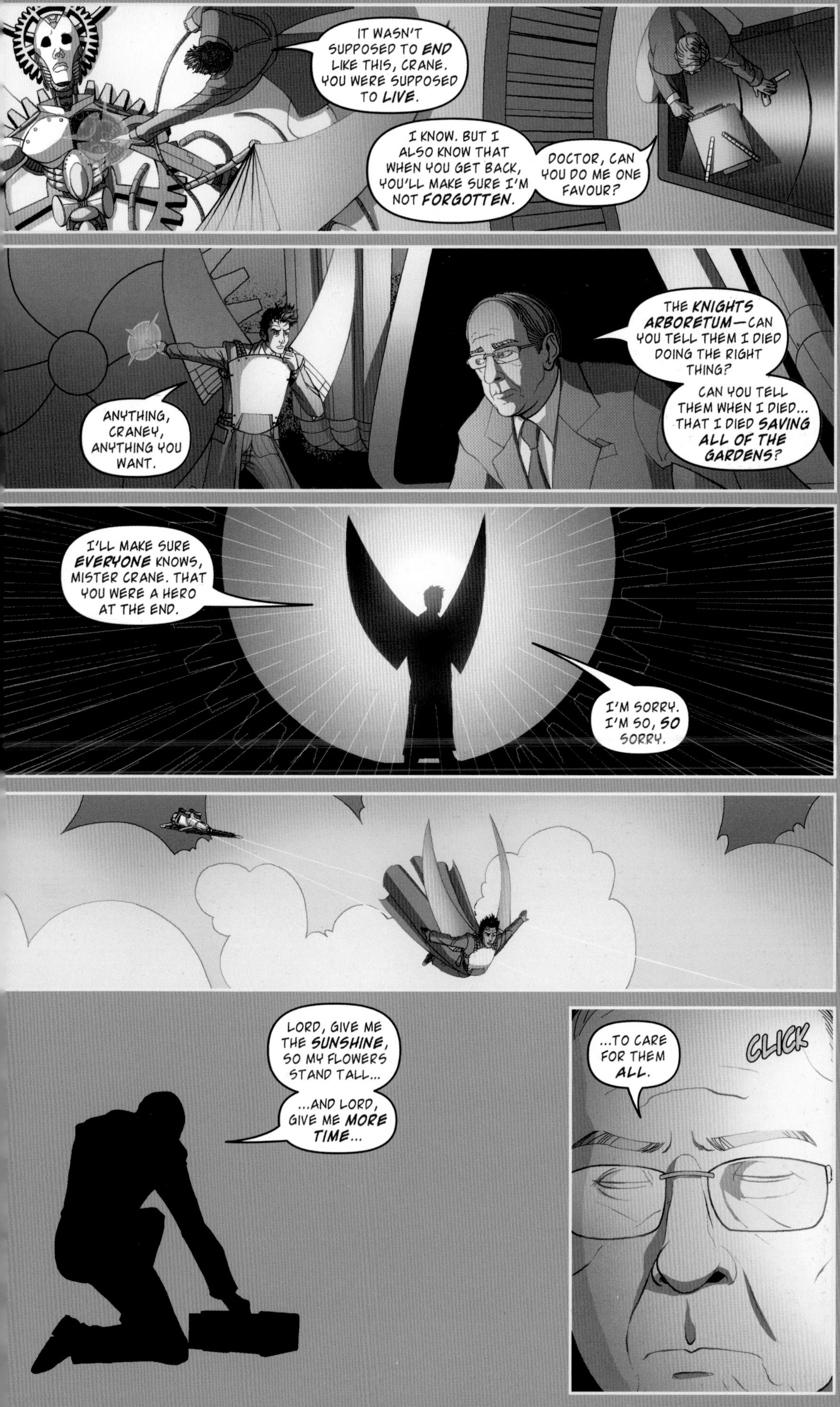
IT WASN'T SUPPOSED TO END LIKE THIS, CRANE. YOU WERE SUPPOSED TO LIVE.
I KNOW. BUT I ALSO KNOW THAT WHEN YOU GET BACK, YOU'LL MAKE SURE I'M NOT FORGOTTEN.
DOCTOR, CAN YOU DO ME ONE FAVOUR?
THE KNIGHTS ARBORETUM—CAN YOU TELL THEM I DIED DOING THE RIGHT THING?
CAN YOU TELL THEM WHEN I DIED... THAT I DIED SAVING ALL OF THE GARDENS?
ANYTHING, CRANEY, ANYTHING YOU WANT.
I'LL MAKE SURE EVERYONE KNOWS, MISTER CRANE. THAT YOU WERE A HERO AT THE END.
I'M SORRY. I'M SO, SO SORRY.
LORD, GIVE ME THE SUNSHINE, SO MY FLOWERS STAND TALL...
...AND LORD, GIVE ME MORE TIME...
...TO CARE FOR THEM ALL.
CLICK

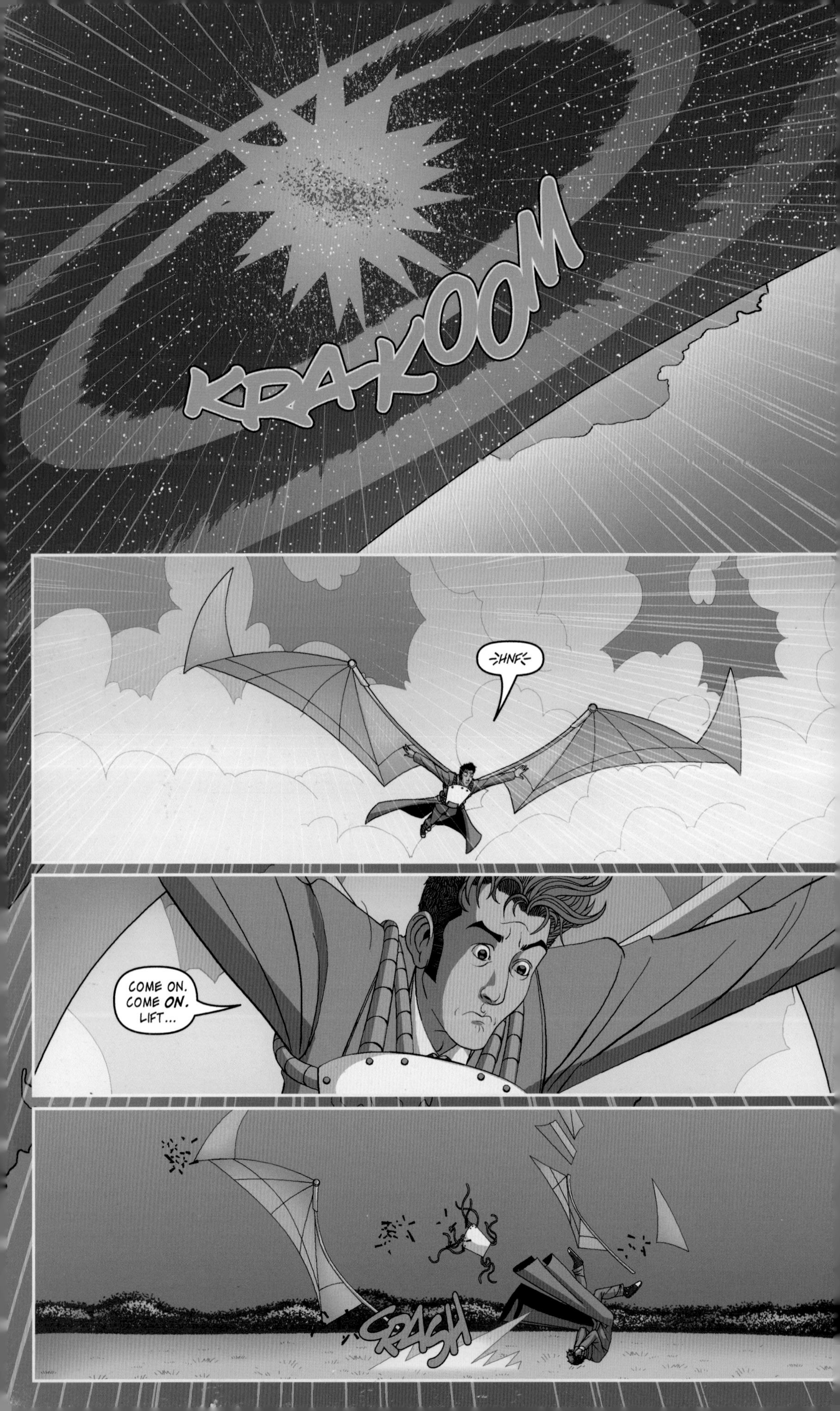
KRA-KOOM
HNF
COME ON. COME ON. LIFT...
CRASH

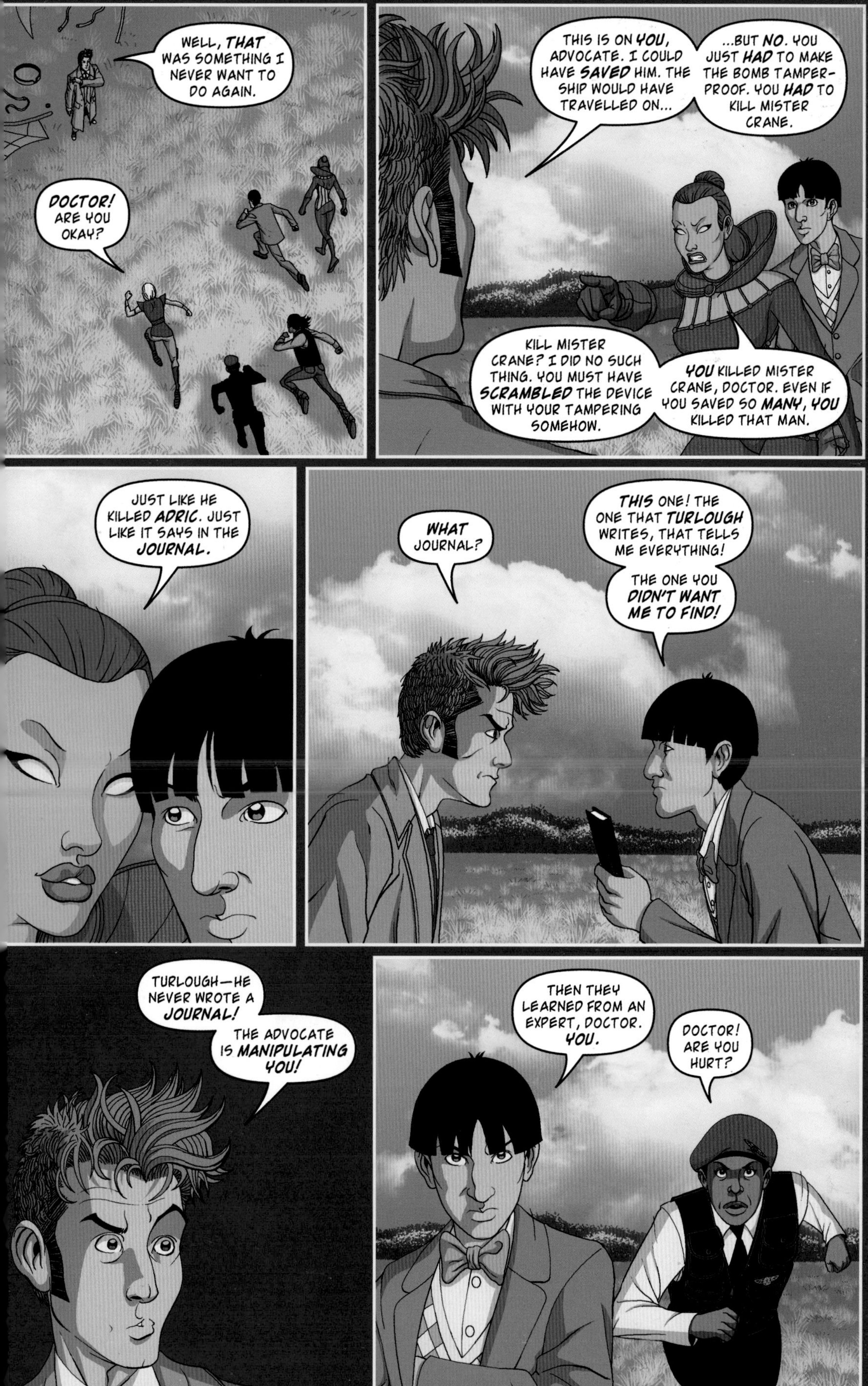
WELL, THAT WAS SOMETHING I NEVER WANT TO DO AGAIN.
DOCTOR! ARE YOU OKAY?
THIS IS ON YOU, ADVOCATE. I COULD HAVE SAVED HIM. THE SHIP WOULD HAVE TRAVELLED ON...
...BUT NO. YOU JUST HAD TO MAKE THE BOMB TAMPER-PROOF. YOU HAD TO KILL MISTER CRANE.
KILL MISTER CRANE? I DID NO SUCH THING. YOU MUST HAVE SCRAMBLED THE DEVICE WITH YOUR TAMPERING SOMEHOW.
YOU KILLED MISTER CRANE, DOCTOR. EVEN IF YOU SAVED SO MANY, YOU KILLED THAT MAN.
JUST LIKE HE KILLED ADRIC. JUST LIKE IT SAYS IN THE JOURNAL.
WHAT JOURNAL?
THIS ONE! THE ONE THAT TURLOUGH WRITES, THAT TELLS ME EVERYTHING!
THE ONE YOU DIDN'T WANT ME TO FIND!
TURLOUGH—HE NEVER WROTE A JOURNAL!
THE ADVOCATE IS MANIPULATING YOU!
THEN THEY LEARNED FROM AN EXPERT, DOCTOR. YOU.
DOCTOR! ARE YOU HURT?

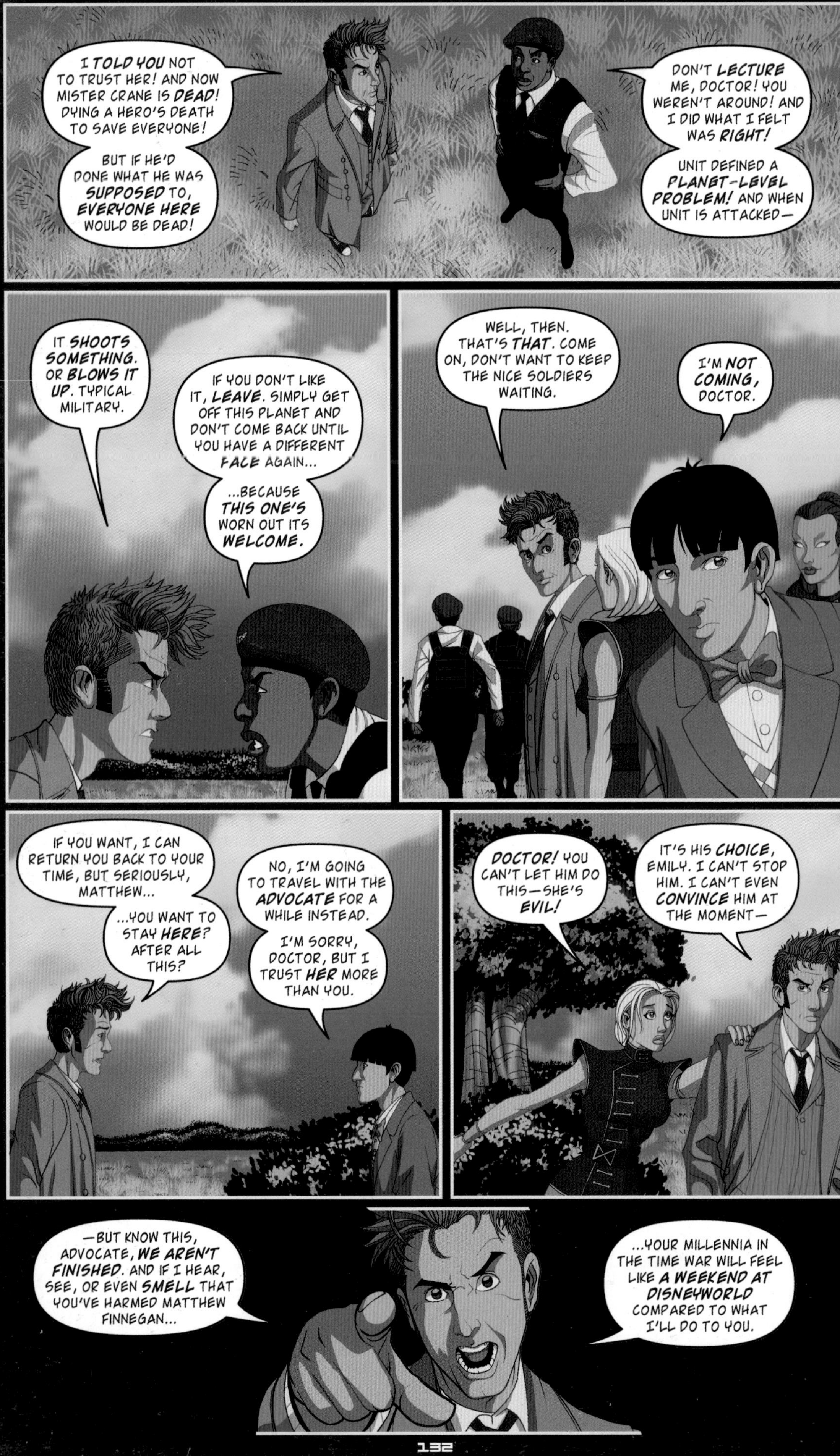
I TOLD YOU NOT TO TRUST HER! AND NOW MISTER CRANE IS DEAD! DYING A HERO'S DEATH TO SAVE EVERYONE!
BUT IF HE'D DONE WHAT HE WAS SUPPOSED TO, EVERYONE HERE WOULD BE DEAD!
DON'T LECTURE ME, DOCTOR! YOU WEREN'T AROUND! AND I DID WHAT I FELT WAS RIGHT!
UNIT DEFINED A PLANET-LEVEL PROBLEM! AND WHEN UNIT IS ATTACKED—
IT SHOOTS SOMETHING. OR BLOWS IT UP. TYPICAL MILITARY.
IF YOU DON'T LIKE IT, LEAVE. SIMPLY GET OFF THIS PLANET AND DON'T COME BACK UNTIL YOU HAVE A DIFFERENT FACE AGAIN...
...BECAUSE THIS ONE'S WORN OUT ITS WELCOME.
WELL, THEN. THAT'S THAT. COME ON, DON'T WANT TO KEEP THE NICE SOLDIERS WAITING.
I'M NOT COMING, DOCTOR.
IF YOU WANT, I CAN RETURN YOU BACK TO YOUR TIME, BUT SERIOUSLY, MATTHEW...
...YOU WANT TO STAY HERE? AFTER ALL THIS?
NO, I'M GOING TO TRAVEL WITH THE ADVOCATE FOR A WHILE INSTEAD.
I'M SORRY, DOCTOR, BUT I TRUST HER MORE THAN YOU.
DOCTOR! YOU CAN'T LET HIM DO THIS—SHE'S EVIL!
IT'S HIS CHOICE, EMILY. I CAN'T STOP HIM. I CAN'T EVEN CONVINCE HIM AT THE MOMENT—
—BUT KNOW THIS, ADVOCATE, WE AREN'T FINISHED. AND IF I HEAR, SEE, OR EVEN SMELL THAT YOU'VE HARMED MATTHEW FINNEGAN...
...YOUR MILLENNIA IN THE TIME WAR WILL FEEL LIKE A WEEKEND AT DISNEYWORLD COMPARED TO WHAT I'LL DO TO YOU.

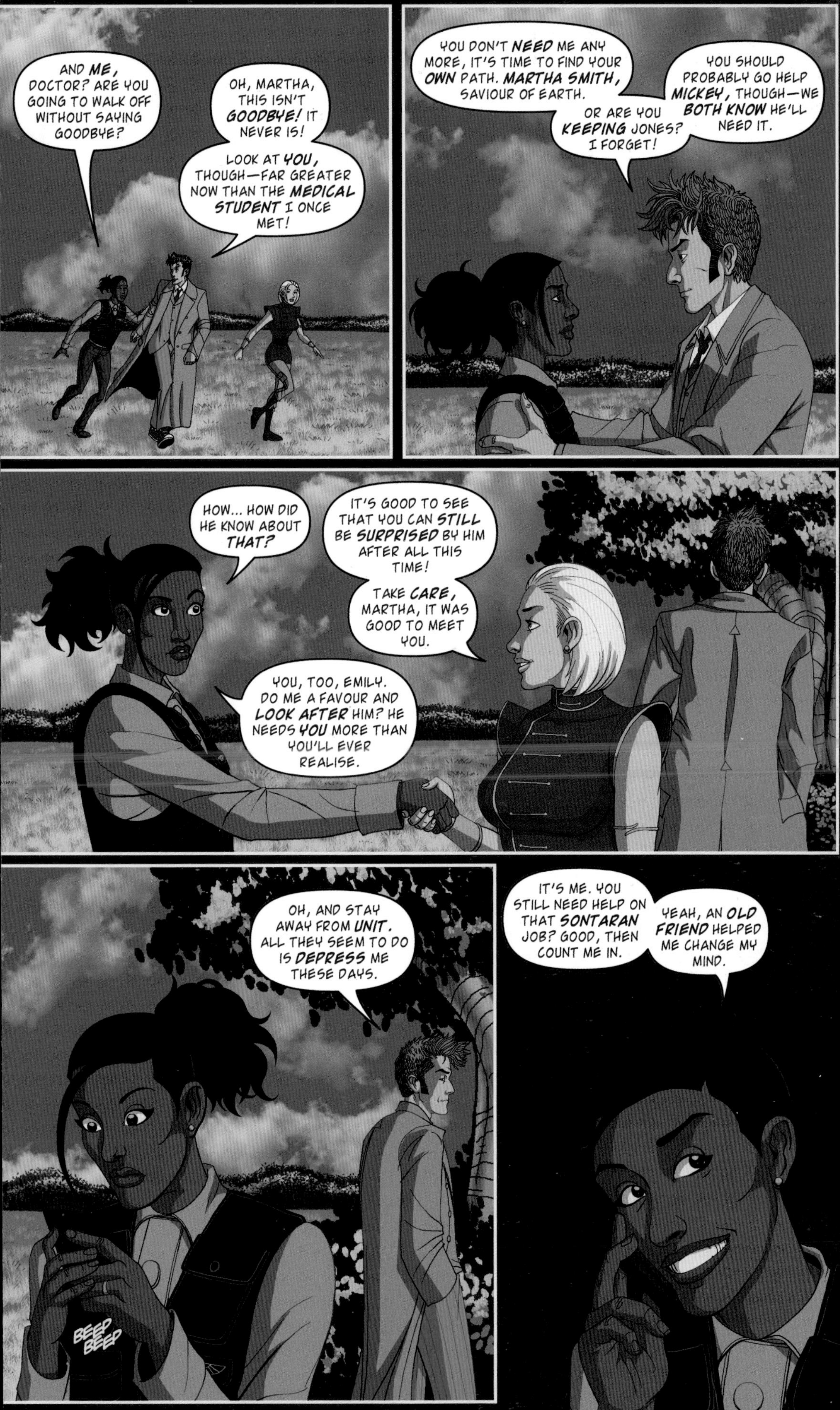
AND ME, DOCTOR? ARE YOU GOING TO WALK OFF WITHOUT SAYING GOODBYE?
OH, MARTHA, THIS ISN'T GOODBYE! IT NEVER IS!
LOOK AT YOU, THOUGH—FAR GREATER NOW THAN THE MEDICAL STUDENT I ONCE MET!
YOU DON'T NEED ME ANY MORE, IT'S TIME TO FIND YOUR OWN PATH. MARTHA SMITH, SAVIOUR OF EARTH.
OR ARE YOU KEEPING JONES? I FORGET!
YOU SHOULD PROBABLY GO HELP MICKEY, THOUGH—WE BOTH KNOW HE'LL NEED IT.
HOW... HOW DID HE KNOW ABOUT THAT?
IT'S GOOD TO SEE THAT YOU CAN STILL BE SURPRISED BY HIM AFTER ALL THIS TIME!
TAKE CARE, MARTHA, IT WAS GOOD TO MEET YOU.
YOU, TOO, EMILY. DO ME A FAVOUR AND LOOK AFTER HIM? HE NEEDS YOU MORE THAN YOU'LL EVER REALISE.
OH, AND STAY AWAY FROM UNIT. ALL THEY SEEM TO DO IS DEPRESS ME THESE DAYS.
BEEP BEEP
IT'S ME. YOU STILL NEED HELP ON THAT SONTARAN JOB? GOOD, THEN COUNT ME IN.
YEAH, AN OLD FRIEND HELPED ME CHANGE MY MIND.

THAT'S IT? WE JUST *LEAVE* HIM WITH... WITH *HER?*

NOTHING WE CAN DO, *YET.*

BUT MATTHEW'S PART OF HER *MASTER PLAN,* WE'LL SEE HIM AGAIN SOON. AND THIS'LL GIVE ME TIME TO *PREPARE.*

DON'T WORRY. WE'LL GET MATTHEW BACK.

SO, WHERE TO THEN? ANCIENT CHINA? THE *MOON?*

WHEREVER YOU WANT TO GO, MISS WINTER! *ALLONS-Y!*

OH, I KNOW A PLACE OUT THERE—DOES THE BEST *CHOCOLATE MILKSHAKES* IN THE UNIVERSE!

WELL, YOU DID PROMISE ME A VISIT TO *CAMELOT,* I BELIEVE!

OR MAYBE EVEN SOMEWHERE OUT *THERE?* DEEP IN SPACE?

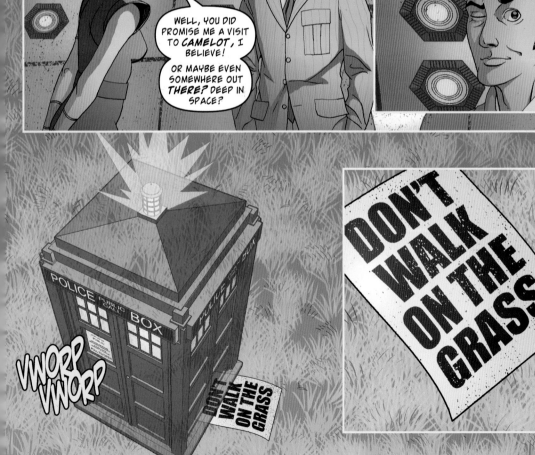

POLICE PUBLIC CALL BOX

VWORP VWORP

DON'T WALK ON THE GRASS

DON'T WALK ON THE GRASS

ART GALLERY

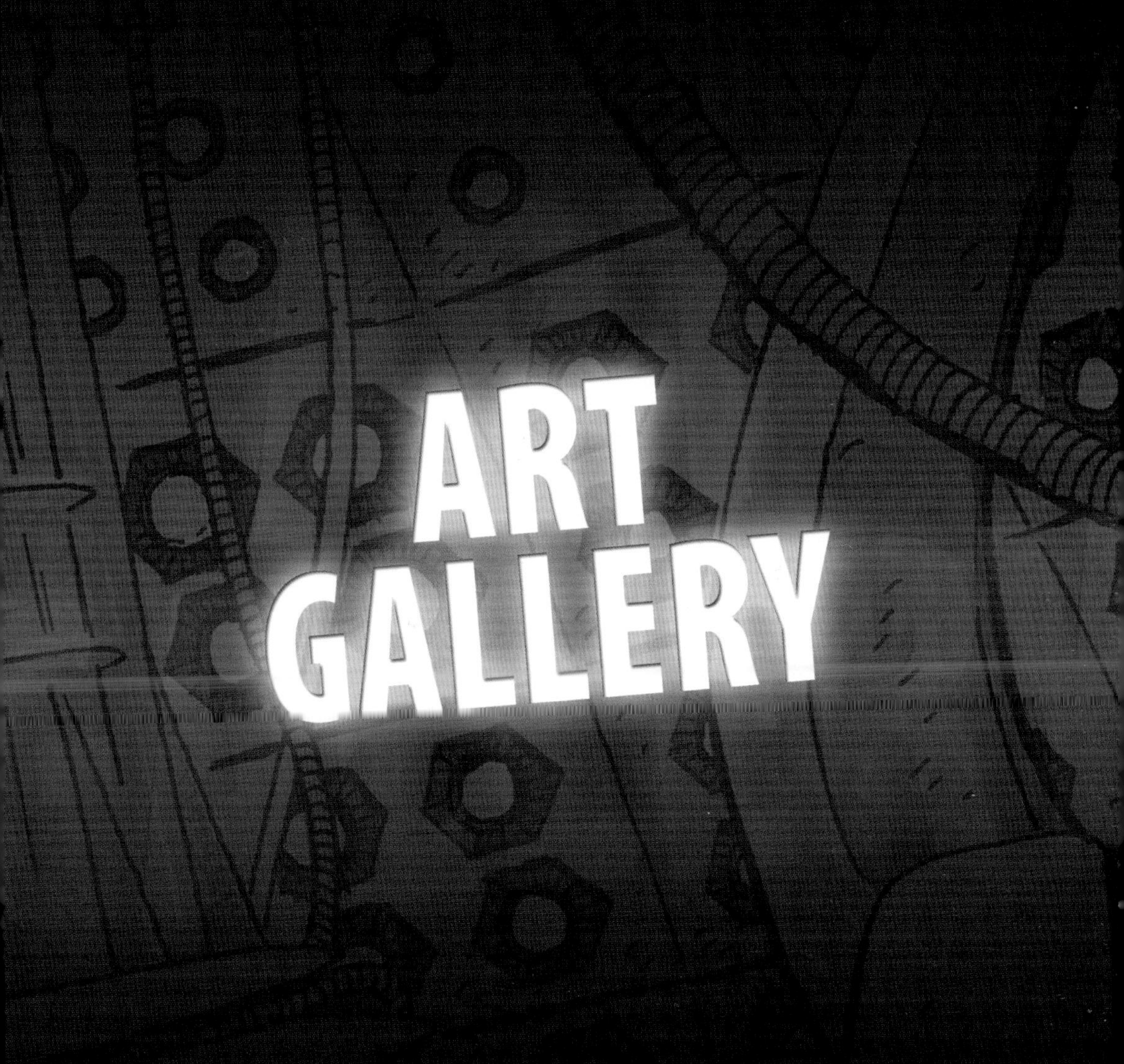

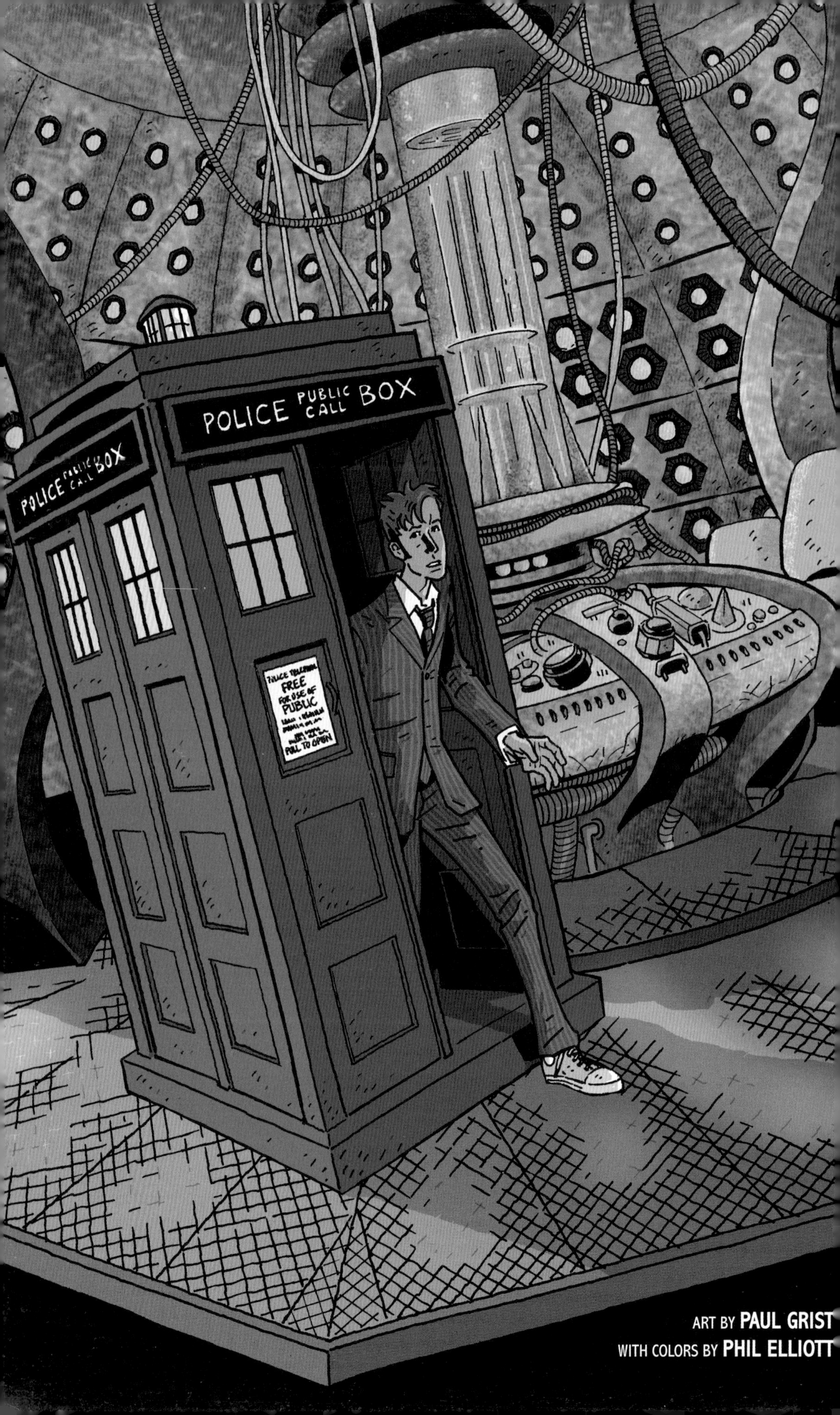
POLICE PUBLIC CALL BOX
POLICE PUBLIC CALL BOX
FREE
FOR USE OF
PUBLIC
PULL TO OPEN

ART BY **PAUL GRIST**
WITH COLORS BY **PHIL ELLIOTT**

ART BY **AL DAVISON**

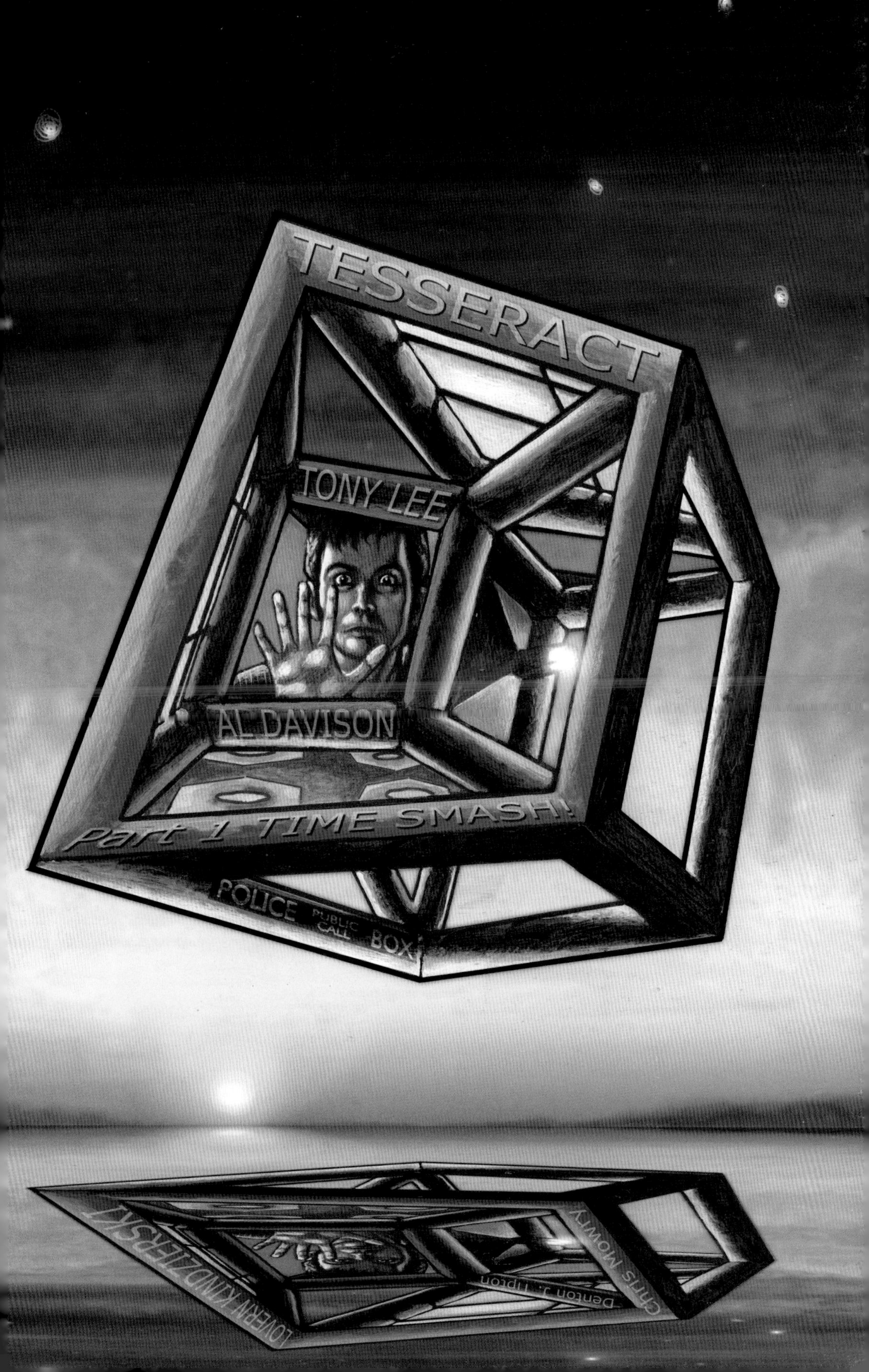
TESSERACT
TONY LEE
AL DAVISON
Part 1 TIME SMASH!
POLICE PUBLIC CALL BOX
LOVERN KINDZIERSKI
Chris Mowry
Denton J. Tipton

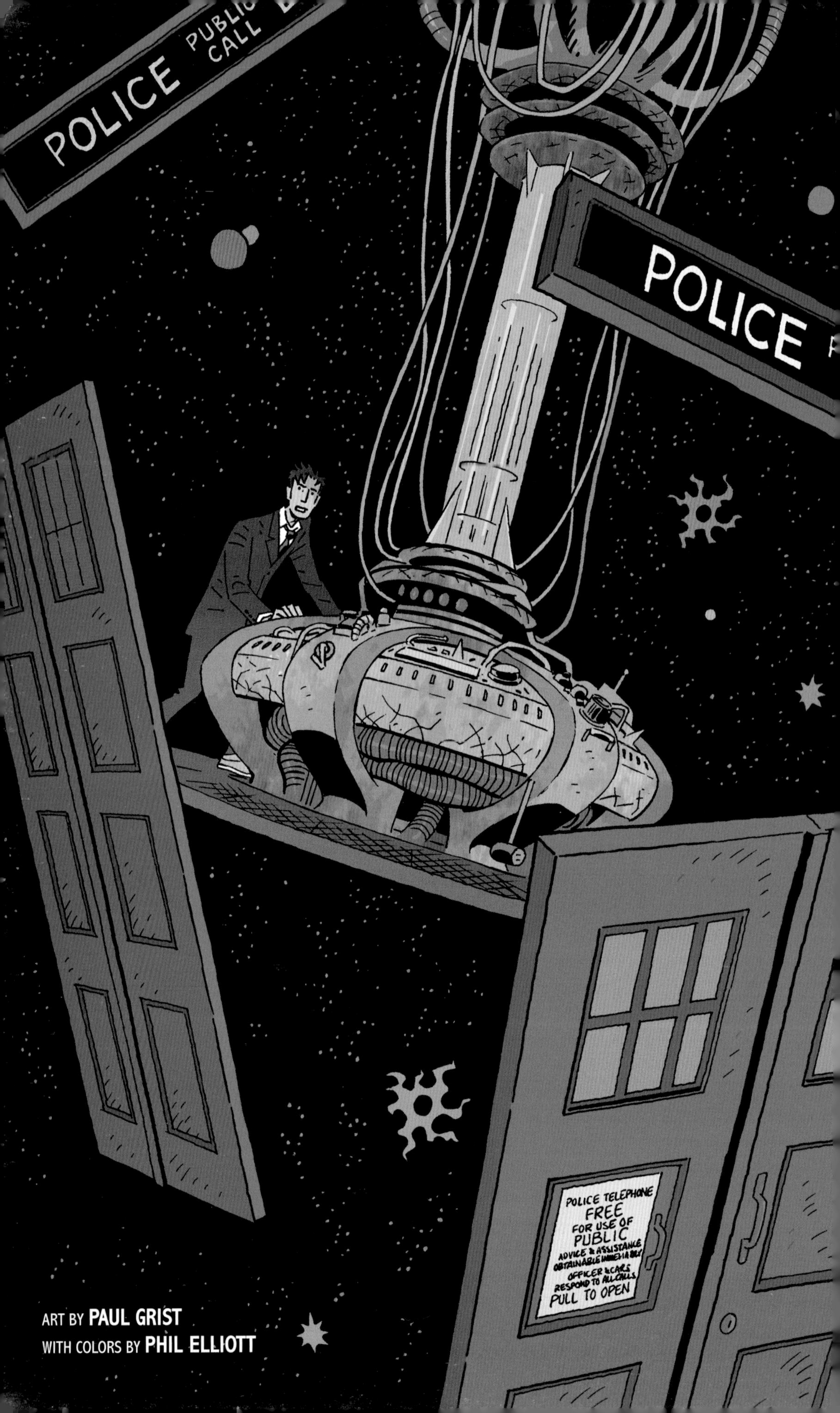
POLICE PUBLI
CALL
POLICE
POLICE TELEPHONE
FREE
FOR USE OF
PUBLIC
ADVICE & ASSISTANCE
OBTAINABLE IMMEDIATELY
OFFICER & CARS
RESPOND TO ALL CALLS
PULL TO OPEN

ART BY **PAUL GRIST**
WITH COLORS BY **PHIL ELLIOTT**

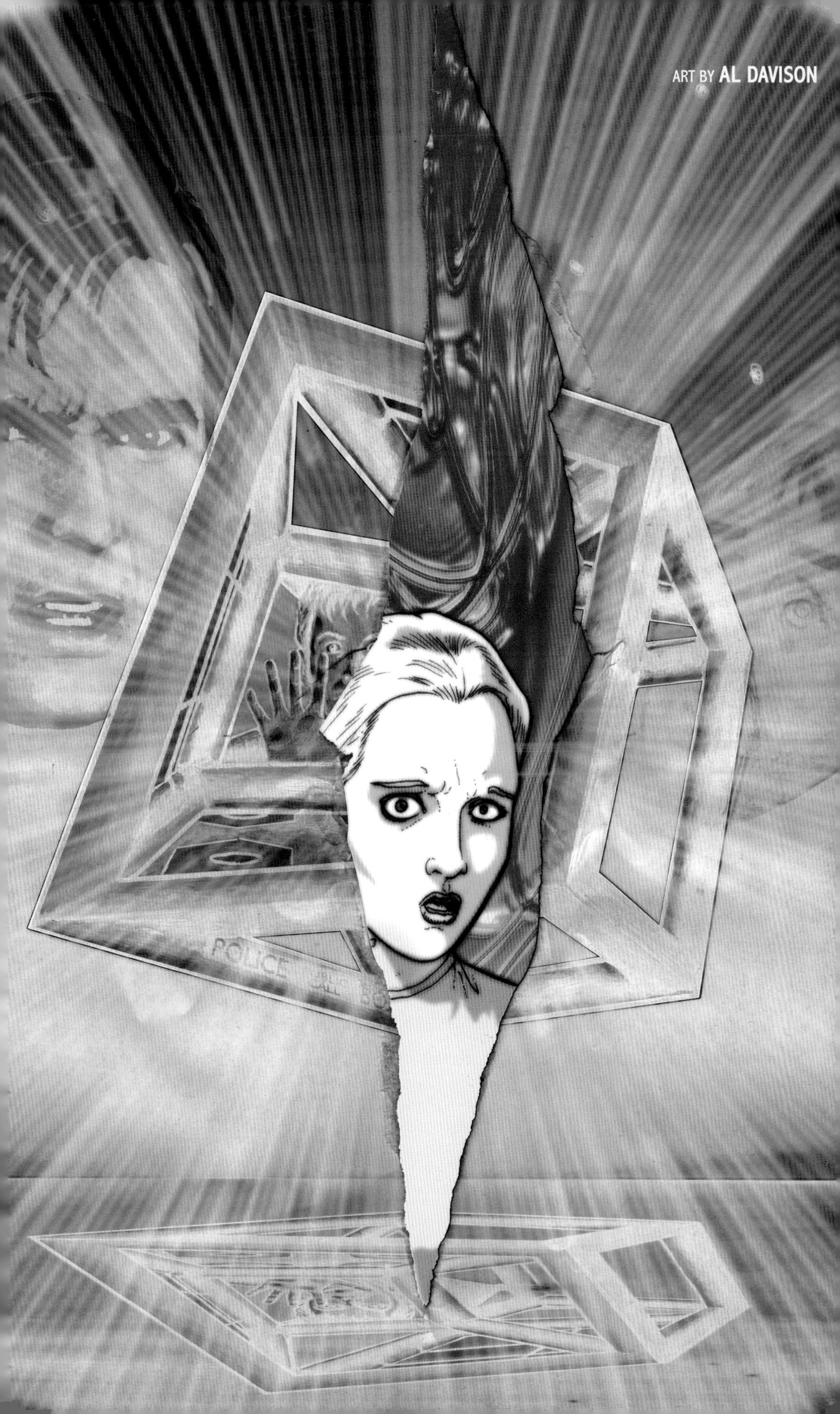
POLICE
ART BY **AL DAVISON**

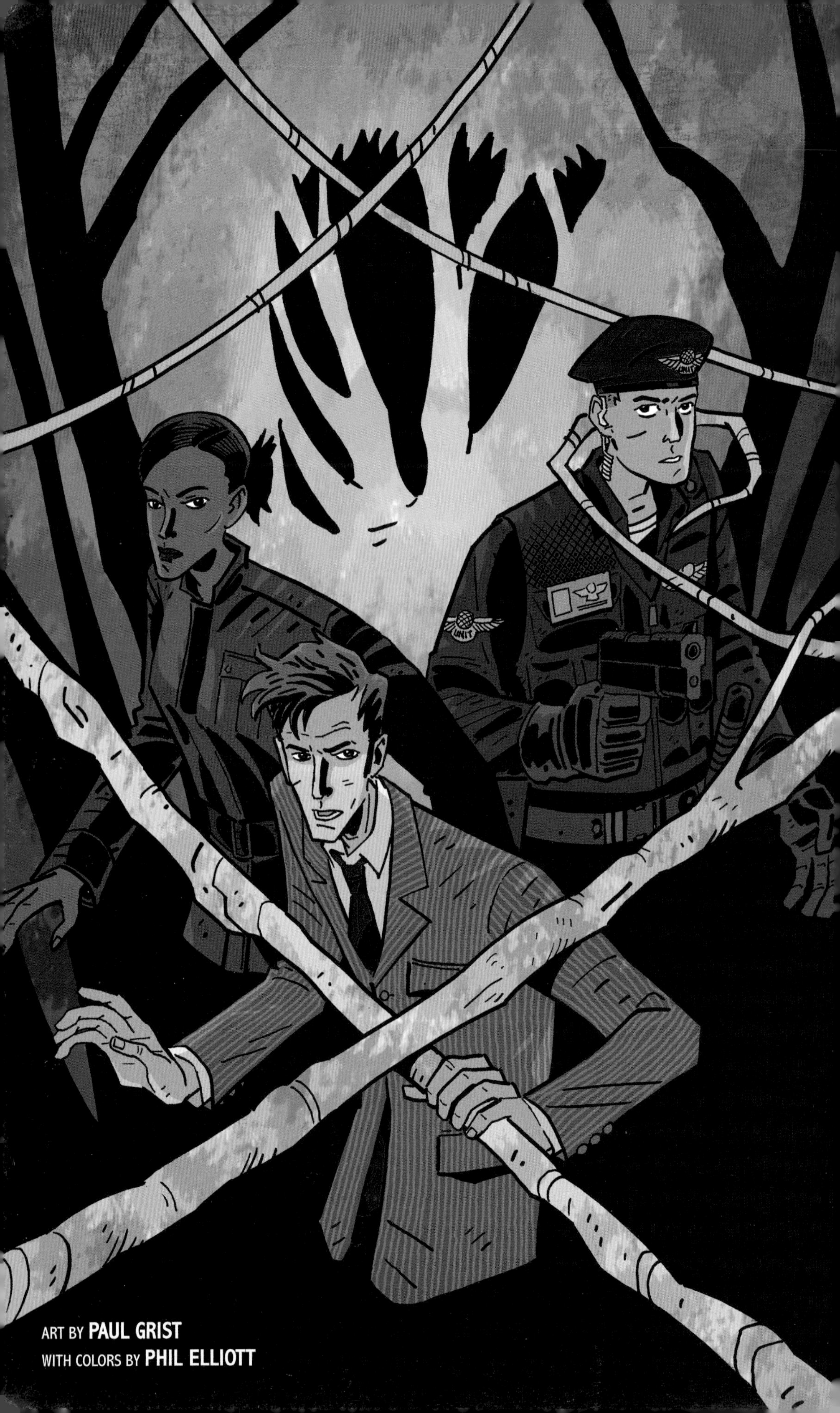

ART BY **PAUL GRIST**
WITH COLORS BY **PHIL ELLIOTT**

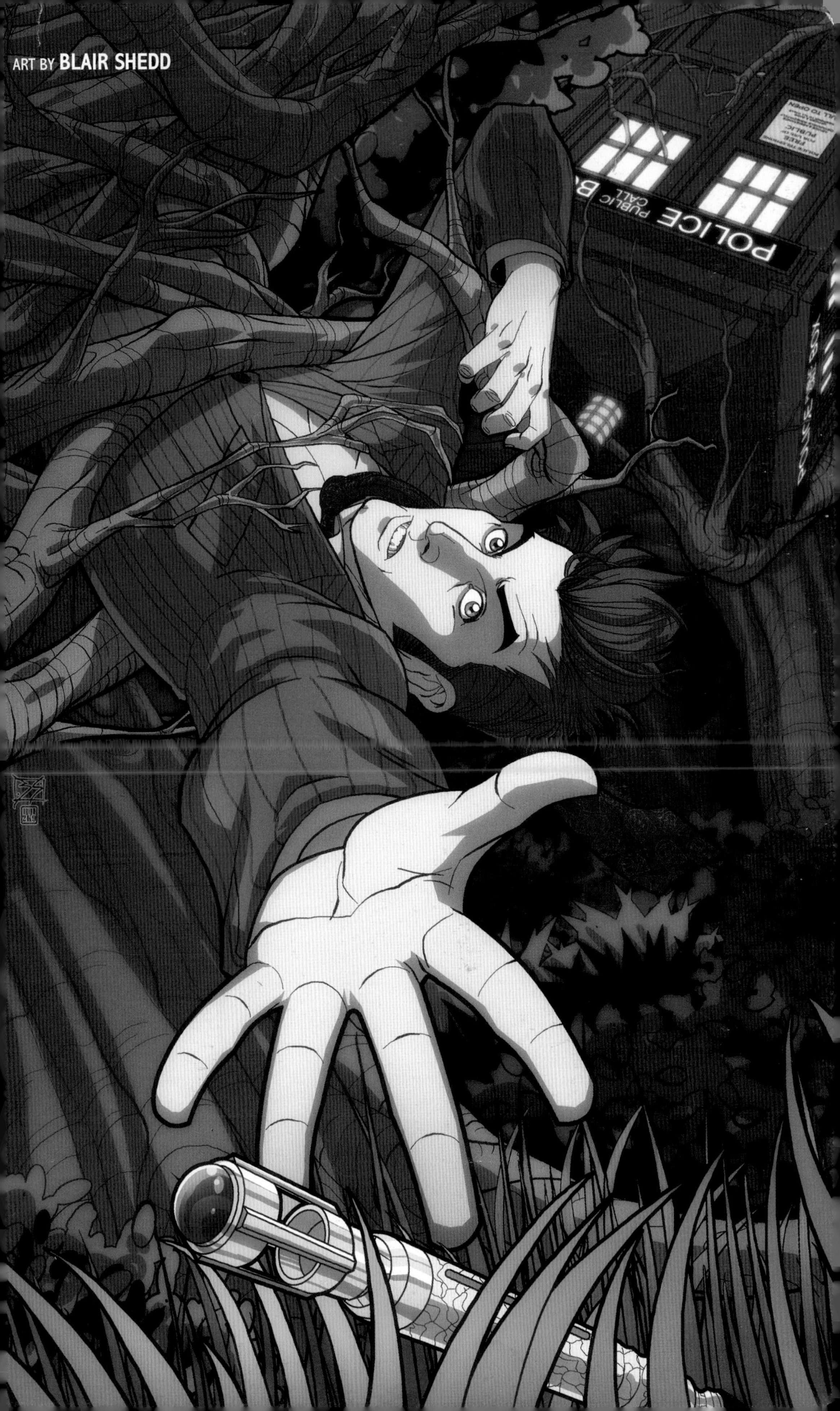
POLICE
PUBLIC
CALL
ART BY **BLAIR SHEDD**

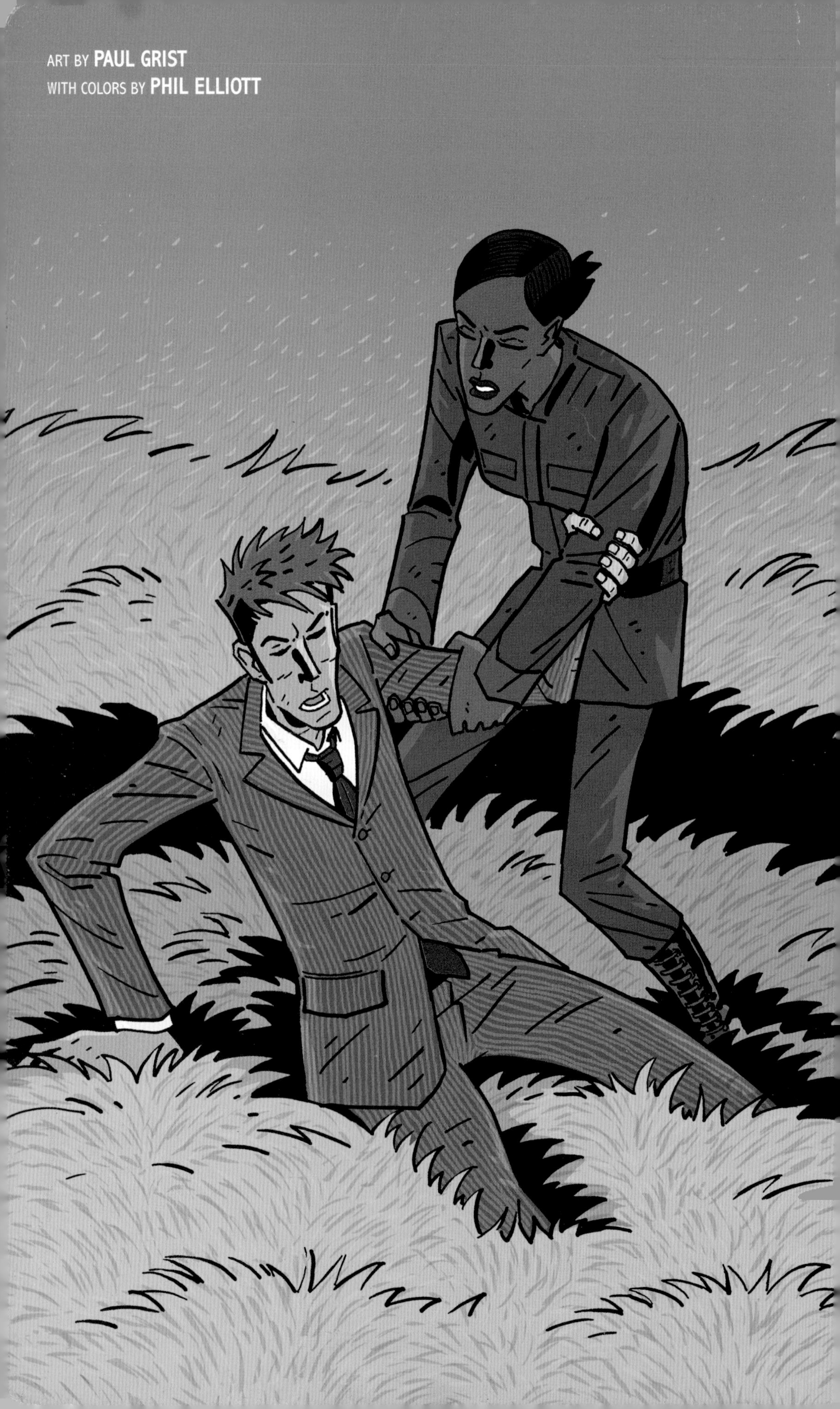

ART BY PAUL GRIST
WITH COLORS BY PHIL ELLIOTT

ART BY **PAUL GRIST**
WITH COLORS BY **PHIL ELLIOTT**

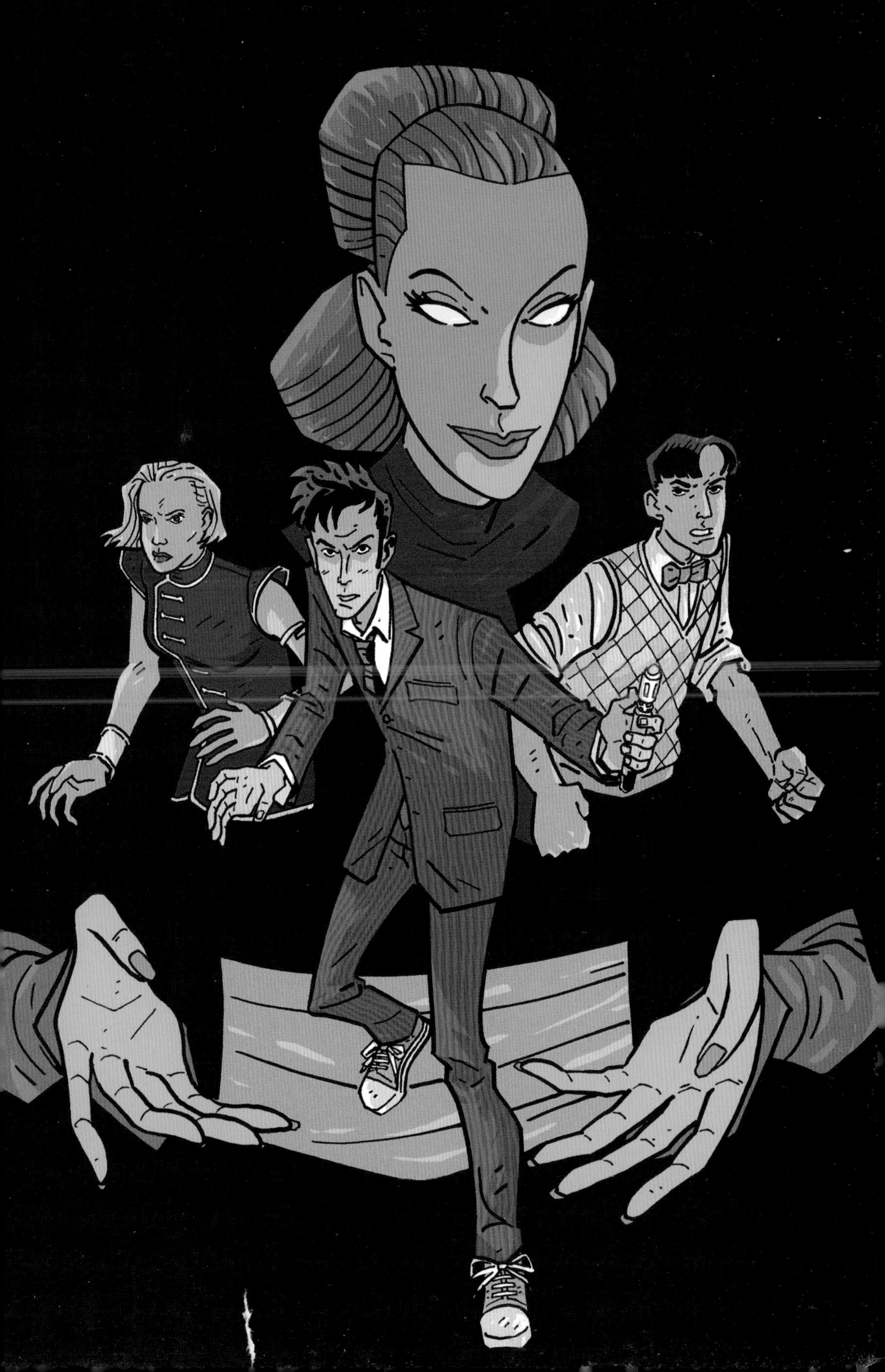

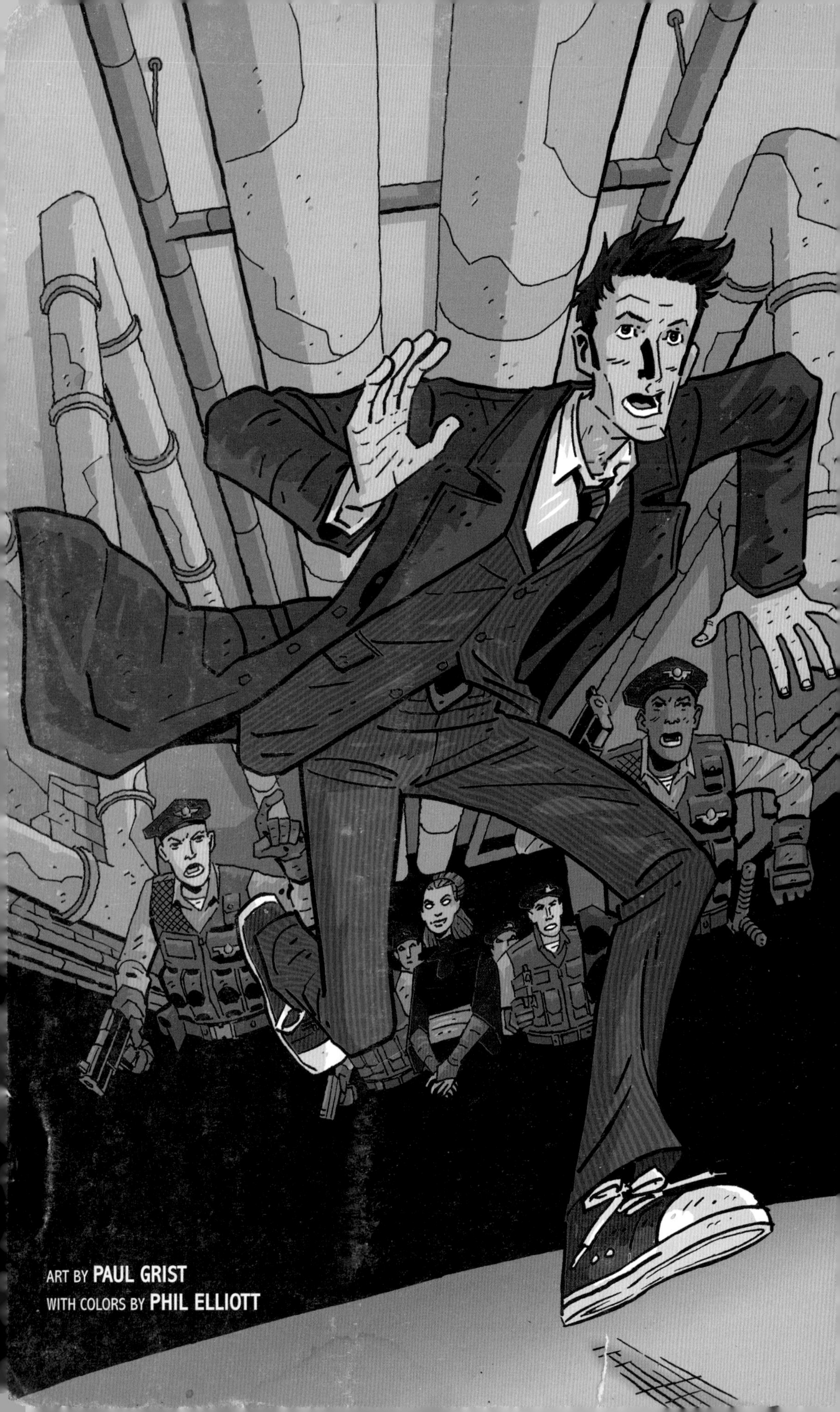
ART BY PAUL GRIST
WITH COLORS BY PHIL ELLIOTT